THE BLUEPRINT

Fire Your Job and Get Rich Building Your Business Empire

By Charles Gentry

Dedication,

To Those Who Mean Everything To Me...

Firstly, I want to thank God above for allowing me to still be here, sharing with readers and trying to do my small part to make the world a better place. I cannot thank my wife Patina Paulette Gentry enough for nursing me back to health when I was fatally sick, taking amazing care of me each day, and loving me always, with all her heart. I Love You with all my little heart Mrs. P. You will forever be my Big Pretty.

My love and appreciation to my beloved wife Sharon, and my beloved Carmelitta, who now watch on from heaven. I would not be who I am without the love and encouragement you gave me on every day we were blessed to share. I thank my wonderful children Milan, Latrice, Keena, Ricky, and my new girls, Kiya and Shauni. You are the best children any father could ever ask for and I love you all dearly. To my new mom, Mother Gibbons, my sister Inez and brother Alonzo, and my new siblings Elaine, Levon, and Debra, thank you for welcoming me to the family. I Love You all. To my cherished family, Latanya, Stacey, Alana, Kee, Tisa, Jordan, Sierra, Manu, Karnesha, Will, Al, Travis, Bennett, and Taneeka, thanks for the love and support. I love you back. To my grandbabies Kingston, Coy, Emilia, Khomani, Leelee, Samiah, and the new grandbaby on the way, your Big Daddy loves you dearly. To my wonderful little family Chasity, Trinity, Charity, Isaiah, Elijah, Michael, Tobbi, and Keesha, Love ya. To my friends Gregory, Reggie, Big Ray, Michael, Thomas, Johnnie ("Hop"), Lajuana, Kevin, Dana, Terry & Laura, Faith, Troy, Kitty Kat, Cindy Lou, John & Ruth, Meardis, Connie, Linda & Richard, Tim, mother Mary, Sista, and my buddy Tyrone, All Love, forever and ever my friends. To my mentors, Dr. Gordon Johnston, Sue Johnston, Bert & Addie, and T.C. Boyle, I strive every day to make you proud. Finally, to my fantastic doctor whose skilled hands saved my life, thanks to you Dr. David Lim, and your medical team, you're the absolute best! To all my readers, friends, and family, All Love. I dedicate this book to each and every one of you.

Table   of   Contents

pages

INTRODUCTION

The clock is ticking. Look around you and you will quickly see that it is a brand new world, a world different than the one that existed 100 years ago, 50 years ago, 10 years ago, even a year ago. Technology and the innovation it enables are creating new ways of doing business, communicating, learning, and living. A world of new opportunities exists today. But those opportunities won't last forever. Tighter restrictions on business, escalating costs for social media marketing, and a consolidation of industry power by the major companies mean a shrinking window of opportunity for those who want to reach financial independence through entrepreneurship. The best time to fire your job and start a new business is now.

Ways of conducting business and even our daily affairs that have been trustworthy for decades are being overturned, or at the very least turned inside-out, to the point they are no longer recognizable. New methods, metrics, and processes are shaking up every industry and every household. Disruption is the new norm. Those brave souls who embrace these technologies and innovation will find it easier to thrive moving forward but those who refuse to let go of the old ways and close their doors and minds to the onslaught of changes pressing in on them will soon find it hard to even survive in this modern world. No industry, finance, education, music, security, sports, health, medicine, entertainment, fast food, manufacturing, publishing, art, retail, insurance, real estate, hospitality, grocery, transportation, or any other will escape the reach of this brave new world. As a result, hundreds of thousands of jobs and many industries will disappear. Most of these poor souls don't even see it coming.

You may soon be faced with a choice between unemployment and becoming your own boss. If you choose the latter, there is a ton of information you need to know if you want to be successful. Perhaps, enough information to fill four years of college and then some. But, Don't Panic! I've packed all the important stuff into this book. To keep you ahead of the curve here's a valuable hint: The best time to start your own business is while you still have a job you can use to inject cash into your own start-up.

The answer to being pushed out of the job market by new technologies should be more than obvious to you. It's entrepreneurship. It's estimated that 27 million Americans will leave the traditional workforce in favor of full-time self-employment by 2020. Those perceptive enough to see the writing on the wall will not wait for their job to evaporate or the need for their skills to be snatched away by emerging technologies like artificial intelligence (AI). They will instead use these new technologies to strike out on their own and become their own boss. As a successful entrepreneur the reward can be more job satisfaction and more income.

Some of the reasons people have been afraid to give up a regular paycheck to venture out on their own are vanishing with the old economy. The rate at which American entrepreneurs had to close failed businesses has fallen by 30% since 1977. Also, certain myths like starting new businesses is only for the young, like millennials, are being debunked. According to research from Massachusetts Institute of Technology, the average entrepreneur who starts a business and hires at least one employee is 42 years old. For those who believe people can't start a successful business and build wealth anymore statistics prove otherwise. After surveying 585 billionaires in 2016, Wealth X determined that 362 or 62% were self-made, and another 18% reached billionaire status through a combination of inheritance and making their own wealth. Furthermore, if you think you need to have a company building and dozens of employees to be a real business you should know that world-renowned companies like Apple, Amazon, Google, Microsoft, and Disney all started in a garage or basement. Currently, 51.6% of companies are started in someone's garage or basement. According to the SBA, 60.1% of firms without paid employees are home-based.

Think you don't have enough education to be successful in business? Lack of education is not a barrier to entrepreneur success either. In fact, most business owners either never went to college or dropped out before they could obtain a degree. According to a CNBC/Survey Monkey survey, only 26% of small business owners said they had a bachelor's degree. Only 17% went to college, 20% graduated high school but did not go to college, and 5% didn't graduate high school at all.

However, if your goal is to be a successful entrepreneur there are some things you need to know and do. According to CB Insights, a surprising 42% of businesses fail because there is no market need for their products or services. Around 29% fail because they run out of cash. Some 23% don't surround themselves with the right team to help them succeed. Another 17% fail because they don't have a strong enough business model. Fads come and go but if you are going to be successful you need a business that is built to last. The Small Business Administration (SBA) states that while nearly 80% of small businesses survive their first year, only 50% have survived five years or longer during the past decade. Only one-third of small businesses survive 10 years or longer.

Wisdom says, it's almost always better to learn by using the other guy's money. Research shows that entrepreneurs are much more likely to be successful if they've held a previous job in the same field their new business is in. The reason for this is obvious. The experience you gain from working a job is valuable when you start a business in the same field, as are the business connections you were able to make with employees, managers, suppliers, vendors, and customers. In all likelihood, a more experienced entrepreneur can provide more value to customers and clients.

If you are going to be a successful entrepreneur, you need to know business success is a result of hard work. A survey of entrepreneurs found that 17.7% claim they work every weekend. About 31% of entrepreneurs work 50 hours per week and 11.8% work 60 hours per week. As an entrepreneur working longer hours means that you may have to miss important family or lifestyle events, celebrations, and other joyful experiences.

It's hard to do better, unless you know better, and that is what this book is all about. We live in The Age of Information, information that has increased from a mere drip to a flood, turned from a light drizzle into a deluge. How can you keep pace with this brave new world without knowing where the world is headed? Where is business, industry and commerce headed? Where is employment, management, and entrepreneurship headed? Where is housing, recreation, and family life headed? And, most importantly, where are you headed without a reliable blueprint to help you get there? These are not the old days when a high school diploma or college degree could guarantee you a job in a warehouse, factory, or office somewhere. In this brave new world, many businesses don't even need warehouses, factories, or offices. Some don't even need employees.

Don't get caught flatfooted as all these new business models and changes rain down, spelling the end of hundreds of thousands of jobs. As you go from page to page, and chapter to chapter of The Blueprint: Fire Your Job And Get Rich Building Your Business Empire; you will be equipping yourself not only to survive in this new economy but to thrive amidst the rapid changes taking place. That tomorrow you've been anticipating, even fearing, is here and success will now come down to survival of the fittest. Who is capable of using the apps, cloud technologies, web-based solutions, artificial intelligence, robotics, and other technologies to thrive in spite of the global competition that awaits everyone not tomorrow, but today? My friend, tomorrow is not coming, it is here. The Blueprint provides you with a map to successfully navigate these technologically choppy waters and still come out ahead.

You will learn methods to increase your brain power, improve your health, start a profitable business, build wealth, understand how technology will affect tomorrow, and how to get from where you are to where you want to be. And, each lesson learned will be supported with case studies and valuable insights to guide you every step of the way. This brave new world holds brutal consequences for those who choose to bury their heads in the sand and ignore the changes that are taking place in public and privately.

No part of your life will go untouched by these changes, from the way you do banking to the way you prepare your food, from the way you earn a living to the way you travel from point A to point B. Hard work and company loyalty will no longer determine your success or failure. How much knowledge and information you possess and how completely you are able to understand and utilize it are the new keys to success. Whether you unlock the doors to opportunity and success or get coldly shut out of this prosperous but selective new economy and culture, is your call. Wealth is almost exclusively the result of entrepreneurship and there has never been a more exciting time to start a business. Technology, and the business tools it has created, now make it possible for you to fire your job and get rich building your business empire. In great detail, The Blueprint, has compiled the information and guidance you'll need to succeed. The clock is ticking. THE NEXT STEP IS UP TO YOU.

Chapter1: Everything You Know Is Wrong

You are searching for answers. Answers for why your life is not what you want it to be. Answers for how you can change it for the better. Answers for how you can have more of what you want and less of what you don't want. If you truly want answers for how you can have better relationships, more success in business or school, how you can upgrade your lifestyle, and get your life moving in the right direction, keep reading. If you are looking for answers to how you can do, have, and be everything you've always dreamed, keep reading. If the preceding statements describe what you hope to gain from life, congratulations. You've stumbled upon the right book.

However, if you're looking for a get rich quick scheme or some over-night solution for all your problems this book is not it. Keep looking. The Blueprint, is designed to help you build your own highway to success. It is not worthless hype to fuel some pipe dream you may have about success. It is a road map to help you actually reach your destination... SUCCESS... through your own efforts.

Without further delay let's get to the point. You have hundreds, possibly thousands of thoughts in your head about what is and is not true. These thoughts have become your truths, or facts you now believe to be unshakeable. As a matter of fact you swear by them and would gladly bet the family farm if someone wagered with you on the validity of these truths. So, it is with a big cup of kindness that I present to you an infallible fact: Just because you believe something doesn't make it true.

Step #1 on the road to success is Get Your Mind Right. Discoveries are being made every day that disprove things that were once widely believed to be true. To support this fact here are 12 such myths that were once thought to be true. Even today some people still believe these myths.

The Earth Is Round and A Perfect Sphere Myth: Scholars have known the Earth is round for thousands of years. A Greek philosopher first suggested the idea around 500 B.C., though his thought process had to do with his belief that spheres were the most perfect shape. Still, Aristotle actually found physical evidence backing up his predecessor's theory. By the time the first century A.D. rolled around, any educated Greek or Roman believed in a round planet. When Christopher Columbus began his voyage the fear was that the oceans would be too big to cross, not that he'd fall off the face of the earth. Less you get cocky here's another truth, the Earth isn't round (a perfect sphere); the North and South Poles are slightly flattened.

The Brain Myth: The idea of unlocking hidden brain power might make a compelling storyline for a movie, but it simply won't happen in real life. One fact playing into the myth is that 90 percent of brain cells are "white matter" that help neurons survive, and only ten percent is the "grey matter" of neurons in charge of thinking. Therefore, some people wrongly believe that white matter could never be used for brain power. But claiming 90 percent of our brain is wasted is like saying you waste watermelon when you spit out the seeds. Any fMRI scan will show you that even saying a few words lights up way more than ten percent of your brain. Scientists haven't uncovered any area of the brain (much less 90 percent) that doesn't affect thought, movement, or emotion in some capacity.

The Genes Determine Race Myth: You might think people who look superficially different would have big differences in their genes, but that's not the case. According to the National Human Genome Research Institute, humans share 99.9 percent of their genes with each other. Even that 0.1 percent doesn't have any racial markers. In fact, a groundbreaking 2002 study revealed there is more genetic diversity between people of African descent than between Africans and Eurasians. You can use your genes to trace your ancestors' geography, but that doesn't directly tie into race. Case in point: Sickle cell anemia isn't a general "African" disease, as it's normally described; it's more common in West Africans, but also in Mediterranean, Arabian, and Indian populations.

The Great Wall of China Myth: Interestingly, this myth has been around at least since 1932, when a Ripley's Believe it or Not! cartoon proclaimed the Great Wall of China is "the mightiest work of man—the only one that would be visible to the human eye from the moon." Of course, that was over 30 years before a machine would touch down on the moon, so the claim was entirely unfounded. Astronauts have now confirmed that even the Great Wall actually can't be seen from space, except at low altitudes. Even at those (relatively) low heights, it's actually easier to see roads and plane runways, whose colors don't blend into the ground like the Great Wall does.

The Lightening Myth: Anyone familiar with lightning rods could probably already tell you there's nothing stopping lightning from hitting the same spot twice. The Empire State Building, for example, once endured eight strikes in 24 minutes during a storm. Even without a lightning rod, there's nothing keeping lightning away from the spot that just got hit. In fact, the features that made the spot likely to get hit once—height, presence of standing water, or terrain shape, for example—would be just as attractive to a second bolt, according to the National Severe Storms Laboratory.

The California Myth: From the 16th century, European experts in geography were convinced that California was an island separate from the North American mainland. Maps of the time show a large island on the left of the land mass and California continued to appear this way even into the 18th century. The matter was finally put to rest indisputably on the 1774-1776 expeditions of Juan Bautista de Anza. Interestingly, it is likely that within 25 million years, Baja California and part of Southern California really will separate from North America due to tectonic plate movement.

The Falling Penny Myth: The story goes that even an innocent penny dropped from the 1,250-foot-tall Empire State Building would build up enough speed on the way down to kill a bystander below. In reality, it wouldn't do much damage, if any. First of all, air resistance called "drag force" would mean the penny would stop accelerating at some point and reach its max speed about 50 feet from its drop point, according to Scientific American. By the time it reached the ground, it would be moving just 25 miles per hour. That might sting, but it wouldn't be enough force to break your skull. MythBusters took the theory to an extreme and shot a penny at 3,000 feet per second, but even that wasn't strong enough to break bones.

The Water Conducts Electricity Myth: While this is a science myth, it doesn't mean you should bring your toaster into the bathtub with you. The reason you shouldn't swim in a lightning storm doesn't have to do with the water itself. Pure water is actually an insulator, which means it doesn't conduct electricity. The danger comes from the minerals and chemicals in it called ions, which have an electric charge. While pure water is theoretically safe around electricity, it is nearly impossible to find it in the real world. Even distilled water has ions.

The McDonald's Hamburger Myth: It's a myth that McDonald's burgers don't rot. Actually, they will rot if the right conditions exist with enough water and warmth for the microbes that break food down.

The Ostrich Myth: The birds would die of suffocation if they actually stuck their heads underground when scared. Instead, they actually lie with their head and neck flat against the ground if a predator is approaching. Their light-colored head and neck blend in with the ground, which could explain why people assumed their heads were underground from faraway, according to the San Diego Zoo.

The Sugar Myth: Don't blame the cake if your kid is acting out at a party. The "sugar high" theory started in 1978, when one study found that kids with hyperkinesis, a hyperactivity disorder, had low blood sugar, which, weirdly enough, can be a sign of eating too much sugar. That study was later discredited when researchers realized the "abnormally low" blood sugar was actually considered normal. Since then, double-blind studies have shown sugar doesn't make kids any more hyper than a placebo. If anything, it's probably your own expectations. One 1994 study found that after five- to seven-year-old boys took a placebo, the moms who were told their sons had eaten a large dose of sugar were more likely to say their kid was acting hyper. More than likely if your kid is acting more energetic he or she might just be excited to play with their friends at the party.

The Sun and Planets Revolve Around the Earth Myth: Because we live on Earth, and we see objects passing across our view of the skies, it's natural to assume that the Earth is the center of the Universe. In fact, this perspective – known as geocentrism – was the default for all ancient civilizations. The Sun, the Moon, the planets and the stars appeared to move around the Earth each day. And because the Earth itself didn't seem to be moving, astronomers like Ptolemy assumed that Earth was the center of the Universe. In fact, they went so far as to create very detailed models for predicting the motions of objects with a high degree of accuracy, using this completely inaccurate model of the Solar System. The predictions made by Ptolemy were used to make astrological predictions for more than 1500 years, until a much better model came along. A new, more accurate model of the Solar System didn't come around until the 16th century, when the Polish astronomer Nicolai Copernicus published his Universe-changing book: On the Revolutions of the Heavenly Bodies. Copernicus accurately reorganized the Solar System, putting the Sun at the center in a heliocentric model. And the Earth took its proper place, as just another planet orbiting the Sun – one of the 6 known to astronomers at that time. Copernicus' model helped answer two questions which had troubled astronomers for centuries: why the planets brighten and dim over the course of several months (because they're getting closer and further away), and why the planets seem to reverse and move in a retrograde direction. Easily explained because of the changing positions of the Earth, planets and the background stars.

Once upon a time people (in some cases even scientists) swore all these myths were true. They even had evidence that they thought proved these myths to be facts. Today, we'd probably laugh out loud if someone tried to convince us these myths were true. But, don't laugh too hard because some of the things you believe to be facts will someday be disproven and shown to be nothing more than myths based on conjecture or faulty science. So, as we enter into this book and begin this journey to re-engineer your life for success the mindset that will allow you to get the absolute most good out of this book is a mindset that begins with the theory: Everything You Know Is Wrong. If you allow that mindset to be your starting point you are truly ready to significantly change your life for the better. Remember this key point, change is inevitable but changing for the better is a choice. Now, if you choose to do so let's begin the process of helping you to become the best YOU that you can possibly be.

Information Is Still King

The Age of Information

We are now living in the Age of Information. On the surface that seems to be a good thing. But for those looking for solutions having the abundance of information that is available today can cause some serious information overload. It can be like looking for a specific needle in a room full of needles. Further complicating the decision-making process is the amount of misinformation available today. Not having the right information can be harmful. But, having the wrong information can be disastrous.

As of 2019, there are approximately 4,383,810,342 people using the internet. That means the internet is now used by more than half the people in the world. That is a growth of 1,114 % between the years 2000 and 2019. Naturally more users mean more people sending information across the internet. Consider the sum total of data (information) held by all the big online storage and service companies like Google, Amazon, Microsoft and Facebook. Estimates are that the big four store at least 1,200 petabytes between them. That is 1.2 million terabytes (one terabyte is 1,000 gigabytes). As of May 21, 2018, more than 3.7 billion humans were using the internet (that's a growth rate of 7.5 percent over 2016). On average, Google now processes more than 40,000 searches EVERY second. That's 3.5 billion searches per day! That is a lot of information to try and process. What part of that information is truthful and what part is not? How much of that information is helpful and how much of it is harmful? How much of it should you explore and consume and how much of it should you ignore?

With Chapter 1, of this book entitled, Everything You Know Is Wrong, we want to get you off on the right foot by teaching you the difference between information that can help you and misinformation that will harm you. It also shows you how information you received in your past (and how you processed that information) can be a major roadblock that keeps you from achieving success. The goal in life is not just to succeed but to reach your full potential as a person. The information you learn, how you process that information, and what decisions you make as a result of that processing will have everything to do with whether you are successful, the level of that success, and the longevity of that success. The first time you hear the statement, "Everything You Know Is Wrong", you may think, 'that can't be true. How can everything I know be wrong?' But once you finish reading this chapter you'll not only know why that statement IS true, you'll also come to understand how knowing that truth can empower you to reach dizzying heights of success you never even dreamed of.

Understanding What Information Is

INFORMATION: Facts provided or learned about something or someone. That definition is our guidepost in determining whether the information you may be receiving is actually information or misinformation. Success is achieved by making the right life decisions. So, basing your important decisions on misinformation is the surest way to torpedo your own success.

A clue to getting this decision-making process right is to closely examine the definition of the word information again. FACTS PROVIDED or LEARNED about something or someone. The first word in that definition is the word FACTS. Facts is defined as: A thing that is known or proved to be true. We live in a time and a culture where a mere "opinion" or "viewpoint" or "preference" is passed off as a fact when in reality it is not. And when you base your decision upon something you believe is a fact when it is actually not a fact that decision will most likely be doomed to failure. Needless to say, because of this very common occurrence many people are making faulty decisions that are negatively impacting if not altogether ruining their lives. Secondly, information is a fact provided by someone. That should automatically trigger an instinct inside you to ask questions: Who is providing this information? What is their expertise on the subject? and, what is their motive for providing this information? Again, there are a ton of people and institutions passing off conjecture, myth, or even lies as absolute facts when they are not. If you want to win, if you want to be successful, you must make it an imperative to base your decisions on real facts provided by sources that have no motive except to provide you with truth.

Lastly, Facts are LEARNED. If you truly want to make good decisions, decisions that lead to success, you owe it to yourself to LEARN whether the information you have been provided is factual or not. Too many people are lazy and don't do their own research to find out what's true. Or, they are biased to the point of believing something because it lines up with what they want to believe. If I'm basing my decision on whether I can outfight a lion or outrun a cheetah based on what I choose to believe I place myself in a dangerous situation, a situation where my decision has no other outcome than failure.

As contrary to your nature or against the grain as it may be you must learn to question and examine every source, be it an individual or an institution. Schools, churches, religions, businesses, governments, political parties, mentors, celebrities, family members, friends and foes. Everyone, everything, and certainly every idea must be examined and scrutinized for accuracy and worth. We live in a day and time when you should take nothing at face value.

Providers of information such as family, friends, teachers, bosses, law enforcement, politicians, the media and others all have their own reasons for providing you with the information they are giving you. Those reasons or motives will play a role in what information they provide and just as importantly how they may choose to shade the information they provide to you. You MUST take that under consideration. Don't allow laziness to cause you to make bad decisions. Don't allow biases or emotions to trick you into making bad decisions. Bad decisions will always hurt you in the end. Like boats with holes in the bottom "bad decisions" will surely sink your chances for success.

Don't Be Misled By Misinformation and Disinformation

The dictionary defines misinformation as "false information that is spread, regardless of whether there is intent to mislead." And it describes disinformation as "deliberately misleading or biased information; manipulated narrative or facts; propaganda."

These twin nemesis Misinformation and Disinformation are now commonly used as a reactive tactic to change the narrative or throw conversations or discussions off course when governments, powerful corporations, or dictatorial individuals want to control the people, i.e. You. Dealing with misinformation and disinformation has become a major problem for anyone hoping to make good decisions today. Information posted by the National Endowment for Democracy clearly points out the way disinformation can be used as a weapon in today's social media driven society:

In the short term, disinformation can be utilized reactively by different entities: for example, when Russian-backed fighters in Eastern Ukraine shot down a commercial airliner, Russian state media went into overdrive proposing multiple, often conflicting alternative explanations for the plane's crash.

Disinformation's applications have also been evident in Syria, where Russian diplomats, media, and intelligence services have falsified evidence, pushed misleading narratives, and spread falsehoods relating to the role of Russia's airstrikes, as well as to obscure evidence of the Syrian government's use of chemical weapons.

Another common technique is to react to a crisis by flooding the information space and drowning out discussion. After opposition protests broke out in Syria during 2011, newly-created Twitter accounts began harassing Syrian users, and social media researchers allege that the Assad regime paid a public relations firm to flood opposition hashtags with photos of nature scenery and sports scores. You may think these large-scale political incidents have nothing to do with you and your smaller scale personal problems but that would be an error on your part. Misinformation and disinformation can be scaled up to disrupt and confuse large groups of people or scaled down to disrupt and confuse individuals. The 2016, presidential election in the United States is a perfect example.

Here are excerpts from an article that appeared in Wired magazine.

The bombshell 37-page indictment issued Friday by Robert Mueller against Russia's Internet Research Agency and its leadership and affiliates provides considerable detail on the Russian information warfare targeting the American public during the elections. And this information makes it increasingly difficult to say that the Kremlin's effort to impact the American mind did not succeed.

The indictment pulls the curtain back on four big questions that have swirled around the Russian influence operation, which, it turns out, began in 2014. What was the scope of the Russian effort? What kind of content did it rely on? Who or what was it targeting, and what did it aim to achieve? And finally, what impact did it have?

Most of the discussion of this to date has focused on ideas of political advertising and the reach of a handful of ads—and this discussion has completely missed the point.

The Mueller indictment permanently demolishes the idea that the scale of the Russian campaign was not significant enough to have any impact on the American public. We are no longer talking about approximately $100,000 (paid in rubles, no less) of advertising grudgingly disclosed by Facebook, but tens of millions of dollars spent over several years to build a broad, sophisticated system that can influence American opinion.

The Russian efforts described in the indictment focused on establishing deep, authenticated, long-term identities for individuals and groups within specific communities. This was underlaid by the establishment of servers and VPNs based in the US to mask the location of the individuals involved. US-based email accounts linked to fake or stolen US identity documents (driver licenses, social security numbers, and more) were used to back the online identities. These identities were also used to launder payments through PayPal and cryptocurrency accounts. All of this deception was designed to make it appear that these activities were being carried out by Americans.

As the indictment lays out in thorough detail, the content pumped out by the Russians was not paid or promoted ads; it was so-called native content—including video, visual, memetic, and text elements designed to push narrative themes, conspiracies, and character attacks. All of it was designed to look like it was coming from authentic American voices and interest groups.

The indictment mentions that the Russian accounts were meant to embed with and emulate "radical" groups. The content was not designed to persuade people to change their views, but to harden those views.

Confirmation bias is powerful and commonly employed in these kinds of psychological operations (a related Soviet concept is "reflexive control"— applying pressure in ways to elicit a specific, known response). The intention of these campaigns was to activate—or suppress—target groups. Not to change their views, but to change their behavior.

Mueller's indictment shows that Russian accounts and agents accomplished more than just stoking divisions and tensions with sloppy propaganda memes. The messaging was more sophisticated, and some Americans took action. For example, the indictment recounts a number of instances where events and demonstrations were organized by Russians posing as Americans on social media. These accounts aimed to get people to do specific things. And it turns out—some people did.

This passage consists of excerpts from the brilliant article that appeared in Wired magazine February 16, 2018, written by Molly K. McKew (@MollyMcKew) who is an expert on information warfare and the narrative architect at New Media Frontier. To read the entire story search for the Wired article "Did Russia Affect the 2016 Election? It's Now Undeniable".

In addition to misinformation and disinformation more and more groups or entities are beginning to use BOTS AND TROLLS TO SHAPE POLITICAL CONVERSATION ONLINE.

Online trolling, harassment, and distraction—especially by highly active automated accounts—are a key component of the modern disinformation purveyor's toolkit. These techniques push independent voices out of public spaces and are sometimes considered a new form of political censorship. The Chinese Communist Party (CCP) was an early pioneer of this approach: for at least a decade, Beijing has deployed a "fifty-cent party" (apocryphally named for posters' going rate per post) to "astroturf" support for the government and derail online political conversations that could spark mass mobilization. Recent estimates suggest this effort encompasses two million individuals, many of them state employees, and produces nearly 450 million social media posts per year.

Over time, similar approaches became a common aspect of authoritarian information manipulation and were later amplified through automation. In the early to mid-2000s, the Russian government began recruiting human commenters before later adopting the use of automated "bot" accounts. One study suggests that on Twitter more than half of tweets in Russian are produced by automated accounts. Aiming to avoid detection, many disinformation campaigns now avail themselves of accounts that are partially automated, partially controlled by human users; these are often referred to as cyborg or sock puppet accounts.

In recent years, the use of bots and trolls to shape online discussion has become so common across countries that it could be considered a widely exploited bug in the digital public square extending far beyond conflict or authoritarian settings. In Mexico, paid political consultants orchestrated the theft of campaign secrets and the large-scale distribution of disinformation to voters. Such activity continues to this day, as pro-government accounts swarm political hashtags, threaten the lives of activists, and marginalize protesters.

In the Philippines, where the public square faces significant threats both online and off, interview-based research has explored a sophisticated "underground" public relations industry in which digital strategists, social media influencers, and paid commenters compete to deliver their clients the greatest degree of control over political narratives on the internet. In a stroke of market innovation, the subcontracting of digital disinformation in the Philippines has tied the financial and career incentives of competing freelancers to the objectives of national political parties, to devastating effect.

The Danger of No Information

Along with misinformation and disinformation there is another roadblock that keeps you from making good decisions and that is having "No Information". When it benefits you to have information to base an important decision on but you don't have that information it can be detrimental if not catastrophic. Probably one of the most historical examples of this is an incident that happened during the Civil War.

One of the most brilliant of General Robert E. Lee's officers was his cavalry commander Major General James Ewell Brown Stuart, famously known as Jeb Stuart.

Stuart has been justly criticized for his role in allowing the fateful clash at Gettysburg to occur when neither General Robert E. Lee nor his Army of Northern Virginia were properly prepared for the battle. Students of the American Civil War know the story well. While conducting another one of his glorious foraging maneuvers around the enemy Federal army, Stuart strayed too far from Lee, leaving his General blind to the enemy's movements. Parts of the Army of Northern Virginia then while out seeking to find a supply of shoes stumbled into the Federal troops at Gettysburg, thereby initiating a battle that Lee had not planned or prepared to fight.

If Stuart and his cavalry had been doing their job and providing reconnaissance Stuart would have been able to alert Lee that the Federal troops were near him and also let him know the strength in numbers of those troops. Armed with this information Lee could have made a decision to avoid engaging the Federals in battle or at least better prepared his army for the conflict. As a result of Stuart's blunder the two armies wandered right into each other's path and were left with no choice except to fight. In three days of fighting the costs would be horrendous. Casualties at Gettysburg totaled 23,049 for the Federal Union army. That was 3,155 dead, 14,529 wounded, and 5,365 missing. Lee's Confederate army casualties were 28,063, with 3,903 dead, 18,735 injured, and 5,425 missing. That total meant that more than a third of Lee's army would end up as casualties because Lee failed to receive the information that could have helped him decide to avoid one of the bloodiest battles in the history of warfare. After his mistake Stuart's cavalry arrived on the battlefield so late that his troopers could not significantly contribute to the outcome of the battle. The battle of Gettysburg (July 1-3, 1863) is considered the turning point of the Civil War. General Robert E. Lee's defeat by the Army of the Potomac forced his Confederate forces into a retreat from which they would never recover.

You too are fighting battles daily. Battles for your family, for your marriage, for your business, for your friendships, for your education, for your investments, for your retirements, and dozens of other strategic battles that will determine if you will be victorious in this war called life. Make sure that you have all the information you need to make the important decisions that will decide the outcome of these battles. How much money will you need to operate your business the first year? How much money will you need to complete your music project? What permits will you need to legally run you're your business? When you add in insurance, gardening costs, utilities, taxes, home-owners association fees, repairs, and your monthly mortgage how much is this house really going to cost? As history has shown time and again going into battle without the information you need is one of the surest paths to disaster.

Beware of Misleading Information

Having a low unemployment rate is surely a good thing. Right? Politicians love to use unemployment statistics to show that things are getting better. But are they? Don't be misled. A story written for the Observer by Sissi Cao in 2018 explains in simple terms why the improving unemployment rate for the United States is misleading.

The current stage of America's economy is hard to define. While some economists claim we've moved past the post-recession period and entered another pre-recession time, others doubt the recovery is complete.

Per estimates by the Federal Open Market Committee, the economy is considered running at full-speed when the unemployment rate drops to 4.5 percent. However, despite the unemployment rate falling from the 2009 peak of 10 percent to 3.9 percent as of last month, an 18-year low, the average wage has barely grown accordingly. Neither has inflation.

Neel Kashkari, president of the Federal Reserve Bank of Minneapolis (one of the 12 regional Federal Reserve banks), believes the error lies within the unemployment calculation itself.

"The U.S. unemployment rate captures only those who are actively looking for work. For example, it ignores people who are out of the labor force because they have given up looking for a job," he wrote in an op-ed for the Financial Times.

The Great Recession pushed many working-age Americans out of the labor market. Although the economic recovery has brought some of these people back to the workforce, it's unknown how many are still left behind.

According to recent months' statistics from the Labor Department, the "marginally attached" group, defined as people who had not looked for jobs in the four weeks before the Labor Department's monthly job survey, has been slowly rising.

"Backward-looking statistics show nearly a third of these marginally attached Americans are now aged over 55," Andrew Hunter, co-founder of job search engine Adzuna, told the Observer.

That means a lot of people who are still unemployed have simply stopped looking for jobs.

"It could be that the 3.9 percent measure does not capture the true slack in the labor market and that additional, hidden slack explains today's modest wage growth," Kashkari explained.

A more reliable measure of workforce robustness, Kashkari suggested, is the employment-to-population ratio of prime age workers (aged 25 to 54).

"By focusing on prime-age adults, this measure of how many people are actually working helps adjust for demographic trends such as aging," he added.

This ratio, as of today, is 79.2 percent, down from 80 percent in 2007. The difference represents one million people.

"That drop suggests that approximately one million additional prime-age Americans would be available to work if the U.S. labor market recovered to its pre-recession strength," Kashkari wrote.

The prime-age labor participation has also been declining in recent years. Although in some sectors the decline of human labor has been a result of technological advancement, which is actually good news, to the broader economy, this is an alarming sign—particularly when this rate is rising in other developed countries.

According to the most recent data from the San Francisco Fed, prime-age labor participation rates in Germany, Canada and the U.K. all exceeded 85 percent as of 2015.

"Each of these countries is experiencing falling fertility rates and an aging population, just like the U.S." Kashkari noted. "The truth is, we don't know how much slack still remains in the U.S. labor market. But international labor markets offer a hopeful sign that many more Americans might choose to work if wages picked up."

As the article illustrates, beware of how statistics can be used to pretend things are great when they really aren't great at all. Misleading information is bad information that can lead you to make a bad decision. Don't just listen to a bunch of numbers being spouted at you. Investigate those numbers to see how they are measured and research them to understand how significant they are, or if they are relevant at all to your circumstances. Generally, if you are still making what you were making 5 years ago that's not progress because while your pay is stagnant the costs of living rises each year.

Capitalism: The Problem and Solution

Here is the great challenge. Democracy, when it is correctly carried out is a beautiful thing. To have a government "Of the people, By the People, and For the people" would be the ultimate government if that ideal were a reality rather than just an ideal. But, be that as it may our version of democracy may still be the best shot on the planet any ordinary citizen has of succeeding big.

Half Lies and The Whole Truth

Now that you have an idea about some of the tools you will need to elevate your standing in the world it is time to introduce you to your opponent. Like every boxer who dreams of being champion, every business that wants to be top dog, every army that wants to win the battle, every baker who wants to win the bake-off, there are opponents also trying to win that brass ring and few of them are going to just roll over and hand you the prize. Life, whether you like it or not, whether you are prepared to face it or not is about competition. Therefore, competing is something we must seriously address. However, before we talk about competing we must first talk about what arena or game we are competing in.

There is an old saying which says: "A lie is as good as the truth if you can get people to believe it". Spouting half truths (formerly known as lies) seems to be an acceptable behavior for people these days from the President on down. Indeed, it seems to have become the new norm, a preferred strategy even.

The motto for everyone trying to pull something shysty today is "Admit nothing, deny everything, make counter accusations." This phrase is often attributed to embattled American political advisor Roger J. Stone, but most say the phrase was coined by the CIA.

Tell those who are getting rich and richer off that wonderful economic system called Capitalism that they are only using it to enrich themselves while paving the way for the huddled masses to live their lives hopelessly mired in poverty and they will indeed, "Admit nothing, deny everything, and make counter accusations".

The truth is capitalism does not work for the majority. In fact, not only does it not work, it will not and cannot work for the masses, not now, not ever. Truthfully, the only way that capitalism can succeed is for the masses to stay poor therefore providing the labor force needed to keep the wheels of capitalism grinding.

Think of this simple scenario. If everyone in the nation had billions of dollars in the bank like Jeff Bezos, Bill Gates, Warren Buffet, Alice Walton, Robert F. Smith, Oprah Winfrey, and other one-percenters, or were the children of these billionaires, who would be working at the drive-up window to supersize your fries, or collecting your garbage each week, or washing the windows of skyscrapers, or working as crossing guards for your school children, or working all the other necessary jobs it takes to keep the country humming? The fact is, capitalism only works and thrives if there is an underclass (translated: poor folk) to work those everyday, laborious, some say menial jobs that the rich are no longer forced to work to survive. Therefore, when it comes to the plight of the working poor capitalism is part of the problem. As long as capitalism exist and businesses measure success by the amount of profits they make "the poor will always be with you."

Why? Because paying workers a decent wage cuts into profits. So, having Chinese workers produce a product for you at .30 cent an hour leaves more money for profit after sells than paying American workers $15 an hour to produce the same product, even after the cost of importing those products. Long as profits are the name of the game in business many companies are going to outsource their production work to countries that can produce their products cheaper. That is the problem globalization has created for us. You may love the cheaper prices you see in stores but those cheaper prices come with a hidden cost and that cost for you equals lower wages or even unemployment. Capitalism is the game you are playing my friend and your opponent is globalization (i.e. the world). Unfortunately, what's good for capitalism may be bad for you. That is why you need to understand how to play the game and play it to win. That is why you must re-engineer your life if you want to succeed.

It would be easy to paint capitalism, or business, or specific corporations as "The Enemy" or the Death Star but it's not that simple. That would be like a player saying football, baseball, basketball, tennis, soccer, or hockey are the enemy. They are just games. How you relate to these games or more importantly how you play these games, and how well you are compensated to play these games determines whether they are beneficial to you or detrimental. Some players make millions for playing these games while others make only thousands. Others don't get paid at all to play these games because they don't have the required skills or level of talent to play the game at a high enough level to warrant compensation. More on that later.

Paradoxically, even though capitalism is a major part of the problem for the masses of poor people in the world it is also a major part of the solution. Examine the philanthropic generosity that some of the world's most profitable companies have displayed over the past few years. Their charitable donations have certainly helped to improve the lives of many. Here is a list of such companies and their contributions courtesy of CareerAddict:

1. Gilead Sciences Total cash donation in 2015: $446.7 million (£333.2 million)
2. Walmart Total cash donation in 2015: $301 million (£224.5 million)
3. Wells Fargo Total cash donation in 2017: $286.5 million (£213.7 million)
4. Goldman Sachs Total cash donation in 2015: $168.5 million (£125.7 million)
5. ExxonMobil Total cash donation in 2015: $168.5 million (£125.7 million)
6. JPMorgan Chase Total cash donation in 2017: $250 million (£186.5 million)
7. Chevron Total cash donation in 2015: $168.5 million (£125.7 million)
8. Microsoft Total cash donation in 2017: $169 million (£126 million)
9. Bank of America Total cash donation in 2015: $168.5 million (£125.7 million)
10. Alphabet (Google) Total cash donation in 2015: $167.8 million (£125.1 million)
11. Citigroup Total cash donation in 2015: $142.8 million (£106.5 million)
12. Merck Total cash donation in 2015: $132.5 million (£98.8 million)
13. Coca-Cola Total cash donation in 2015: $117.3 million (£87.5 million)

If all companies made it a policy and a goal to include philanthropy as part of their purpose it would surely help to make the world a better place. By supplying more money and resources to fight the ills of the world it would give charities and organizations dedicated to working for the social good more ammunition to fight things like hunger, disease, genocide, crime, natural disasters, and other problems plaguing the world. Looking at some of the social issues these companies address and hope to alleviate it's clear to see what an impact a socially conscious form of capitalism could have on the world.

The good corporations do of course does not erase the bad some of them choose to do. Pollution, global warming, harmful products, destructive methods and ingredients, unfair wages, discrimination, unsafe workplaces, sexism, racism, and a host of other problems can still be found in various places of business. These practices must be weeded out before any business can truly be proclaimed as a benefactor to society. However, seeing the rise of socially responsible companies is a start. As an example, here's some of the ways the above-named companies positively impact society.

Few companies are as socially conscious or prolific as pharmaceutical giant **Gilead**. Through their foundation, they are responsible for the funding of numerous national and international public health campaigns (especially HIV and Hepatitis awareness and prevention), as well as working closely with non-profits and medical professionals in areas where their products are more difficult to access.

With a staggering annual revenue of $500 billion (£373 billion), **Walmart** can afford to be generous. As with most other large corporations, the main thrust of their philanthropy is focused towards economic development, environmental sustainability and the advancement of communities through construction and engagement projects. Their 2.3 million employees are also active, having contributed well over a million hours of their own time to charitable causes in 2016.

In support with its sister organization, the **Wells Fargo** Foundation, the financial services provider is fully committed to its philanthropic contribution. The company focuses on funding non-profit organizations that are aligned with its own values, specifically in the social, economic and environmental sectors. Aside from donating monetary funds, Wells Fargo also offers a willing workforce of volunteers, as well as the pro bono provision of its own services.

Through its internal foundation, **Goldman Sachs** Gives, the New York-based investment giant claims to have provided a total of $1.25 billion (£932.4 million) in grants since its inception, partnering on projects with thousands of organizations including the United Nations. Most recently, this has seen the bank donate heavily to those affected by the Syrian refugee crisis, although the majority of funding destinations are recommended by a dedicated board of current and retired senior employees.

With a culture of giving that stretches as far back as the 1950s, the **ExxonMobil** Foundation – rebranded in 2000 – has targeted a variety of areas in which it donates significantly. Currently, this includes the development of STEM education programs, women's economic initiatives and, increasingly, funding into the research of malaria.

Having established its own dedicated trust, **JPMorgan Chase** has been hugely proactive in donating money in recent years; in 2017, this sum reached $250 million, with a commitment to invest $1.75 billion (£1.35 billion) overall by 2023. If you want to get your hands on some of that money, the firm currently prioritizes donation requests within four specialist sectors: jobs and skills, small business expansion, financial health, and neighborhood revitalization.

As a major global oil and energy conglomerate, **Chevron**'s reputation is of vital importance for investors. One of the ways in which they seek to maintain a positive image is by donating heavily to various charitable causes. Primarily, this takes the shape of supporting economic development in the areas in which it drills, such as the west coast of Africa. Closer to home, Chevron is active in pushing STEM development opportunities within the education sector. According to Forbes, the oil giant also donates to the Clinton Foundation, as well as pursues economic empowerment for women in Latin America.

Under the guidance of Bill Gates – one of the world's most prominent philanthropists – **Microsoft** has sought to set itself apart from the crowd with its charitable giving; Microsoft Philanthropies was established in 2015 to build on this legacy, with jaw-dropping results so far. Although $169 million in cash was donated by the company itself, Microsoft's employees also raised $149 million (£111.1 million) in matched individual donations in 2017. The company also gave well over $1.2 billion (£895.1 million) worth of free software and hardware to various non-profits during this time. It's not just about the fiscal figures, either; staff gave up nearly 700,000 hours of their own time to work on projects, following the illustrious example set by their legendary co-founder.

Bank of America has initiated two signature development programs within the last 10 years, claiming to have invested over $200 million (£149.2 million) during that time. These programs are targeted at arming external non-profits with the tools they need to build community projects, as well as offering internships and development opportunities to promising high school students.

As you would expect from such a progressive organization, **Alphabet** – **Google**'s holding company – is at the forefront of corporate philanthropy. They established Google.org in 2005 to aid external non-profits through cash donations and the use of Google's many cutting-edge technologies, utilizing data and research to align with the most suitable partners. This sense of efficiency is present at the ground level, too, with employee volunteer opportunities matched to the individual's skillset; Google also matches personal contributions, having done so to the tune of $50 million (£37.3 million) in the last decade.

With the enormous swathes of money circulating throughout the investment banking sector, it's little surprise that many large financial institutions give generously to charity. **Citigroup** is no exception, with the New York-based firm focusing especially on economic opportunities for young people, as well as urban transformation projects that create additional opportunities for low-income workers. Citigroup actively encourages volunteer participation amongst its workforce, too, particularly within its signature Pathways to Progress program where staff work with young people in urban areas to develop key employability skills.

Pharmaceuticals firm **Merck** is consistently active in their philanthropic endeavors, particularly in the fields of science, education and environmental sustainability. The company heavily funds research into disease management, for instance, as well as provides numerous scholarship opportunities and STEM development programs within the education system. Merck also provides donations in lieu of cash, such as providing water filtration devices to areas affected by natural disasters like Thailand and the Philippines, while also matching individual employee contributions up to $1,000 (£745) per year.

Having established a purpose-built company foundation in 1984, the global soft drinks giant claims to have given back more than $820 million (£611.6 million) since. This is supported by its pledge to donate 1% of its previous year's operating income each year. In terms of where the money actually goes, **Coca-Cola** lists three areas of priority. These are the economic empowerment and entrepreneurial development of women; the education and youth development of local communities across the globe; and, finally, access to and the conservation of clean drinking water in deprived areas.

Capitalism has also been the source of the wealth that has allowed some of the world's most generous individual philanthropists to give billions to charitable causes. Names such as Warren Buffett, Bill & Melinda Gates; Michael Bloomberg; The Walton Family; George Soros; Mark Zuckerberg & Priscilla Chan; Gordon & Betty Moore; James & Marilyn Simons; Hansjoerg Wyss; Dustin Moskovitz & Cari Tuna; John & Laura Arnold; Pierre Omidyar; Michael & Susan Dell; and Charles Koch are some of America's leading philanthropists.

Of course, being rich and generous does not automatically qualify you as being a good person. Former CBS Chief Executive Les Moonves is one of the latest high-powered entertainment figures to be ousted from his perch in the #MeToo era. The movie producer Harvey Weinstein has been accused by scores of women of sexual assault and now faces felony charges. Matt Lauer stepped down as the anchor of NBC's most valuable news program, "Today," after several women alleged incidents of sexual harassment. Charlie Rose of CBS and PBS left the airwaves after he, too, was implicated by multiple women. And Fox News saw the departures of its founding executive Roger Ailes and its top-rated host, Bill O'Reilly. You can toss hotel tycoon Steve Wynn, actors Kevin Spacey, Bill Cosby and others on that pile as well. All of those men have denied any nonconsensual sexual activity but the substantial accusations remain.

The point being made is that there are some generous individuals in this non-perfect world who are using the immense wealth they have earned thanks to capitalism to help solve some difficult social problems. It is odd for any entity to contribute to both the problem and solution of world troubles but capitalism continues to do just that. Through raising wages, providing workers with better benefits, and remaining the primary source of resources used for philanthropy, capitalism can make a greater effort to tip the scales toward being more of a solution and less of a problem on the world stage. If you think capitalism and the wealthy are only the problem you're wrong. If you think capitalism and the wealthy are the only solution you're also wrong. Hopefully, by following The Blueprint and re-engineering your life you can become part of the solution to the world's problems.

Rebuilding Your Mental Data Base

Once you access the amount of information stored in your mind you will most likely discover that your mind is packed full with cargo containers of bad information put there by friends, family, teachers, preachers, bosses, politicians, the media, your haters, enemies, and a plethora of other people who had ulterior motives for feeding you the information they sold you. If you truly want to move forward with your life and begin to think and act on a higher level the first step toward this new better life is to wipe your mind clean of this refuge and totally rebuild your mental data base. Why? Because it is seriously unwise to construct a beautiful new building on a bad old eroding foundation.

Decisions

Remind yourself constantly that life, your life, everyone's life amounts to no more than the decisions we make. Make good decisions and you'll have a good life, make bad decisions and you'll have a bad life, make horrible decisions and you'll live a horrible life. Your decisions are the building blocks of your life and those building blocks are made from the information you have acquired over the years. Information that may be helpful or harmful. Making decisions is like cooking a meal. The meal may look good, smell good, even taste good, but if it contains some deadly toxins like salmonella or E. coli it can kill you anyway. You may make decisions that sound good, look good, even feel good but if those decisions are made by using bad or false information it can end up throwing your life into a deadly tailspin that you may never fully recover from. There are cautionary tales aplenty about people who could have lived exceptionally good lives if not for the bad decisions they made. The tragedy of Len Bias is one of the most heartbreaking.

Leonard Kevin Bias was a first-team All-American college basketball player at the University of Maryland. He was selected by the Boston Celtics as the second overall pick in the 1986 NBA draft on June 17, held in New York City at Madison Square Garden. Red Auerbach, the Celtics' president and general manager, had dealt guard Gerald Henderson and cash to the Seattle SuperSonics for the pick in 1984. After the draft, Bias and his family returned to their suburban Maryland home. On June 18, Bias and his father flew to Boston, Massachusetts, from Washington, D.C., for an NBA club draft acceptance and product endorsement signing ceremony with the Celtics' coaches and management. Bias also had discussions with Reebok's sports marketing division regarding a five-year endorsement package worth $1.6 million.

After returning home to Maryland, Bias retrieved his newly leased sports car and drove back to his room on the campus of the University of Maryland. He then dined with some teammates and a member of the football team. He left campus at approximately 2 a.m. on Thursday, June 19 and drove to an off-campus gathering, which he attended briefly before returning to his dorm in Washington Hall sometime between 2:30 and 3 a.m. For the next three to four hours, Bias, longtime friend Brian Tribble and several teammates repeatedly insufflated cocaine in the dormitory suite shared by Bias and his teammates. According to the campus timeline, Bias had a seizure and collapsed between 6:25 and 6:32 a.m. while talking with teammate Terry Long. At 6:32 a.m., when the 911 call to Prince George's County emergency services was made by Tribble, Bias was unconscious and not breathing. All attempts by the emergency medical team to restart his heart and breathing were unsuccessful. After additional attempts to revive him at Leland Memorial Hospital in Riverdale, Maryland, Bias was pronounced dead at 8:55 a.m. of a cardiac arrhythmia related to usage of cocaine. It was reported that there were no other drugs or alcohol found in his system.

Dr. John E. Smialek attributed Bias' death directly to cocaine, "which interrupted the normal electrical control of his heartbeat, resulting in the sudden onset of seizures and cardiac arrest."

Len Bias died of "cocaine intoxication" after ingesting an unusually pure dose of the drug that stopped his heart within minutes, Maryland's chief medical examiner said.

We are left to wonder what were the mistakes that led to this tragedy. Was Bias the victim of misinformation? Did someone perhaps a friend innocently convince Bias that cocaine was harmless? Was it misinformation that led to his fatal decision? Was Bias a casualty of having No Information? Did he participate in what he thought was a harmless celebratory use of cocaine because he had no information that told him how deadly using cocaine could be? Sadly, we'll never know how great Len Bias could have been because the decision he made robbed him and us of all he could have achieved.

Costly decisions happen every day in every aspect of life including business. Today, Google is valued at over $180 billion, which is a lot more than the $750,000 sale price that was offered to Internet portal Excite to purchase Google in 1999. At the time, Excite was a highly-trafficked search engine that was at the forefront of the dot-com boom. Google founders Larry Page and Sergey Brin, had initially attempted to sale their search engine for $1 million but eventually reduced their asking price by $250,000. Excite's CEO George Bell turned down their offer. A few years later, Excite was purchased by AskJeeves following a major decline in the value of its own stock. Like all business decisions you can be sure that this one was preceded by plenty of research. So, what information, misinformation, disinformation, or misleading information led to Bell's terrible decision?

Bad decisions in the form of bad judgement are often at the center of failed relationships. In 2009, America was shaken by reports that Tiger Woods had engaged in multiple illicit sexual affairs. Within a year, Tiger was on the end of a $750 million divorce settlement paid to his wife Elin Nordegren. The total cost of Wood's mistake was even higher if you include the loss of revenue from endorsement deals from Nike, Gatorade, Buick and other sponsors. One professor of economics put the cost as high as $12 billion for Tiger's indiscretions. What faulty information we might ask led Tiger to think his careless decisions would be played out without a cost to his marriage and his wallet?

People cry about misfortune. They bemoan accidents and natural disasters and those bad things that happen to good people but bad decisions spawned from faulty information destroy more lives than all of history's natural calamities put together.

If we want to avoid the mistakes that have befallen others in the past on every level, in every area and aspect of life we must press delete to empty our minds of wrong information, information that sabotages our good efforts and leads us to make bad decisions. Then we must begin to refill our minds with data that is based on truthful, factual, beneficial information from reliable sources who are not skuing or altering information to favor their own point of view.

You are responsible for doing your own research and fact checking information to make sure it is accurate and truthful. You must be hungry to learn, diligent in arming yourself with useful information and not lazy or gullible enough to digest whatever information you are fed. Investigate. Always investigate.

If you are truly striving to better yourself and improve your circumstances you must also value your time and not waste it away watching reality TV, scrolling endlessly through social media sites, gossiping with friends, or having pity parties. You must understand that these various entities were created to consume your time and cash in by turning your eyeball engagement time into advertising dollars. People, companies, and special interest groups are taking advantage of you for their benefit. You have to be invested enough in your own life to make each minute count. You must strive to make each day yield something that moves you closer to being the best version of yourself. That takes harvesting as much useful information as you possibly can and using that information to make the best decisions you can make. Decisions about what you're doing and what you should be doing instead. What your goals are and what your goals should be instead. How you are using your time and how you should be using your time. Who you are spending your time with and who you should be spending time with. How you are using your resources and how you should be using your resources.

Begin with this premise, "Everything You Know Is Wrong." Then step by step look for the proof in every strand of information before accepting its validity. You owe yourself that much. No more betting the family farm on whims or someone else's hunches or faulty facts. Again, no one is coming to rescue you. You are your own liberator. Stop assigning your well-being to everyone else. Accept responsibility for your own welfare. Stop basing your decisions on half lies and refuse to accept anything but the whole truth. Once you know the truth If you remain in captivity it will be because you have chosen to do so. Not because freedom is beyond your reach. Step one is get your mind right. This I know to be true, "You'll never be able to grow a good crop if you're planting it in bad soil."

Chapter 2: Rewiring Your Mind

Restructuring The Mental Landscape

Now it is time to start laying track, to start building on the foundation of sturdy information you have so carefully put in place. We begin this process with Chapter 2: Rewiring Your Mind, where we start the important work of restructuring your mental landscape. Education without learning information beneficial to your goals is useless. It is better to be self-taught than book taught if your formal education yields little or no information that is useful. If your self-learning has yielded a wealth of useful information the value of that learning is obvious. The value of your treasure lay not in where you discovered it but instead in the fact that you discovered riches.

The following names may sound familiar: (writers and artists) August Wilson, Ernest Hemingway, Mark Twain, Ray Bradbury, Leonardo da Vinci, Jean Michel Basquiat, Vincent van Gogh, William Faulkner, Herman Melville, Eugene O'Neill, John Steinbeck, Truman Capote; (musicians) Jimi Hendrix, Keith Moon, Nas, David Bowie, Eminem, Frank Zappa, Bruce Springsteen, Kurt Cobain, Dave Grohl, Errol Garner; (engineers and inventors) Frank Lloyd Wright, Nikola Tesla, Granville Woods, Wilbur and Orville Wright, Thomas Alva Edison, Henry Ford, R.G. LeTourneau, Sean Parker; (Historical Figures) Harry S. Truman, Frederick Douglass, Malcolm X, Booker T. Washington, Benjamin Franklin, and hundreds of other self-taught successes didn't let their lack of a college education stop them. You can add to this list college drop-outs like Bill Gates, Michael Dell, Steve Jobs and other super successful icons.

The above names represent two things: People who achieved great things and people who are for the most part self-taught. You may have dropped out before finishing high school, received no more than a high school education or G.E.D., or dropped out before completing college but don't let that discourage you or keep you from accomplishing great things.

From the day you were born you have been amassing knowledge, sometimes consciously and sometimes unconsciously. That knowledge forms a kind of human data base. A data base you draw information from to make day to day decisions. Some decisions you make are relatively unimportant but others are hugely important. The more useful and relevant information you have in your data base the better decisions you're going to make. It doesn't matter how you acquired that good information. Knowing it and having it at your disposal is what matters. If you learned it at school or through formal education, wonderful. If you learned it through your own research or from someone else, all the better because it shows that you took the initiative to learn something on your own.

Throughout your life you are going to be faced with various problems. You'll be required to make decisions on how to best solve or somehow overcome those problems. In those times you'll need to reach into your data base and pull out information that will help you. Solve problems well and you'll become a success. If you can't solve them... your life is going to be a series of ups and downs, starts and stops, disappointments and failures. That kind of life is usually not a happy one. All things being equal, the more focused and well stocked your data base, the better your decisions. The better your decisions the greater your success. The greater your success the happier your life.

You may ask how important is it for you to make good decisions? Will making good decisions make you any more successful than the next person? To answer that question maybe we should look at the salary compensation of those people who get paid to basically make decisions.

Chief Executive Officers (CEOs) who run major corporations get paid what may seem like ridiculous amounts of money to run giant businesses because of their ability to make good decisions. Decisions that in turn help these companies to earn millions and in some cases billions of dollars. Naturally, other skills like leadership, the ability to organize and motivate workers, the ability to articulate the company vision, and various other abilities factor into why they are valued so highly and compensated so much. But, the key to their worth lay in their ability to process the available information they are given and make good, if not great decisions. That ability leads companies to pay these executives millions of dollars annually. Their compensation amounts to dozens, sometimes even hundreds of times what the average worker at the company makes a year.

Ask yourself this question. If the top corporations in the world value making decisions so highly, why does the average person value decision making so little? If these corporations and CEOs with all their resources and data take sometimes weeks and months to make important decisions, why do we with our limited resources and small amount of information sometimes make important decisions in only hours or minutes?

Here is a list (courtesy of USA Today) of the **top 10 paid CEOs for 2018,** what they make annually, and how many times greater their salaries are than the average workers at their companies. Maybe this list will inspire you to esteem good decision making more highly in your own life.

10. Stephen Kaufer: Company: TripAdvisor (TRIP), Annual compensation: $43.2 million, Company revenue: $1.6 billion, CEO pay vs. median employee salary: 481x greater.

9. Ron Clarke: Company: FleetCor Technologies (FLT), Annual compensation: $45.1 million, Company revenue: $2.2 billion, CEO pay vs. median employee salary: 1,517x greater.

8. Jeff Bewkes: Company: Time Warner (TWX), Annual compensation: $49.0 million, Company revenue: N/A, CEO pay vs. median employee salary: 651x greater.

7. Dexter Goei, Company: Altice USA (ATUS), Annual compensation: $53.6 million, Company revenue: $9.3 billion, CEO pay vs. median employee salary: N/A

6. W. Nicholas Howley: Company: TransDigm Group (TDG), Annual compensation: $61.0 million, Company revenue: $3.8 billion, CEO pay vs. median employee salary: N/A

5. Gregory Maffei: Company: Liberty Media & Qurate Retail Group (FWONA & QRTEA), Annual compensation: $67.2 million, Company revenue: N/A, CEO pay vs. median employee salary: N/A

4. Leslie Moonves: Company: CBS (CBS), Annual compensation: $68.4 million, Company revenue: $13.7 billion, CEO pay vs. median employee salary: 595x greater.

3. Michael Rapino: Company: Live Nation Entertainment (LYV), Annual compensation: $70.6 million, Company revenue: $10.3 billion, CEO pay vs. median employee salary: 2,893x greater.

2. Frank Bisignano: Company: First Data (FDC), Annual compensation: $102.2 million, Company revenue: $12.1 billion, CEO pay vs. median employee salary: 2,028x greater.

1. Hock E. Tan: Company: Broadcom (AVGO), Annual compensation: $103.2 million, Company revenue: N/A, CEO pay vs. median employee salary: N/A

Go ahead and scream, "These salaries are ridiculous!" Possibly so. Why should anyone be paid millions of dollars a year to run any company? Especially when the workers who labor for that company under that CEO make so little in comparison? All things considered maybe paying a CEO millions to help a company earn billions is all relative. Whatever your thoughts on the subject of CEOs and their salaries the point I hope to make is this: what value should you be placing on your decision making and how carefully should you be compiling the daily information that will help you make great decisions for your own benefit?

Now that you are a little more enlightened about the importance of gathering information and decision making you may ask what is the best way for you to fully stock your mental data base? Glad you asked. Here are some important things to consider.

Programming

Information floods into your mind every day. The internet, television, radio, magazines, mail, billboards, flyers, books, menus, conversations, what you see, what you taste, what you touch, what you hear, what you smell, these and dozens of other sources deposit information into you. Your brain is one of the most complex systems in nature. In essence, it is like a super-computer. To understand how your brain processes all this information let's take a brief course in brainology and see what we are working with as we build our mental data base. Understanding how the brain works will be helpful to our process.

The Brain And How It Works

If you are not interested in how the brain works you can actually skip this section on the brain. But if you are game to dive deeper here we go. The brain is divided into two halves, called hemispheres. There is evidence that each brain hemisphere has its own distinct functions, a phenomenon referred to as lateralization. The left hemisphere appears to dominate the functions of speech, language processing and comprehension, and logical reasoning, while the right is more dominant in spatial tasks like vision-independent object recognition (such as identifying an object by touch or another nonvisual sense). However, while it is easy to exaggerate the differences between the functions of the left and right hemispheres; both hemispheres are involved with most processes. Additionally, neuroplasticity (the ability of a brain to adapt to experience) enables the brain to compensate for damage to one hemisphere by taking on extra functions in the other half, especially in young brains.

The cerebral cortex, the largest part of the brain, is the ultimate control and information-processing center in the brain. The cerebral cortex is responsible for many higher-order brain functions such as sensation, perception, memory, association, thought, and voluntary physical action.

The two hemispheres communicate with one another through the corpus callosum. The corpus callosum is a wide, flat bundle of neural fibers beneath the cortex that connects the left and right cerebral hemispheres and facilitates interhemispheric communication. The corpus callosum is sometimes implicated in the cause of seizures. Patients with epilepsy sometimes undergo a corpus callostomy, or the removal of the corpus callosum.

The brain is separated into four lobes: the frontal, temporal, occipital, and parietal lobes. The frontal lobe is associated with executive functions and motor performance. Executive functions are some of the highest-order cognitive processes that humans have. Examples include:

- planning and engaging in goal-directed behavior;
- recognizing future consequences of current actions;

- choosing between good and bad actions;
- overriding and suppressing socially unacceptable responses;
- determining similarities and differences between objects or situations.

The frontal lobe is considered to be the moral center of the brain because it is responsible for advanced decision-making processes. It also plays an important role in retaining emotional memories derived from the limbic system and modifying those emotions to fit socially accepted norms.

The temporal lobe is associated with the retention of short- and long-term memories. It processes sensory input including auditory information, language comprehension, and naming. It also creates emotional responses and controls biological drives such as aggression and sexuality.

The temporal lobe contains the hippocampus, which is the memory center of the brain. The hippocampus plays a key role in the formation of emotion-laden, long-term memories based on emotional input from the amygdala. The left temporal lobe holds the primary auditory cortex, which is important for processing the semantics of speech.

One specific portion of the temporal lobe, Wernicke's area, plays a key role in speech comprehension. Another portion, Broca's area, underlies the ability to produce (rather than understand) speech. Patients with damage to Wernicke's area can speak clearly but the words make no sense, while patients with damage to Broca's area will fail to form words properly and speech will be halting and slurred. These disorders are known as Wernicke's and Broca's aphasia respectively; an aphasia is an inability to speak.

The occipital lobe contains most of the visual cortex and is the visual processing center of the brain. Cells on the posterior side of the occipital lobe are arranged as a spatial map of the retinal field. The visual cortex receives raw sensory information through sensors in the retina of the eyes, which is then conveyed through the optic tracts to the visual cortex. Other areas of the occipital lobe are specialized for different visual tasks, such as visuospatial processing, color discrimination, and motion perception. Damage to the primary visual cortex (located on the surface of the posterior occipital lobe) can cause blindness, due to the holes in the visual map on the surface of the cortex caused by the lesions.

The parietal lobe is associated with sensory skills. It integrates different types of sensory information and is particularly useful in spatial processing and navigation. The parietal lobe plays an important role in integrating sensory information from various parts of the body, understanding numbers and their relations, and manipulating objects. It also processes information related to the sense of touch.

The parietal lobe is comprised of the somatosensory cortex and part of the visual system. The somatosensory cortex consists of a "map" of the body that processes sensory information from specific areas of the body. Several portions of the parietal lobe are important to language and visuospatial processing; the left parietal lobe is involved in symbolic functions in language and mathematics, while the right parietal lobe is specialized to process images and interpretation of maps (i.e., spatial relationships).

The limbic system is a complex set of structures found on the central underside of the cerebrum, comprising inner sections of the temporal lobes and the bottom of the frontal lobe. It combines higher mental functions and primitive emotion into a single system often referred to as the emotional nervous system. It is not only responsible for our emotional lives but also our higher mental functions, such as learning and formation of memories. The limbic system is the reason that some physical things such as eating seem so pleasurable to us, and the reason why some medical conditions, such as high blood pressure, are caused by mental stress. There are several important structures within the limbic system: the amygdala, hippocampus, thalamus, hypothalamus, basal ganglia, and cingulate gyrus.

The amygdala is a small almond-shaped structure. There is one located in each of the left and right temporal lobes. Known as the emotional center of the brain, the amygdala is involved in evaluating the emotional valence of situations (e.g., happy, sad, scary). It helps the brain recognize potential threats and helps prepare the body for fight-or-flight reactions by increasing heart and breathing rate. The amygdala is also responsible for learning on the basis of reward or punishment.

Due to its close proximity to the hippocampus, the amygdala is involved in the modulation of memory consolidation, particularly emotionally-laden memories. Emotional arousal following a learning event influences the strength of the subsequent memory of that event, so that greater emotional arousal following a learning event enhances a person's retention of that memory. In fact, experiments have shown that administering stress hormones to individuals immediately after they learn something enhances their retention when they are tested two weeks later.

The hippocampus is found deep in the temporal lobe and is shaped like a seahorse. It consists of two horns curving back from the amygdala. Psychologists and neuroscientists dispute the precise role of the hippocampus, but generally agree that it plays an essential role in the formation of new memories about past experiences. Some researchers consider the hippocampus to be responsible for general declarative memory (memories that can be explicitly verbalized, such as memory of facts and episodic memory).

Damage to the hippocampus usually results in profound difficulties in forming new memories (anterograde amnesia) and may also affect access to memories formed prior to the damage (retrograde amnesia). Although the retrograde effect normally extends some years prior to the brain damage, in some cases older memories remain intact; this leads to the idea that over time the hippocampus becomes less important in the storage of memory.

Both the thalamus and hypothalamus are associated with changes in emotional reactivity. **The thalamus,** which is a sensory "way-station" for the rest of the brain, is primarily important due to its connections with other limbic-system structures. The hypothalamus is a small part of the brain located just below the thalamus on both sides of the third ventricle. Lesions of the hypothalamus interfere with several unconscious functions (such as respiration and metabolism) and some so-called motivated behaviors like sexuality, combativeness, and hunger. The lateral parts of the hypothalamus seem to be involved with pleasure and rage, while the medial part is linked to aversion, displeasure, and a tendency for uncontrollable and loud laughter.

The cingulate gyrus is located in the medial side of the brain next to the corpus callosum. There is still much to be learned about this gyrus, but it is known that its frontal part links smells and sights with pleasant memories of previous emotions. This region also participates in our emotional reaction to pain and in the regulation of aggressive behavior.

The basal ganglia is a group of nuclei lying deep in the subcortical white matter of the frontal lobes that organizes motor behavior. The caudate, putamen, and globus pallidus are major components of the basal ganglia. The basal ganglia appears to serve as a gating mechanism for physical movements, inhibiting potential movements until they are fully appropriate for the circumstances in which they are to be executed. The basal ganglia is also involved with:

- rule-based habit learning (e.g., initiating, stopping, monitoring, temporal sequencing, and maintaining the appropriate movement);
- inhibiting undesired movements and permitting desired ones;
- choosing from potential actions;
- motor planning;
- sequencing;
- predictive control;
- working memory;
- attention.

The Gatekeeper

With so much information flooding into your brain each day it is imperative that you have some type of filter to keep the negative and harmful information out. This filter or Gatekeeper if you will is charged with turning away the bad influences from entering your mental data base. Why a gatekeeper? Remember our detrimental intruders misinformation, disinformation, and misleading information? They only muddy the water when it is decision time. If you can simplify the decision-making process by rejecting or eliminating bad information it helps your decision to be made faster and with a greater chance of being the right decision.

If someone told you to count all the red apples in a barrel and the barrel was full of not only red apples but green and yellow ones as well it would help the process if the apples that are not red could be removed before you start counting. The same goes for information that is detrimental or not useful to you.

It seems today everyone is promising something or selling something. We already had TV, radio, telephone, and the mail trying to deliver information to us. With the internet now added to the fray everyone is accessible, and with access comes excess. Like everyone else you are probably being drowned in a sea of mostly useless information. As far back as 2011 a study by the EMC Corporation found that the amount of data stored on Earth doubles every two years, meaning the amount of data that will be created over the next 24 months will be greater than all the data ever produced in history. There is so much data out there that intelligence agencies like the CIA, FBI, and Homeland Security are now using AI (artificial intelligence) to sift through it all in an effort to catch the bad guys and keep us safe. I'm sure you can't afford to go to those extremes so you will have to be vigilant enough to be your own gatekeeper and block harmful information yourself.

A much-quoted bible passage says, "life and death are in the power of the tongue".

Meaning: words alone are powerful enough to bring you life or death. It is up to you to filter out those words that speak death to you and allow in those words that speak life. This is an almost nonstop process. Words of death are trying to gain entry into your mind through the lyrics of songs, tv commercials and programs, social media sites, telephone conversations, billboard signs, and hundreds of other sources. No wonder you often feel drained at the close of the day even when you haven't participated in any physical activity. It is the ongoing battle for your mind that is wearing you out. As tiring as waging this war of information is you must wage it or become a casualty of it.

Time And Money

Don't Waste Time or Money

You spend hours watching dysfunctional people on reality TV shows and wonder why you seem to be getting more short-tempered week by week, and why your family is showing signs of dysfunction. Why kids appear to have no respect for parents, men seem to have no respect for women, women seem to have little trust in men, and few seem to have any respect for authority after repetitively listening to messages of misogyny, sexism, anger, rage, prejudice and rebellion. How can you expect your mind to have a positive outlook when you are allowing these negative messages to saturate your mind constantly? If you were a world class athlete competing in the Olympic games would you tell yourself daily that "you have no chance of winning, you are the worst athlete on the planet, your coaches are terrible, the referees are cheaters, and everyone hates you?" If you spoke those negative things to yourself constantly how do you think it would affect your performance? You must employ yourself as a gatekeeper to guard your mind. If not this flood of negativity will sweep away your chances for success like a violent flood. When it comes to guarding your mind it really is you against the world.

The main reason you don't want to fall prey to negativity or useless information is it drains your energy. Another reason to avoid people who bring you useless information is because they waste your time. Every time you allow the whiners, complainers, gossips, and soul-sucking time wasters to consume your valuable time and chew on your ear they drain you of energy you could be using to do something productive. Whether you are rich or poor, young or old, a PhD or high school dropout, everyone has the same 24 hours in their day. It's not time that separates those who succeed from those who fail but rather how each person uses their time. There are things we have to do with our time like eat, sleep, work, and travel to and from important activities. These things take time. But, there are other things we don't have to do but do them nonetheless. Sitting on the phone listening to friends complain about the same issues over and over. Reading and commenting daily on social media sites. Watching news cycles repeat the same information again and again. Watching hours of television. These and other activities that do not push you closer to your financial or family goals are time wasters and big drains on your energy that you must avoid if you want to achieve the success you are always talking about. I can't say this enough. You only get 24 hours a day. DON'T LET PEOPLE WASTE YOUR TIME and ENERGY.

Time really Is Money

People who don't have money always think that money is the most precious resource. While people who have money know that time is our most precious resource. These two viewpoints are why people who don't have money usually find it so hard to make some and people who have money find it easier to make more. Money can be increased and multiplied. But time is what it is. An hour is always an hour. And 10 minutes no matter how you slice it is still just 10 minutes. When it comes to time management take a tip from those who have achieved massive success. If you want to achieve massive success you must manage your time wisely. Here are **12 daily time management routines** that successful people find helpful.

1. How you start your day impacts the entire day. Therefore, it is always best to start your day with positivity and energy. Getting up an hour before the rest of the family so you can have some time to yourself is a good routine (especially for female entrepreneurs).

2. Create a morning routine to get your brain started such as listening to motivational tracks as you get dressed. It feeds and motivates your brain during what is usually just dead time. Do some light exercise to get the endorphins going. Then eat a nice light breakfast like oatmeal and fruit. Don't weigh yourself down with a big heavy breakfast that your body will then have to spend a lot of time and energy digesting. If you are having fresh fruit or something that takes prep time do your chopping and cutting at night and store it so you don't waste time preparing it in the morning.

48

3. Your brain works most efficiently during the first couple of hours after you wake. So, use the first few hours to take care of your MIT's (most important tasks). Once you have completed these you have gotten the day off to a great start. Then you can move on to other tasks.

4. Warren Buffett, Chairman of Berkshire Hathaway, one of the greatest investors of all time, and one of the world's wealthiest people says: "successful people say no to nearly everything." They understand every commitment they make may make them lose out on better opportunities. By saying "No" they save their most precious asset, Time, for important things. They don't agree to any requests that will not support their top priorities.

5. To work more efficiently apply The Pareto principle (also known as the 80/20 rule) named after Italian economist Vilfredo Pareto. It states that, for many events, roughly 80% of the effects come from 20% of the causes. Meaning: that a certain 20% of your work leads to 80% of the results you get. Therefore, you will work most efficiently by finding and applying your efforts to that important 20% of your workload that produces the 80% of your results.

6. Many people think they make the most of their time by multi-tasking but successful people understand that multitasking is a time waster. Studies show that humans are not designed to multitask. You will be more efficient and better your performance by focusing on one task and finishing it before going on to the next one.

7. Use your lunch for a midday break to recharge your battery. If there is a gym in the building use it for a quick exercise. Or relax away from your desk somewhere quiet and listen to music to give your mind a break from work. Then you can return to work refreshed with energy to finish the day strong.

8. After lunch is a good time to bunch those tasks that can be done quickly and knock them out. The end of the workday is usually reserved for things that are lower priorities but need to get done. Also, this is time to set up things for the following day.

9. If you are in a leadership position removing a formal meeting from your schedule can save a lot of everyone's time. Set up

meetings only when other types of communication don't work. Steve Jobs was famous for avoiding meetings. Instead, he replaced them with short walks around the workplace. Billionaire Mark Cuban famously said: "don't waste time in meetings. Do them only when someone is writing a check."

10. Successful people are never too busy to read. They make sure reading is a priority. Read newspapers and blogs on the way to work if you are not driving. Or, listen to audible books or podcast if you drive to work. Also, set aside time to read nonfiction (biographies or autobiographies) in the evenings when you return home. A big part of staying successful is staying informed and reading is a sure way to keep informed.

11. Use each night to write out your schedule for the following day. That way you have the following day all planned out and don't waste time doing things out of order. You can then hit the ground running starting each day in high gear instead of wasting time searching for things to do.

12. I personally complete the day with family time. It keeps me grounded by connecting with those who are most important. This is time for the family to talk, share, laugh and play. The wife and I love to close the night by jumping into bed and binge watching our favorite TV series on DVD or streaming while sharing some cuddle time.

Maximize Your Information Intake

Now that you've taken the time to empty your brain of all the garbage that has been taking up space you can fill that space with useful information. Like a computer your brain only has room for so much data. Erasing, deleting and uninstalling unhelpful bad information opens space for your brain to store useful good information. If you want to be at the top of your game every day you must do those things that keep you operating in peak condition mentally, physically, emotionally, and spiritually. Begin your intake of information by equipping your mind with information that can help you achieve peak performance. Let's start with your mental approach.

Mental sharpness involves concentration and understanding but also memory focus. Basically, mental sharpness, is just how well your mind is working. Like a muscle, your brain can run at its peak performance level by being reliable, fast, and effective. Or, it can run at low levels leaving you lethargic, tired, unfocused, and unable to be creative, innovative, or retain information. Here's some info to up your game.

The Wonders of Magnesium

Over 90% of Americans are deficient in Magnesium. Magnesium regulates nerves in the body and is responsible for the relaxation phase of the muscles and the heart.

Magnesium (the relaxer) is required at the center of every cell in the body. When the cells are low in magnesium, calcium (the constrictor) moves to the center of the cell to protect the cell integrity. This causes every cell in the body to be tight. That causes us to suffer from muscle stiffness, headaches, insomnia, rage, anxiety and stress.

Magnesium is required for the proper function of over 325 enzymatic processes in the body. Magnesium is needed to keep the brain, nerves, flexors, motor nerves, spinal nerves and functions throughout the system functioning properly. Proper levels of magnesium can significantly impact both the size and scope of our mental sharpness.

Getting adequate sleep, eating healthy, getting regular physical fitness, and managing stress levels are all important for improving mental sharpness but being low on magnesium will defeat the effects of all these good habits. Before using Magnesium check with a nutritionist.

Improve Your Brain

Neuroplasticity Is Your Friend

They say that you can't teach an old dog new tricks but when it comes to the brain, scientists have discovered this old adage isn't true. The human brain has an astonishing ability to adapt and change, even into old age. This ability is known as neuroplasticity. With the right stimulation, your brain can form new neural pathways, alter existing connections, and adapt and react in ever-changing ways. The brain's incredible ability to reshape itself holds true when it comes to learning and memory. You can harness the natural power of neuroplasticity to increase your cognitive abilities, enhance your ability to learn new information, and improve your memory at any age.

Boost Your Brain Power

By the time you reach adulthood your brain has developed millions of neural pathways that help you process and recall information quickly, solve familiar problems, and execute routine tasks with a minimum of mental effort. However, if you keep doing the things you've always done you aren't giving your brain the stimulation it needs to keep growing and developing. In order for your brain to keep growing and improving you must give it new challenges.

Your memory, like muscular strength, requires you to "use it or lose it." The more you work out your brain, the better you'll be able to process and remember information. The best brain exercises are the ones that break your routine and challenge you to use and develop new brain pathways.

No matter how intellectually demanding the activity if it's something you are already good at, it's not a good brain exercise. The activity needs to be something that's unfamiliar and out of your comfort zone. To strengthen your brain you need to keep learning and developing new and more challenging skills. Learning a new language, learning a strategic game like chess, learning to paint, learning to create pottery, learning computer coding, learning ballroom dancing, any such activity can help you improve your memory, and mental acuity as long as they keep you challenged and engaged. Why do you need to boost your brain power? Because you are going to need that added brain power if you hope to reach the kind of success levels we are talking about in this book.

Get Those Reps In

Physical exercise also helps your brain stay sharp. It increases oxygen to your brain and reduces the risk for disorders that lead to memory loss, such as diabetes and cardiovascular disease. Exercise also enhances the effects of helpful brain chemicals and reduces stress hormones. Perhaps most importantly, exercise plays an important role in neuroplasticity by boosting growth factors and stimulating new neuronal connections.

Aerobic exercise is particularly good for the brain, so choose activities that keep your blood pumping. Remember, anything that is good for your heart is good for your brain. Physical activities that require hand-eye coordination or complex motor skills are excellent for brain building. If you are one of those people who suffers from brain fog in the morning waking your system up by exercising in the morning before you start your day will make a big difference. The best thing about morning exercise is that it serves double duty. It clears the cobwebs out of your mind and prepares you for learning throughout the day. Exercise breaks can also help you break through mental fatigue and those challenging afternoon slumps. Just a few jumping jacks, short walk, or jog can be enough to reboot your brain.

Sleep Is More Important Than You Think

For most people there is a big difference between the amount of sleep you can function on and the amount you need to function at your best. Over 95% of adults need between 7.5 to 9 hours of sleep every night in order to avoid sleep deprivation. Missing out on even a few hours of sleep can make a big difference. Memory, creativity, problem-solving, and critical thinking skills are all compromised when you short-change yourself on sleep. Research shows sleep is necessary for memory consolidation because this key memory-enhancing activity occurs during the deepest stages of sleep.

You will most likely function at your best if you get on a regular sleep schedule. Try to go to bed at the same time every night and get up at the same time each morning. You will be more mentally sharp if you don't break your sleep routine. This includes weekends and holidays. If you are one of those people who have trouble falling asleep be aware that the blue light emitted by TVs, tablets, cell phones, and computers may be the cause. It suppresses hormones such as melatonin that make you sleepy. If you are having bouts of sleeplessness try shutting these devices off an hour before bedtime.

Don't Forget to Feed Your Brain

Your brain needs fuel just like your body does. A diet based around fruits, vegetables, whole grains, "healthy" fats (fish, olive oil, nuts) and lean protein provides an abundance of health benefits. It also improves your memory. The following nutritional tips will boost brainpower and reduce your risk of dementia.

- **Omega-3s:** Research shows that omega-3 fatty acids are particularly beneficial for brain health. Fish is a particularly rich source of omega-3, especially cold water "fatty fish" such as salmon, tuna, halibut, trout, mackerel, sardines, and herring. There are also non-fish sources of omega-3s such as seaweed, walnuts, ground flaxseed, flaxseed oil, winter squash, kidney and pinto beans, spinach, broccoli, pumpkin seeds, and soybeans.
- **Eat more fruit and vegetables:** Produce is packed with antioxidants, substances that protect your brain cells from damage. Colorful fruits and vegetables are particularly good antioxidant "superfood" sources.
- **Drink green tea:** Green tea contains polyphenols, powerful antioxidants that protect against free radicals that can damage brain cells. Among many other benefits, regular consumption of green tea may enhance your memory and mental alertness as well as slow brain aging.
- **Take advantage of resveratrol:** Drink fluids rich in resveratrol, a flavonoid that boosts blood flow in the brain and reduces the risk of Alzheimer's disease. Resveratrol-packed drinks and foods include grape juice, cranberry juice, fresh grapes and berries, peanuts, and red wine.
- **Limit calories and saturated fat.** Research shows that diets high in saturated fat (from sources such as red meat, whole milk, butter, cheese, cream, and ice cream) increase your risk of dementia and impair concentration and memory.

Improve Memory and Learning

It takes about eight seconds of intense focus to process information into your memory. Obviously, you can't memorize something until you first learn it. The act of learning takes paying attention and focusing on what you are trying to learn. If you know you are easily distracted choose a quiet place to study where you won't be interrupted. Turn off TVs, videos, radios, the internet, cell phones, and other distractions. If you are listening to music make sure you turn the volume down low enough that it doesn't pull your attention away from what you are trying to learn. Remember, it takes a lot of learning and memorizing before you can store enough information to compete against the best. Here are 8 learning and visualization tricks to help you bring your 'A' game:

- **Use Repetition:** Repetition is a well-known learning tool. Repeat over and over what you've learned the same day you learn it and do it at various intervals. Repetition is more effective than cramming information especially when it comes to retaining what you've already learned.
- **Use your sense:** The physical act of rewriting information can help you encode it onto your brain. If you are a visual learner try reading out loud the information you want to remember. Reciting information in a rhythmic pattern or rap is also an effective memorization tool.
- **Simplify information:** For very complex information try focusing on understanding the basic ideas rather than trying to memorize isolated details. Also, instead of memorizing something word for word try paraphrasing or explaining the ideas to someone else in your own words.
- **Use rhymes and alliteration**: Rhymes and alliteration (a repeating sound or syllable), are good ways to remember facts and figures. As an example: The rhyme "Thirty days hath September, April, June, and November" is a way to remember the months of the year with only 30 days.
- **Use Acronyms:** An acronym is a word that is made by taking the first letters of all the key words or ideas you need to remember and creating a new word out of them. Example: The word "HOMES" can be used to remember the names of the Great Lakes: Huron, Ontario, Michigan, Erie, Superior.

- **Acrostic (sentence):** Make up a sentence in which the first letter of each word is part of or represents the initial of what you want to remember. Example: The sentence "All Cows Eat Grass": Will help you remember the music notes on a bass clef, which are A,C,E,G.
- **Chunking:** Chunking breaks a long list of numbers or other types of information into smaller, more manageable chunks. Example: Remembering a 10-digit phone number by breaking it down into three sets of numbers: 652-787-3179 (as opposed to 6527873179).
- **Visual image:** If you are a visual learner you can help yourself remember information by associating a visual image with a word or name. The more vivid the image is the easier it is to remember. Example: To remember the name Rosa Parks and what she's known for, picture a woman sitting on a park bench, surrounded by roses, waiting as her bus pulls up.

The Affects Of Food Allergies And Sensitivities

Food Sensitivity and Allergies

In order to do better it is important for you to feel better. Food allergies and sensitivities are on the rise. GMOs, processed foods, late-application pesticides, food coloring, preservatives, and hard-to-pronounce unknown to the public ingredients are listed on a majority of food labels today. Altered and engineered foods are having adverse effects on our bodies and our health. Scientists and researchers are now drawing a direct correlation between what we eat and how we feel. You may be taking medicines for ailments that are not illnesses at all but are actually food allergies or sensitivities.

The symptoms of food sensitivities and food allergies are causing everything from rashes, to sickness, to mood swings. Often these food derived illnesses are mistaken for something else. No matter how these symptoms manifest themselves they are our body's way of letting us know that what we are eating is harmful to us. The best way to be successful at any endeavor is to maximize your potential and maximizing your health, needless to say, is a large part of maximizing your potential.

Getting your health together is a major intersection on the road to getting your life together.

Recognizing Food Sensitivities and Food Allergies

While both food allergies and food sensitivities stem from our body not agreeing with certain ingredients in our foods there are key indicators we should be aware of when it comes to recognizing food sensitivities and food allergies. The timing of symptoms, the severity of each symptom, and how your body reacts are key differentiators. A food allergy will trigger an immediate reaction from the immune system, producing IgE antibodies to neutralize the foreign substance or offending food allergen.

In the case of food allergies symptoms come on quick and strong. They may affect multiple organs. These symptoms may occur with even the smallest exposure to the offending food. Food allergies draw attention because they are now frequently associated with itchy hives, EpiPens, and trips to the hospital Emergency Room. Medical facilities, schools, employers, even airlines have had to alter the way they do business because the frequency of these allergic reactions are on the rise. Between 1997 and 2007 one medical study found that food allergies had increased by a highly noticeable 18%.

Reactions that arise from food sensitivities are your immune system's response mediated by IgG antibodies. These symptoms are commonly isolated in the digestive track often causing chronic inflammation, and the reaction can be delayed by up to 48 hours. These symptoms are often mistaken for something else which makes a correct diagnosis especially tricky. Sufferers of food sensitivities can spend a lifetime treating their symptoms with over-the-counter medications never diagnosing the root cause of their problems. Such misdiagnosis increases the risks of running into serious illnesses later in life. The best way to avoid these food ailments is to pinpoint trigger foods and avoid them. In order to do that you must pay attention to your symptoms and understand what they mean.

Food Allergy Symptoms

When your body has an allergic reaction to food the immune system kicks in. These symptoms can be life-threatening and can happen almost immediately after a trigger food is ingested. It's difficult to miss the symptoms of a food allergy which is why they are easier to diagnose than food sensitivities. Once you have felt the agony of hives, bloated skin, and swollen lips you never forget it.

Understanding the warning signs and knowing when to get help are important for those who suffer from food allergies, especially severe ones. It's important to remember that mild reactions can become serious in a short period of time. It's possible for you to have a trigger food a few times with only mild reactions before a major reaction occurs.

Food Allergy Symptoms include:

Your skin becomes flushed, red, swollen, dry, itchy or can develop hives or eczema. Your eyes may become itchy, watery and red. The insides of your ears may feel itchy. Your mouth may feel tingly, itchy or have a funny taste. Your face, tongue or lips may swell. You may start coughing, wheezing, sneezing, or have a runny nose. You may suffer with an upset stomach, vomiting, cramps, diarrhea, feel dizzy or lightheaded. You may have a drop in blood pressure. You may have constricted airways due to swelling of your tongue, throat or vocal cords. You could suffer from chest pains or a weak or uneven heartbeat. You may become weak, feel confused or pass out. You may go into shock.

Anaphylaxis, the most serious acute allergic reaction

Each year in the United States, there are approximately 30,000 ER visits, 2,000 hospitalizations and 150 deaths due to anaphylaxis which makes it a relatively rare occurrence. Still, if you suffer from anaphylaxis the best thing to do is to undergo testing to find out what food allergies you have. Also, you should carry two EpiPens wherever you go. Remember, food allergy deaths are preventable.

Foods Most Likely to Cause Serious Allergic Reactions

There are over 160 foods that can trigger food allergies but eight foods in particular account for nearly 90% of all food-related allergic reactions that can cause serious side effects. These serious reactions can be so dangerous that laws have been enacted to protect those who suffer from them. The following eight foods and any ingredient that contains proteins derived from one or more of them are designated as "major food allergens" by The Food Allergen Labeling and Consumer Protection Act (FALCPA). That means manufacturers must include specific disclaimers on their packaging to let you know whether or not their product contains these foods. The eight foods most likely to cause serious allergic reactions are milk, eggs, peanuts, tree nuts such as walnuts, cashews or almonds; fish, shellfish, soy, and wheat.

Foods that cause the most common adult allergies include fish, shellfish, fruits like peaches, plums and apricots; nuts, seeds, and peanuts. Foods that are slightly less common to cause allergic reactions are corn, gelatin, beef, chicken, pork, seeds like sesame, sunflower and poppy; and spices like caraway, coriander, garlic and mustard. Be aware that no food can be ruled out when it comes to potential allergens. So, if you show any symptoms you should be tested. Here is a watch list of things to be aware of in regards to the most common causes of serious food allergies.

Peanut Allergy

Technically peanuts are a legume not an actual nut. They are the leading cause of severe reactions to food, including anaphylaxis. Even a microscopic amount of peanut dust can potentially trigger severe reactions and it seems to be on the rise. One 2010 study concluded that peanut allergies in children had more than tripled between 1997 and 2008. This is a troubling statistic considering the severe reactions associated with this very popular food and products that use it as an ingredient.

Egg Allergy

Egg whites are more likely to cause reactions than the egg yolk but it is possible for you to be able to tolerate the yolk and not the white or vice versa. Egg allergies are more common in children than adults. Symptoms can range from mild to severe and common reactions include nasal congestion, rash, hives, vomiting and other digestive issues and in rare cases anaphylaxis. Cutting eggs out of a diet is a challenge since eggs are so essential. This versatile ingredient is in so many foods. They serve as an emulsifier in products like mayonnaise, a binder in recipes like meatloaf, and an aerator in cakes.

You should also know that some vaccines contain egg proteins, including measles-mumps-rubella. The vaccine is generally considered safe for those with egg allergies. The flu vaccine, which also contains egg proteins is considered safe for most allergic people. However, the yellow fever vaccine is highly advised against for those with egg allergies. If you have food allergies it is advised that you speak with your doctor before you get any immunization.

Milk Allergy

It should be noted that milk contains 25 different molecules identified by scientists to cause reactions. Milk proteins such as lactoglobulin, lactalbumin, casein, and whey, are some of the problem causing ingredients present in milk. Obviously, those allergic to milk products should avoid things like ice cream, milk chocolate, and cream-based sauces. But you need to also be aware that a milk protein like casein is found in soy products which are a common dairy substitute. Milk allergy symptoms include digestive issues, abdominal pain, hives, itching and even colic in babies. Milk allergies are the third most common cause of anaphylaxis, after peanuts and tree nuts. These ailments are in addition to those that result from being lactose intolerant.

Wheat Allergy

How can you tell if you have a wheat allergy or if you are allergic to gluten? A wheat allergy means that you have an allergic reaction to the proteins in wheat. If you eliminate wheat from your diet and your symptoms disappear you have a wheat allergy. If your allergic symptoms continue even after you cut out other grains it is more likely you are having a bad reaction to gluten. Those with wheat allergies should cut your carb intake and avoid foods like pasta and bread. If you do this and are still having symptoms be aware that things like cosmetics, bath products, and even that kiddie favorite Play-Doh, can have wheat-based ingredients that will cause a reaction upon contact.

Food Sensitivity Symptoms

If you are experiencing a range of digestive issues food sensitivities are an obvious place to look since our digestive track is the first to come into direct contact with the food we eat. How about if you have lower back pain from indigestion, or, if you suffer from chronic sinus congestion or brain fog? Would you suspect food sensitivities are the cause? Food sensitivity symptoms and the foods that cause them are common. Remember too that reactions to food sensitivities can be delayed and that symptoms can be very deceptive and it's easy to see why food sensitivities can be the cause of so much confusion. A few of the many symptoms associated with food sensitivities are:

Digestive Issues

The digestive tract is the first line of contact with food, so it's not surprising that the most common response is noticed in the digestive system. A bloated stomach after eating, reflux, diarrhea, difficulty losing weight, excess gas, stinky gas, and respiratory Issues are all symptoms of food sensitivity.

Respiratory problems are commonly associated with sensitivities to milk products and milk products are known to increase mucous production. Food sensitivity problems can show up in your respiratory system in the form of a runny nose, chronic sinus congestion, asthma and skin Issues.

"Inflammation in other areas of the body can often be seen first on the skin," says Jeffrey Bland, PhD, author of The Disease Delusion: Conquering the Causes of Chronic Illness for a Healthier, Longer, and Happier Life.

It has been said that your immune system speaks through your skin. As your largest organ, the skin reflects your overall health. Some food sensitivity symptoms that show up on the skin are:

Acne, eczema, dry and itchy skin, and dark circles under eyes.

It should be no surprise that what we eat can affect how we feel physically and psychologically. Depression, moodiness, fatigue, hyperactivity, anxiety, and brain fog may all be the results of food sensitivity. Again, if you want to maximize your potential it begins with optimizing your health. Identifying trigger foods and paying attention to what they are doing inside your body is a critical first step on your road to great health. Inflammation, joint pain, headaches, migraines, chronic ear infections (these are common for children with sensitivities to milk products) may all be due to food sensitivities.

If you want to perform at your best you would do well to tweak your diet to eliminate foods that you are sensitive to and foods you are allergic to. The following foods may be triggers that cause you illness and keep you from achieving optimum health and peak performance.

Dairy products, gluten-containing foods like wheat, rye, and barley; corn, soy, eggs, shellfish; beef, pork and lamb (a lot of livestock is raised on corn and soy), plus food additives like sulfites and artificial color.

If you suffer from problems with your gut or digestive system you should get to know the word FODMAP. The term FODMAP is an acronym, derived from "Fermentable Oligo-, Di-, Mono-saccharides And Polyols". They are short chain carbohydrates that are poorly absorbed in the small intestine. Fodmap is one of a group of compounds thought to contribute to the symptoms of irritable bowel syndrome and similar gastrointestinal disorders. The term is used mainly with reference to a diet that is low in these compounds (which are mainly carbohydrates).

High FODMAPs foods, or fermentable oligosaccharides, disaccharides, monosaccharide and polyols, are certain carbohydrates found in common, often healthy foods that are fermentable, osmotic, and poorly absorbed, resulting in digestive distress and intestinal gas buildup. Some examples are: dried fruit, stone fruit, cherries, apples, mango, papaya, cottage cheese, sour cream, yogurt, milk from cows, sheep or goats, beans, lentils, squash, garlic, mushrooms, broccoli, cabbage, onions, coffee, high-fructose corn syrup, agave, chocolate and artificial sweeteners.

Finally, This Brings Us to The Great Gluten Debate

One study suggests that up to 30% of adults in the United States are trying to cut down on gluten for health reasons. The gluten-free trend is causing controversy between some nutritional experts and doctors, especially when it is used as a tool for weight loss. The gluten-free product industry is now a multi-billion-dollar industry. How curious that with many gluten-free products the calorie count, fat content and prices are higher than regular products that contain gluten. That means these particular gluten-free products offer no real nutritional advantage over gluten-containing products. Many experts agree unless you have a condition that is aggravated by gluten intake—like Celiac Disease or Hashimoto's Disease—a gluten-free lifestyle is not necessary. Both of these autoimmune diseases are relatively rare, with 1% of the U.S. suffering from Celiac Disease and 5% of the population is affected by Hashimoto's Disease (also known as Hashimoto's Thyroiditis).

Though those figures are low still it seems a third of the public believes they should be eating a gluten-free diet? The problem with many people who believe they have a sensitivity to gluten can be traced to Non-celiac gluten sensitivity (NCGS). Research indicates 18 million Americans have a gluten sensitivity. That figure is six times higher than Celiac Disease. For those with NCGS, non-celiac gluten sensitivity gluten may spur any number of sensitivity symptoms, including ADHD-like behavior, brain fog, inflammation and digestive issues. If symptoms disappear when gluten is eliminated from your diet and you have tested negative for diseases like Celiac Disease and Hashimoto's Thyroiditis, signs point to you having a non-celiac gluten sensitivity.

So, is the gluten-free trend a result of fad diets, industry marketing, gluten-free enthusiasts, or perhaps "amateur" nutritionists? To be fair research is showing that some people for whatever reason can't tolerate gluten and their numbers are on the rise. If you believe you are sensitive to gluten speak to a professional and get tested for this sensitivity.

Want to Get Tested For Food Allergies and Sensitivity?

If you are thinking of self-diagnosis you should think twice. When it comes to the relationship between your body and food self-diagnosis can be dangerous, especially when it comes to overlooking serious underlying issues. You may think a gluten sensitivity is to blame for your symptoms when it could be a more serious condition like Celiac Disease, that would require a different treatment. Your self-diagnosis could also lead you to start unnecessary and potentially harmful diets that might deprive your body of much needed nutrients.

Consulting your primary care physician or allergist is a crucial first step. Since symptoms can be life-threatening, this isn't something that falls into the category of self-diagnosis. After going over your medical history with you, your doctor can use some of the following methods to help test for food allergies and food sensitivity.

Skin test: Small amounts of allergens are applied to skin, followed by a small prick with a needle. If the prick becomes red or itchy it indicates that you are, in fact, allergic.

Blood test: Checks the number of igE antibodies produced in your body. In an igE test, elevated levels of certain antibodies help identify reactions to specific foods.

Food diary: Document what you eat and the possible symptoms that follow. Use an elimination diet to remove suspected culprits one at a time for two to eight weeks (the longer the better).

The Affects Of Music

Add Music to Your Brain Boosting Toolkit

Since the first note was song and the first instrument played music has played an important part in shaping culture. Now, thanks to advances in neuroscience we can measure how music affects the brain. This interest in music and its effects on the brain has led to the creation of a new branch of research called neuromusicology. Based on findings from this latest science we now know that music activates every known part of the brain. (Source: Suomen Akatemia (Academy of Finland), December 6, 2011)

Research shows that both listening to and playing music can actually make you smarter, healthier, happier and even more productive. And, the best thing about these positive effects is they can take place no matter what age you are. So, music can play a significant role in helping your brain to function better and that means it should be added to your toolkit as another tool you can use to reach that next level of performance. Let's see how you can use music to help reach your success goals.

Why Do Musicians Have Healthier Brains?

A team of researchers from Heidelberg University in Germany have found professional musicians have bigger, better connected, more sensitive brains than non-musicians. They learned this fact through the use of brain scans. Professional musicians who perform regularly showed 102% more activity in their auditory cortex than non-musicians. Even activity in the brains of amateur musicians was on average 37% higher than in those who did not play an instrument, the researchers said in a report published in Nature Neuroscience.

This discovery suggests musicians have superior working memory, auditory skills, and cognitive flexibility. Research results showed their brains to be more symmetrical and respond more symmetrically when listening to music. The areas of their brain that are responsible for motor control, auditory processing, and spatial coordination are larger.

Another significant finding showed that the corpus callosum the band of nerve fibers that transfer information between the two hemispheres of the brain is larger in musicians. This increased size indicates that the two sides of the brain of musicians are better at communicating with each other. If you are not a professional musician you may ask how these findings impact you. The average person listens to an average of 32 hours of music each week. Listening to that much music also has a significant and positive affect on your brain.

The Positive Effects of Playing and Listening to Music

Science has found that listening to and playing upbeat music reduces chronic stress by lowering the stress hormone cortisol. The reduction of this hormone makes you feel more hopeful, powerful, and in control of your life. In addition to this finding about the effects of upbeat music studies show that listening to sad music also has some positive effects when you are dealing with grief and sadness. It finds listening to sad music is cathartic and helps you get in touch with your emotions which helps in the healing process.

Music Releases Beneficial Brain Chemicals

Music also affects your mood by stimulating the formation of specific brain chemicals like the neurotransmitter dopamine. Dopamine is known as the brain's "motivation molecule" and plays an integral part in the brain's pleasure-reward system. It is also the brain chemical responsible for the euphoria we feel from eating chocolate, experiencing orgasms, and experiencing a runner's high. Whenever you hear a song you like it triggers a small dopamine boost.

Dopamine isn't the only beneficial brain chemical music helps us produce. Playing music or enjoying some live music stimulates the brain hormone oxytocin. Oxytocin is known as the "trust molecule" and the "moral molecule" because it helps us bond with and trust others. An increase in oxytocin can make you a more generous and trustworthy person.

The Power Of Music

Did you know that Nobel Prize-winning theoretical physicist Albert Einstein was an accomplished violinist? William J. Clinton the 42nd president of the United States of America is a good saxophone player. The man known as the world's most successful investor, Warren Buffett, Berkshire Hathaway CEO, also one of the world's wealthiest people, stays mentally sharp by playing the ukulele. Maybe that's what keeps this icon now in his late 80s at the top of his game.

The power of music is undeniable. Research shows that restaurant's that play music with positive messages during meals get bigger tips from their customers. Music plays a role in how people see and relate to others. Listening to positive song lyrics helps people become less prejudiced and fearful of those different than themselves. There are companies that design music for businesses that help employees be more productive. They also design music for stores that encourage customers to purchase more.

Researchers have linked music to prosocial behaviors such as kindness, generosity, compassion, empathy, and cooperation. Listening to positive music makes people more willing to use their time and energy helping others and this prosocial effect of music happens with adults and children.

Music In The Workplace

According to the National Center for Biotechnology Information background music enhances performance on cognitive tasks, enables the completion of repetitive tasks more efficiently, and improves the accuracy of workers. Studies show that workers who are allowed to listen to their choice of music complete tasks more quickly and present better ideas than those who have no control over the music they listen to at work. These employees are also happier and more productive.

Studies have also been done on the effects of music on productivity within specific occupations. For instance, software developers are happier, produce better work, and work more efficiently when listening to music. Surgeons who listen to music while operating are less stressed out, work faster and more accurately. Plus, all these added efficiencies increase if the music they listen to is of their own choosing. For decades athletes have been using music to "psyche themselves up" before games. Studies confirm that listening to upbeat music before a game can keep athletes from choking in high-pressure situations.

To get even more specific, test study participants who listen to music that is "happy," find that their creativity goes up, they come up with more creative solutions to problems, and they submit a greater amount of ideas than participants who listen to other kinds of music or no music at all. Studies also show that this effect remains true whether students like the music they are hearing or not.

The Benefits of Early Music Development On Brains

Parents of the 1990s, remember the craze of having their babies listen to the music of Mozart, Beethoven, or classical music in general to improve their brains. Sometimes parents started their babies listening to classical music even before they were born. The theory was listening to music composed by Mozart made kids smarter. This effect of music on young brains became popularly known as the Mozart effect.

While taking music lessons as a child does enhance brain function and structure, scientists now say there is nothing uniquely beneficial about the music of Wolfgang Amadeus Mozart.

In spite of the Mozart effect being false research does show that children with musical backgrounds do better in language, reading, and math and have better fine motor skills than their non-musical peers. Early music lessons encourage brain plasticity. Plasticity is the brain's capacity to change and grow. Studies show just a half hour music lesson increases blood flow in the left hemisphere of the brain which is extremely beneficial. Research shows when exposure to music training begins before the age of seven the beneficial affect on the brain can last a lifetime. Even when tested 40 years later as little as four years of music lessons have been found to improve certain brain functions.

It's never too early to involve children with music and reap its benefits. Studies have shown babies who play drums and sing nursery rhymes before they can walk or talk show brain improvement. Babies who have music lessons communicate better, smile more, and show earlier and more sophisticated brain responses. Music taught in schools or outside schools helps students improve language development and test scores, increase brain connectivity and spatial intelligence, and adds a small increase to their IQ. Such skills are critical for careers like architecture, engineering, math and computer science.

Seniors Also Benefit from Music

Research shows it's never too early to take advantage of the benefits of music and never too late. Seniors who play an instrument, sing, or dance reap physical, psychological and social benefits from music. Seniors who have musical backgrounds score higher on cognitive tests and show greater mental flexibility than their non-musical peers. More than other activities music protects against memory problems and cognitive decline.

The Healing Qualities of Music

There is extensive research to show music has healing qualities. Mental health disorders or neurological diseases including anxiety, depression, insomnia, attention deficit hyperactivity disorder (ADHD), post-traumatic stress disorder (PTSD), schizophrenia have all been treated and improved through music therapy. Music therapy also shows promise in treating stroke, autism, Parkinson's, dementia, and Alzheimer's. Music therapy has brought about positive changes in neurotransmitter levels in Alzheimer's patients positively affecting their brains. Patients suffering from cancer, dementia, Parkinson's and various types of chronic pain can improve their quality of life by tapping into the beneficial psychological aspects of music. Before and after surgery listening to music reduces the stress experienced by patients. Elderly patients run into their own problems when recovering from surgery and music can decrease their postoperative confusion and delirium. With all its positive affects you must still use the power of music wisely because it can also have negative effects. Patients that have undergone heart surgery should not listen to heavy metal music or techno sounds because doing so can lead to stress and life-threatening arrhythmias.

Music Affects Each Brain Differently

Neuroscientists can now see that music affects each person's brain differently. By using functional magnetic resonance imaging (fMRI), researchers have found that listening to music you like increases blood flow to the brain and brain connectivity more than listening to music you don't like. Interestingly, the number of areas in the brain activated by music varies depending on your musical background and tastes. Researchers say the best kind of music to increase focus and productivity is music you enjoy. Music that rates highest for this purpose is instrumental music, with an upbeat tempo, played at medium volume. According to the University of Birmingham, England you can receive added benefits if you listen to that type of music with nature sounds.

Improve Your Focus with Focus@Will

If you are particularly interested in using background music to increase your productivity and ability to concentrate, check out Focus@Will. According to Focus@Will's website, employees at corporations like

Microsoft, Google, Apple, and Amazon use their service to increase productivity. Focus@Will offers scientifically engineered music channels for enhancing focus based on your personality type. Their playlists works by altering brainwave activity to enhance focus and attention. Focus@Will's research says listening to their music channels can quadruple focus and productivity.

Music to Enhance Your Brain

If you want to listen to music specifically to improve your mood, learning or concentration, check out Spotify. Among its millions of songs this music streaming service boast an entire section of brain-enhancing music. You can find it by creating a free Spotify account. Use the "Browser" function to access the "Genres and Moods" tab. That's where you'll find playlists created specifically to improve your mood and enhance your focus. If you browse the "Mood" genre you'll find playlists for increasing happiness and confidence as well as dozens of other brain and mood enhancing categories.

The Affects Of Colors

How Room Colors Affect You

Feeling some kind of way sometimes and don't know why? Sometimes it may be because of something that happened, or because of something that was said, or a memory that was triggered, or because of something you ate. Or, maybe it's simply because of the color of the room you are in. Colors are everywhere, on the walls of your home, in stores, on clothing, on cars, on the ground, in the sky, in the trees, on oceans, rivers, and lakes, surrounding you at work and at play, on your TV, phone, even on the faces of every one you meet. Colors, all colors affect you in one way or another. Some are positive and some are negative. Here are some clues that may explain why you feel how you do when you don't know why. Once you understand the affect various colors can have on you use this knowledge to control how you and others feel. Colors are more tools to add to your mental toolbox. You can use colors to create moods and emotions that benefit you.

As an example, Red raises a room's energy level. The most intense color, it pumps the adrenaline like no other hue. It is a good choice when you want to stir up excitement, particularly at night. In the living room or dining room red draws people together and stimulates conversation. In an entryway, it creates a strong first impression. Red has been shown to raise blood pressure and speed respiration and heart rate. It is usually considered too stimulating for bedrooms, but if you're typically in the room only after dark, you'll be seeing it mostly by lamplight so the color will appear muted, rich and elegant.

Orange evokes excitement and enthusiasm and is an energetic color. While not a good idea for a living room or for bedrooms, this color is great for an exercise room; it will bring out all the emotions that you need released during your fitness routine. In ancient cultures orange was believed to heal the lungs and increase energy levels.

Yellow captures the joy of sunshine and communicates happiness. It is an excellent choice for kitchens, dining rooms and bathrooms where it is energizing and uplifting. In halls, entries and small spaces yellow can feel expansive and welcoming. Even though yellow is a cheery color it is not a good choice for main color schemes. Studies show that people are more likely to lose their temper in a yellow interior. Babies also seem to cry more in yellow rooms. In large amounts yellow tends to create feelings of frustration and anger. In chromotherapy, yellow is believed to stimulate the nerves and purify the body.

Green is considered the most restful color for the eye. Combining the refreshing quality of blue and the cheerfulness of yellow, green is suited for almost any room in the house. In the kitchen, green cools things down; in a family room or living room it encourages unwinding but has enough warmth to promote comfort and togetherness. Green has a calming effect when used as a main color for decorating. It is believed to relieve stress by helping people relax. It is also believed to help with fertility making it a great choice for the bedroom.

Blue is said to bring down blood pressure and slow respiration and heart rate. That is why it is considered calming, relaxing and serene. It is often recommended for bedrooms and bathrooms. Careful though, a pastel blue that looks pretty on the paint chip can come across as unpleasantly chilly on the walls and furnishings, especially in a room that receives little natural light. If you opt for a light blue as the primary color in a room balance that choice with warm hues for the furnishings and fabrics. To encourage relaxation in social areas such as family rooms, living rooms or large kitchens consider warmer blues such as periwinkle, or bright blues such as cerulean or turquoise. Blue is known to have a calming effect when used as the main color of a room but it is best to go for softer shades. Dark blue has the opposite effect. It evokes feelings of sadness. You may want to refrain from using darker blues in your main color scheme.

Purple, in its darkest values (eggplant, for example), looks rich, dramatic and sophisticated. It is associated with luxury and creativity. As an accent or secondary color it gives a scheme depth. Lighter versions of purple such as lavender and lilac bring the same restful quality to bedrooms as blue does but without the risk of feeling chilly.

Learn How to Use The Psychology of Color

Though there has not been a great deal of scientific research on the subject the concept of color psychology has over the past decade become a hot topic in marketing, art, design, and other areas. While not having the majority of its findings based on hard science researchers and experts in various fields have nonetheless made some important observations and discoveries about the psychology of color and the effect it has on moods, feelings, behaviors, and consumerism.

Perceptions of color are for the most part subjective. Still there are some color effects that are felt universally. As an example, colors in the red area of the color spectrum are known as warm colors. They include red, orange, and yellow. These warm colors evoke emotions ranging from feelings of warmth and comfort to feelings of anger and hostility. Colors on the blue side of the spectrum are known as cool colors and include blue, purple, and green. These colors are often described as calm but can also call to mind feelings of sadness or indifference.

The next time you visit a grocery store look at the colors of laundry detergents. An overwhelming majority are blue and orange. Blue symbolizes cleanliness and orange is dynamic energy. Therefore, a blue and orange package would clearly communicate industrial strength and cleaning power.

Marketing experts have increasingly begun to use colors to draw certain responses from consumers. Color has been known to have a powerful psychological impact on people's behavior and decisions. Savvy branding experts have used colors to successfully promote products and shape how consumers feel about their company or brand. Sales analytics have shown that color can often be the sole reason someone purchases a product. One survey showed 93% of buyers said they focus on visual appearance, and close to 85% claim color is the primary reason they make a purchase. Research has reinforced that 60% of the time people will decide if they are attracted or not to a message based on color alone. A University of Loyola, Maryland study found color increases brand recognition by up to 80%. Apple cleverly introduced colorful iMac computers into a marketplace where color had not been seen before. Apple was the first to say, "It doesn't have to be beige". Those iMacs reinvigorated a brand that had suffered $1.8 billion in losses over two years. Let's take a look at why and how various colors are used commercially.

Red – Creates a sense of urgency which makes it the perfect color to put on tags for clearance sales. It also encourages appetite and that's why it is frequently used by fast-food chains. Red physically stimulates the body, raises blood pressure and heart rate, and can be associated with movement, excitement, and passion so companies use it when they want to stimulate customers to execute these particular actions. McDonald's uses high-energy colors like red and yellow which appeal to children, stirs appetites and creates a sense of urgency.

Orange & Yellow – Are cheerful colors that promote a sense of optimism. Yellow can make babies cry, while orange can trigger a sense of caution. They are also used to create a sense of anxiety that can draw impulsive buyers and window shoppers into stores. With its iconic yellow frame representing a window or portal to the world National Geographic's

73

yellow is best associated with knowledge and wisdom, characteristics that create optimism and draws readers in.

White – Is linked with feelings of purity, cleanliness and safety. It is also used to project neutrality. White space sparks creativity since it can be viewed as representing a clean canvas. Whether it's the soothing simplicity of its packaging, the simple purity of its logo or the fact iPhones and iPads are available in white, the way Apple uses white is nothing short of iconic.

Blue – Is the preferred color of men. It is associated with peace, water, tranquility, and reliability. Some other characteristics of blue are that it provides a sense of security, curbs the appetite, and stimulates productivity. Blue is the most common color used by conservative brands looking to promote trust in their products. Blue is the most universally preferred color and Dropbox the file sharing service uses it to reflect reliability, trustworthiness, and communication which works well for a collaboration tool.

Green – Is associated with health, tranquility, power, and nature. It is used in stores to relax customers and for promoting environmental issues. Green stimulates harmony in your brain and encourages a balance that leads to decisiveness. One of the few major global brands to use green as its primary color is Starbucks. By using green Starbucks hopes to promote a sense of relaxation in their cafes.

Purple – Is commonly associated with royalty, wisdom, and respect. It stimulates problem-solving and creativity. Purple is frequently used to promote beauty and anti-aging products. Purple and Cadbury's have been associated with each other since 1914. Pantone 2685C is now officially Cadbury Purple.

Black – Is often associated with authority, power, stability, intelligence and strength. However, use it cautiously because it can become overwhelming if it is used too frequently. Using black as a primary brand color, adds a bold, powerful, classic effect that feels confident and sophisticated for more expensive products. A perfect example is premium

British confectionery company Hotel Chocolat, which coats its stores, packaging and branding with black like the darkest of dark chocolate.

Gray – Promotes feelings of practicality, old age, and solidarity. When overused grey can lead to feelings of nothingness and depression. Gray can be conservative, boring, drab and depressing but it can also be seen as "elegant and formal" when used properly. It is often used in logos because it goes well with many other colors but it is not as bold as black or white. The logo for the luxury brand Swarovski, maker of lead crystal glass, is gray. Though gray could be viewed as representing the lead that is a part of the product the company makes, it also represents the respect and authority that comes from the history of a company that has been around for over 100 years.

Color and Brand Identity

The link between color and brand identity is strong. In the Journal of the Academy of Marketing Science, researchers Lauren Labrecque and George Milne explain that "like a carefully chosen brand name, color carries intrinsic meaning that becomes central to the brand's identity, contributes to brand recognition, and communicates the desired image."

In their research on color differentiation in the marketplace, Labrecque and Milne highlighted how certain industries frequently use particular colors. For instance, they found that blue is used in over 75% of credit card brand logos, and 20% of fast food brand logos. Red, meanwhile, is found in about 0% of apparel logos—but over 60% of retail brands.

For consumers confronted with advertising thousands of times a day these visual cues are an unconscious message about what they're being sold, and who is selling it. For budding entrepreneurs about to create their own business here is some pertinent information about colors courtesy of EPC Group that may be helpful.

The number of Colors used by Fortune 500 company logos.

- 38% use one color
- 44% use two colors
- 14% use three colors

- 2% use four colors
- 2% use five colors

Most popular logo colors

- #1 Blue, #2 Black, #3 Red, #4 Green

The Most Popular Colors for 2-Color logos

- #1 Black & Red 18%, #2 Blue & Red 11%, #3 Black & Blue 10%

The most popular 3-Color logos

- Blue, Black, Green/Blue, Black, Gray/Red, Black, Gray/Red, Yellow, Green/Red, Black, White

Armed with this knowledge of color and its effects, you should be ready to paint your bedroom with the color that will allow you to get a good night's sleep, wear the color dress or suit that will score big at your job interview, turn window shoppers into customers, keep visitors to your website engaged, and do hundreds of other things to give yourself a competitive advantage in your race to success.

Now that you know how entities like food, music, color, and your daily routine can affect you and your quest to be successful it's up to you to put this information to good use. Knowledge is power, only if you use it.

Chapter 3: You Are Your Miracle

Some people think of themselves as castaways stranded on a deserted island waiting for a cargo ship to happen by or a low flying plane to appear overhead and rescue them. Or, worse they envision themselves adrift on a vast ocean of problems and misfortune, their lives wasting away as they sit waiting to be rescued by somebody, anybody. The truth is that maybe they will be rescued. Maybe like a wayward cargo vessel someone will sail close enough to them to throw a lifeline and pull them out of whatever murky ocean they are drowning in. Reality being what it is, there is of course a greater chance no one is coming. If you don't want to end up wasting your entire life waiting on that miracle you'd best pull it together and rescue yourself. How, you may ask? When you are buried by your circumstances rescuing yourself may sound like an impossible thing to do. However, if you want to live your best life you should, you can, and if you follow the prompts detailed in this chapter you will rescue yourself. By having the right strategy, living by design, and avoiding pitfalls you will find that you are your miracle.

Strategy

Success Begins with Having The Right Strategy

Employing the Wrong Strategy: Having a strategy is good but having a good strategy is better. Too many people believe they will succeed just because they have a plan. In the words of former baddest man in the world and former heavyweight champion Mike Tyson, "Everyone has a plan until they get hit in the face."

Ok, you have a plan. So does the next person. So does your competitor. So does everyone else fighting and scratching for their piece of the pie. If life has taught us anything it has taught us this, not all plans are equal.

If you are old enough to remember the dotcom boom that occurred between 1994 and 2000 you will remember the poster child of the dotcom bust that followed it. During those days the Pets.com sock puppet was everywhere. He was on the Pet.com commercials. He was doing interviews on television programs like Nightline, Good Morning America and Live with Regis and Kathie Lee. A likeness of the puppet made from a balloon even appeared at the 1999 Macy's Thanksgiving Day Parade. If that wasn't enough exposure the sock puppet was famously featured in a $1.2 million advertisement during the 2000 NFL Superbowl. Pet.com obviously had a plan. Unfortunately for them it wasn't a good plan. Just a year later the company was out of business.

Their plan was to flood the airwaves with the cute little sock puppet mascot and customers would lovingly flock to their website and order dog toys, leashes, cat litter and all the other pet products they sold. Pets.com's owners, Hummer Winblad Venture Partners, made a costly strategic mistake by failing to do market research before it moved forward with its initial public offering (IPO) cashing in by selling stock in the company. What Pet.com found out was that there were few customers out there who wanted to buy pet products from their company. Once the dust had settled their investors had watched $50 million of their money vanish into thin air. That's 50 million reasons why it's not enough to simply have a plan.

If you haven't done your market research before you develop a business plan your plan is highly likely to be full of holes. Don't procrastinate. Do the research you need to do. Do the advance work that needs to be done. Make the decisions that need to be made. You can't develop the right strategy until you perform your due diligence so that your strategy is based upon concrete information.

Never choose short-term rewards over long-term benefits: Would you rather have $10 today or $300 next year? Individuals and companies who chase instant gratification at the expense of long-term gains rarely end up on the list of most successful companies. Yes, sometimes you must strike when the iron is hot. But if you believe the iron is always hot that's a problem.

Patience Is Still A Virtue

The millennial generation, born during the 1980s and 1990s, grew up on technology. Unlike previous generations instant gratification is a natural desire for them. About 60 percent of 18-to-34-year-old respondents to a Pew Research Center survey said they sleep next to their cell phones so they don't miss calls, texts, or updates during the night. As a measure of how conditioned they are more than three-quarters of millennials check their phones for messages or missed calls even when they didn't hear a notice alert or their phones ringing.

Over 70% of elementary, middle and high school teachers claim constant media use has hurt students' attention spans. According to Common Sense Media more than 40% of teachers surveyed believe it has interfered with the critical thinking of students and their ability to engage with subject matter. Among the biggest distractions for students cited by teachers are video games at 68% and texting at 66%.

Diagnoses of attention deficit disorder for children and teenagers has soared. Even older adults are increasingly getting prescriptions for ADD medications. Some Teachers say they rarely assign complete book assignments anymore. Most opt to assign short stories or book excerpts instead because of shorter student attention spans.

Millennials find it more difficult than previous generations to delay not just the gratification of the trivial but also the more important aspects of their lives. Many young professionals today want their careers to be super-charged for rapid advancement. They want the gratification of getting pay raises or job promotions every few months. When they don't get what they expect they feel frustrated and sometimes end up quitting their jobs. This behavior is creating retention headaches for employers, some of whom see the impatient, job-hopping millennials as unappealing employment prospects.

If this pattern is a predictor of future results the need for instant gratification is likely to become an even bigger problem for the generation born after 2000 where more than 70 percent of children age 8 and under had already used a mobile device to connect with some type of media activity like playing games, using apps or watching videos in 2013. That number was up from 38% in 2011, according to a parent survey by Common Sense Media, a nonprofit group that provides information and recommendations about the media use of young people. Today, even babies and toddlers are being given access to tablets and smartphones.

Around 38% of children under 2 have used a mobile device for media activity. That figure was a rise of 10% from two years earlier.

Patience has long been considered a virtue but in the future people may see it as an unnecessary nuisance. We now live in a world where DVRs have eliminated the need to waste time watching commercials. Viewers can instantly summon the latest movies on-demand. No more standing in lines at theaters. No more waiting at restaurants to be seated. Smartphone apps give consumers the ability to buy movie tickets in mere seconds and book dinner reservations immediately. Thanks to location-based technology seekers of companionship don't even have to wait on dates. They can instantly connect people who are hanging out in the same neighborhood.

Instant gratification is now baked into the marketing pitch and services offered to today's consumer. Internet service providers promise faster connections for an uptick in price. If you are looking for fast, faster, and fastest, Verizon offers its Quantum FIOS service in several different speeds. Verizon's "rocket fuel" speed promises to download a high-definition movie in 2.2 minutes or upload 200 photos in 31 seconds for around $200. And, if that's still too pedestrian for you their "supersonic" speed will finish the video download in 1.4 minutes and the photo upload in 20 seconds for about $300 a month.

Also playing on the instant gratification theme Amazon offers same-day delivery in some cities, which means packages ordered early in the day will arrive by 8 p.m. and even that rapid delivery schedule will soon be eclipsed by their Prime Air unmanned delivery drones that the company is currently working on blanketing the skies with. These drones will deliver packages to Amazon customers in 30 minutes or less. Amazon tells customers on its website:

"One day, Prime Air vehicles will be as normal as seeing mail trucks on the road today."

Dopamine and The Pleasure Principle

So, what is the root problem that millennials and possibly you face that is causing so many to sell out their tomorrows for instant gratification?

"The promise of technology was that it would make us masters of time," says Harold Schweizer, Professor of English at Bucknell University. "It has, ironically, made us into time's slaves."

Most of the major social media platforms are free and rely on revenue from advertisers to make a profit. This business formula has created a social media eco-system that is dependent upon attracting visitors to the platform to boost their advertising value and thereby capitalize on turning those eyeballs on the page into revenue. The company that can best use its platform to attract visitors, and because of those visitors revenue, is the winner. How does a social media platform assure itself of becoming a winner? By effectively exploiting that brain chemical that keeps visitors coming back for more, Dopamine.

Dopamine is a neurotransmitter, a chemical messenger in the brain. It is responsible for sending signals from the central nervous system. It is the chemical that allows information to be passed from one neuron to another. Dopamine is influenced by other types of neurons it combines with and while scientists originally thought that this substance is the cause of the pleasure we experience it is now believed dopamine is more related to anticipatory pleasure and motivation. In the prefrontal cortex, the main part of the brain associated with higher-ordered thinking, dopamine secretions help to improve your working memory. Dopamine levels are extremely delicate so even slight increases or decreases to the normal amount can cause your memory to malfunction.

Since dopamine affects your memory it also affects your learning processes and how you retain information. When dopamine is present in the brain during an event or experience, you will remember that event. But, if dopamine is absent, you usually won't remember it. Dopamine works in union with your brain's reward center. If you don't feel interested in specific activities or in learning certain subjects dopamine levels will decrease in your prefrontal cortex. If this happens, your brain will not feel the motivation to remember the information presented to you.

Dopamine aids you in keeping focused and paying attention. It does its work by responding to vision (the optic nerves), which causes you to direct your attention to any specific task or activity. The neurotransmitter dopamine may be responsible for what content stays in your short-term memory, a portion of your prefrontal cortex associated with immediate attention. When the dopamine concentration is too low it could lead to Attention Deficit Disorder (ADD).

When you increase your motivation you increase your levels of dopamine. What is the best way to increase your motivation and thereby increase your dopamine level? By having content presented to you in a new way. Remember the acronym NERF. When the content or information that is presented to you is a New, Exciting, and Rewarding, Formula, it will release dopamine helping you to remember it. Don't just try to receive content and information in the same old routine and possibly boring way.

Use new techniques, new technology, new sources, or new instructors to feed you content or information. Make it Exciting by trying a different location for receiving content in, trying to make learning more hands-on, or applying it to an exciting activity as you learn. Reward yourself for learning by treating yourself to something you like each time you reach another level of learning, shortening your study session if you learn the material faster. Once you discover a more effective way to learn turn it into a Formula. Use the same learning methods just changing the variables like using different locations, rewards, technologies etc. to keep the dopamine coming, to solidify the memorization process.

Dopamine is also the central chemical in your brain that regulates how you perceive and experience pleasure. During pleasurable moments or situations dopamine is released. Searching for this euphoric feeling again is what causes a person to seek out a desirable activity again and again. Eating, especially foods with high levels of sugar, is such an activity. Having sexual intercourse is another such activity. Both activities stimulate dopamine to be released in the brain which is why we find them so enjoyable and continue to engage in them.

On the negative side, most addiction-causing drugs work by targeting the dopamine neurotransmitters in your brain. Drugs like cocaine and amphetamines inhibit the re-uptake of dopamine in each synapse available. A synapse is composed of a neuron that is releasing a specific neurotransmitter and another neuron that is receiving the said neurotransmitter. The gap between the two neurons is called a synaptic cleft. Neurons communicate with each other in different ways and one of these ways involves the process called reuptake. Reuptake refers to what happens after the neurotransmitter is released from the first neuron. In order to recycle the neurotransmitter the first neuron will absorb what it has released after the neurotransmitter's job has been completed then re-use it again when necessary. Re-uptake also controls the amount of the neurotransmitter that is available for the brain's use to ensure an excessive amount is not being used.

What does all this mean? Research in reward learning and addiction have recently focused on a feature of dopamine neurons called reward prediction error (RPE) encoding. These prediction errors serve as dopamine-mediated feedback signals in our brains. This neurological feature is a trick gambling casinos have used for years to rake in profits. While playing slot machines you've most likely experienced intense anticipation as you watched those cherries and other icons spinning. In the seconds between your pull of the handle and the bars lining up when you see whether you have won or not dopamine neurons increase their activity creating a euphoric feeling from the anticipation. However, if loses keep mounting up the slowing of dopamine activity and loss of that pleasurable feeling encourages us to stop playing. It is this balance between positive and negative outcomes that allow our brain to find a normal equilibrium.

Social media apps take advantage of this same dopamine-driven strategy? Similar to slot machines, many apps implement a reward pattern optimized to keep you engaged as long as possible. The concept of variable reward schedules was introduced by psychologist B.F. Skinner in the 1930's. In his experiments, he found mice responded most frequently when the activity used reward-associated stimuli and the reward was administered after a varying number of responses. This left the mice unable to predict when they would be rewarded. Humans are no different than mice in this regard. If we believe the reward is rewarded randomly, and if checking for the reward cost little or nothing, we will check habitually just like someone with a gambling addiction. You are probably in the habit of checking your phone whenever you feel bored. It has become a habit. Why? Because the social media programmers have worked very hard to create a platform that keeps you doing just that.

When you first joined Facebook your notification center revolved around your initial set of connections, and friends, etc. That is what created the link between your notifications and social rewards. As you used Facebook more and began interacting with various groups, artists, and events your notification center became more and more active. After a while you had enough notifications to check your app at any time and expect to be rewarded with likes or other activities. Since there is such a low cost for checking your phone, mainly just time itself, it presents you with a strong incentive to check in whenever you have an opportunity.

Instagram, which is owned by Facebook, has implemented a variable-ratio reward schedule. Its notification algorithms will sometimes withhold "likes" on your photos to deliver them in larger bunches. Because of this you may post a picture and caption and receive little or no feedback which of course is disappointing. You check later and find a bunch of responses. Your dopamine centers have been primed by those initial negative outcomes to respond pleasurably to the sudden rush of social media approval. The variable reward schedule they use takes advantage of our dopamine-driven desire for social validation optimizing the balance of negative and positive feedback signals turning us into habitual users. Realizing this is the game being played with our brains it is up to us to decide how much of our valuable time we want to spend or waste with these social media activities.

Design

Succeeding in Life By Design

Step One: Figure out why you are where you are. Though we love to blame things on luck and attribute other things to happening by accident the truth is that neither luck nor accidents are the cause for anything that exist. Rather, all things are the result of cause and effect. Good, bad, or indifferent everything happens for a reason. It may not happen the way you planned. It may not be what you hoped for or prayed for. But, everything happens for a reason. Nothing is random.

Jan. 28, 1986, The Challenger Space Shuttle exploded 73 seconds after liftoff, killing all 7 crew members. It was discovered that a rocket booster leak ignited the fuel, causing the explosion.

Feb. 1, 2003, The Columbia Space Shuttle: broke up on reentering Earth's atmosphere on its way to Kennedy Space Center, killing all 7 crew members. The cause of this disaster was foam insulation fell from the shuttle during launch damaging the left wing. On reentry, hot gases entered that wing leading to the disintegration of the shuttle.

On occasion, freak lightning strikes from thunderstorms may spark wildfires like the ones that seem to ravage California each year. But, many of these fires have been traced to human actions such as motorists throwing cigarettes out their car windows, campers failing to completely put out their campfires, sparks coming from car mufflers setting fire to dry grass along the road, or even electrical wires in need of maintenance sparking and catching the surrounding vegetation on fire.

What were the causes of recent commercial airline crashes? Those crashes caused several airlines to ground the Boing 737 Max jets, the same kind of jets as the ones involved in 2 of the crashes. Technology installed in both planes is being investigated as a probable cause that contributed to the crashes.

How about disastrous oil spills that dump thousands of gallons of oil into our oceans killing wildlife, ruining commerce for business sectors like the fishing industry, contaminating the environment, and even causing loss of life?

What about nuclear power plant disasters at 3 Mile Island in California, or Chernobyl in Russia, or the Fukushima Daiichi nuclear plant in Japan? It's easy to just write disasters and so-called accidents off as bad luck but each of these incidents has a cause.

The negative incidents and unfortunate accidents that occur in your life also have a cause. That is why one of the first things you must do to turn your situation around or improve your life is make an accurate assessment of exactly why things happened to you the way they did. Don't just blame someone, or blame something like the economy, or conclude that you just happened to be in the wrong place at the wrong time. Do some intensive research that will help you pinpoint the exact causes that explain what happened and how it resulted in a negative outcome for you. You cannot put together a foolproof plan to repair your life until you truly understand what is broken, and how it got that way. Only then can you put together a strategy to undue things that are keeping you from reaching your goals.

Things that stop you from achieving success no matter how much you want it:

Lack of Preparation: What does it really take to build a house? A hammer and nails? No, it takes much more than that. You need a developer to develop the land. An architect has to draw up the blueprint. A builder is needed to read the blueprint and start construction. You need a contractor to hire the sub-contractors to do the electrical, plumbing, drywall, HVAC, and other jobs. You need landscapers to do the yards. And on top of all this you need dozens of other craftsmen and skilled workers to actually complete the building of the house. Bottom line, if you think knowing how to use a hammer and nails is all you need to know to build a house you are going to find yourself woefully unprepared to successfully complete the task.

You need to exhaust yourself in researching all the things you will actually need to know, be, and do to successfully reach your goal. What education and certifications will you need? How much capital and what resources will you need? How much time will you need? What things will you need to pass up or sacrifice to put yourself in a position to succeed? There are probably 100 questions you need to ask yourself before preparing to go after your goals. Once you get the answers to these questions you need to follow through with putting together a strategy based on the answers to those questions.

Falling Prey to Procrastination: Don't put off until tomorrow what you should do today. Good advice for anyone looking to achieve great things.

One trait that separates those who do from those who don't is doing what needs to get done, when it needs to get done. While many people who dream of success but never achieve it often procrastinate, those who have a track record for being successful are decisive and never allow important duties to be pushed aside or delayed. The successful person does not shy away from duties big or small because he or she knows that success is not the result of one decision but a series of decisions that lead to a triumphant result.

An author must decide to sit down and write, day after day, page after page until a manuscript is completed to give those words and pages a chance to become a best-selling book. A basketball player must train for long days, weeks, months, years to hone skills and elevate his or her talent to the point where those skills and talents can succeed on the biggest stage when the stakes are highest. Before you can make the shot, you must take the shot, and a lot of sweat equity must be paid before that shot takes flight. One does not become successful by putting work off until another day. A person becomes a success by embracing work as a necessary rung on the ladder that leads to success. You must not only fall in love with the rewards that come from success but with the day to day process that results in that success. When you delay decisions you also are making a decision to delay success. For anyone striving to succeed procrastination is a dirty word.

Good Ideas Can't Overcome Bad Execution: You can have a fantastic idea. You can put together a great business plan. But, these things mean nothing if you don't follow up with excellent execution. Dreaming and planning are wonderful but it's the doing that determines your level of success.

How easy success would be if all you had to do was come up with brilliant ideas. The videotape format war was a period of intense competition or a "format war" of incompatible models of consumer-level analog videocassette and video cassette recorders (VCR) in the late 1970s and the 1980s, mainly involving the Betamax and Video Home System (VHS) formats. VHS ultimately emerged as the preeminent format. The main determining factor between Betamax and VHS was the cost of the recorders and recording time. Betamax is, in theory, a superior recording format over VHS due to resolution (250 lines vs. 240 lines), slightly superior sound, and a more stable image; Betamax recorders were also of higher quality construction. But these differences were negligible to consumers, and thus did not justify either the extra cost of a Betamax VCR (which was often significantly more expensive than it's VHS equivalent) or Betamax's shorter recording time. What does all this say? The best product doesn't always win.

To succeed you must have a plan and not only a plan but also a plan for how to implement your plan. To gain an understanding of what an implementation strategy is, we must first define what a strategic plan is. A strategic plan is the process of defining the strategy by which you (or a team or organization) will accomplish certain goals or make decisions. Organizations make strategic plans to guide organizational direction, a particular department's efforts, or how to go about completing any project or initiative.

An implementation strategy is the process of defining how to bring the strategic plan to life. To execute the objectives outlined in the strategic plan you must define how you will implement each aspect, from funding and personnel to organization and deliverables. Therefore, without an implementation strategy, it can be difficult to identify how you will achieve each of your stated goals and objectives.

4 Steps That Lead to Project Success

There are four key steps involved in a project implementation strategy:

1. Build a project plan: When building your project plan you must first define what your core goals are. To define your core goals ask yourself these questions:

First, what are you trying to accomplish? Your goals and objectives should all tie right back into what you have defined as your end game. If one of your goals or objectives doesn't, why are you doing it?

Second, do you have the internal resources to execute and accomplish your goals and objectives? Internal resources can include project managers, logistics management, business management, finances, etc..

Third, what are the cost implications for achieving your goals and objectives? Determine the costs of all the resources you'll need so you can tie these cost projections back to the company budget. As your project moves forward stay focused on the core goals that support the objectives of the business as a whole. Don't stray from what your goals and objectives are or allow your budget to be siphoned off for things that fall outside of your stated goals and objectives.

2. Manage your resources: Do you have the resources it will take to achieve your project goals? Do you presently have the staffing or help to manage the process without additional help? If not, you may need to work with an outside vendor or outsource work. If you outsource work also consider sending one of your managers or staff to help the vendor or outsource partner get up to speed on training or logistical details such as: selecting training venues; required technology, hardware or software choices, training materials, etc. Select a vendor or contractor who has a strong track record in the area you need help in.

3. Set A Timeline and Stick To It: Remember, most things that occur in business are time sensitive so make it a goal to stay on schedule. Unless a very necessary detour must be made that throws you off schedule don't get bogged down on any one thing to the point where it throws your schedule off. If you made a realistic assessment of what resources and human capital were necessary to achieve your goals and objectives there should be no big surprises. Follow your plan and make adjustments when necessary but do not allow things or processes to disrupt your timeline. In most cases finishing on or ahead of time is just as important as finishing. Stay focused on your core goals and objectives and don't allow distractions to derail you. Be vigilant every day and every step of the way. Do your best to anticipate problems before they arise and have the solution ready and waiting.

4. Evaluate the End Results Of Your Work: Once you complete a project and reach all of your goals and objectives it's important to evaluate what worked and went according to plan and what did not. Be sure to evaluate what impact the results had on your business. This information will be extremely valuable as you refine your design process and strategy before embarking on your next project. Did your systems work as you expected or did they fall short of expectations? Were your resources enough or do you need to add some resources before your next project? Assess your performance frequently. A good way to find this out is to send out a short evaluation form or survey to your managers or core leaders. As you end projects make sure the payment for your work has been made or your billing arrangements have been acknowledged and payment is forthcoming as agreed upon. Your business needs working capital so don't leave payments for work completed dangling out there. Reel it in. Also, value your vendors and pay them on time so when it's time for the next job they will want to work with your company or organization.

The 7 Deadly Modern Day Sins

Being A Victim of Distractions: There is no doubt that we are a distracted society. People walk the streets staring at their phones. They stumble through airports, sit at restaurants, muddle through family gatherings, even pass their time at events with heads bowed and eyes glued to the screen. We are so distracted we have lost the ability to connect with each other. We don't even pay attention to our surroundings anymore. We spend the majority of our day on auto-pilot glancing up just long enough not to bump into an oncoming pedestrian or tumble off a curb into oncoming traffic. Most of the time our minds are so preoccupied that we drive from point A to point B and don't remember any of the scenery along the way. Nor do we remember how we got to our destination once we arrive. Life is no longer passing us by, we are passing it by. Distracted drivers are killing people on our highways. We get more excited about answering emails, checking alerts and notifications, and texting than we do about checking in with family and friends to see if they are in good health. Research shows that our distracted lives are eroding our ability to maintain healthy relationships, properly manage our time, focus on the things that are important, put time and energy into planning out our lives, or do the important things that add value to our lives. We have become a victim of our distractions.

Attaching to the Wrong Friends: How do you know when you're attached to the wrong friends? Perhaps when they constantly gossip and backstab you and others. If they talk about others they're probably talking behind your back as well. If you have friends that are always too busy to be with you, you don't have a friend. When it's always you making time for them you probably need to move on. If your friends have no problem borrowing money but always seem to have problems paying it back, you need new friends. If they tell you to pick up the tab whenever you go out, it means they don't see you as a friend, they see you as a wallet. If you have friends that are great at making promises but terrible at keeping their promises, they are taking your friendship for granted. And who needs friends like that? If your friends always want you to be there for them but are rarely there for you, that's not much of a friend. If your friends fill your life with drama instead of wisdom and chaos instead of peace the cost of their friendship is too high. A friend is someone who not only makes your life better, they make you better. They are always looking out for your best interests, always supportive of you doing positive things, and always celebrate your growth. If your friends are all about the preceding sentence congratulations. But, if they are toxic it's time to say adios.

Being A Slave to Your Emotions: How do you know that you are a slave to your emotions? if you find yourself reacting to situations before you even take time to think about it, you're probably a slave to your emotions. The term amygdala hijack refers to the phenomenon that happens when the emotional parts of your brain have completely taken over the thinking parts of your brain. When you fly off the handle and react to a situation before you even have all the information, often hurting yourself and others because you get so overwhelmed with emotions that you are no longer capable of being reasonable, that's a pretty good sign that you're a slave to your emotions. When you keep reacting impulsively instead of learning from your mistakes and changing your behavior it is a sign that you have not mastered your emotions, which means you are still a slave to them. If you find yourself unable to be rational and solve your problems without getting all worked up it will always end up hurting you, your relationships, your career, and finally your health. Of this you can be sure. Nothing positive will ever emerge from being a slave to your emotions.

The Curse of Being Unfocused: Even with all the talent in the world you can't get far if you are unfocused. Imagine trying to drive across the country to a state on the opposite coast while looking at every billboard on the side of the road, constantly changing the radio station, talking on your phone, steering with one hand and eating with the other, ignoring the gas gauge and speedometer, paying no attention to the navigation system, and wondering what your best friend is doing today. Truth is, you could end up anywhere. Probably, anywhere but where you intended to go. So many people live their lives that way, focusing on anything and everything except reaching their goal as though things will somehow miraculously fall in place for them. Things don't just happen. You must make them happen. Life doesn't manage itself. You must manage it. Your goals won't just fall into your lap. You have to pursue them and overcome obstacles to achieve them. You must plan, strategize, and execute that plan to succeed, and none of this can be achieved without staying focused on your tasks. You must lock onto your goal and stay in hot pursuit of it like a heat seeking missile. If you want success you can't allow yourself to be distracted, or take shortcuts, or quit when things get tough, or fail to give at least 100%, or wander off track, or waste time, or allow hours, days, weeks, to pass without making progress toward your goal. Don't let the curse of being unfocused stop you cold. You must get your mind on your goal and keep it there until the task is completed.

Thinking Failure Is Not An Option: Why do people fear failing so much? Show me anyone who has succeeded greatly without failing at some point in their lives. How do you recover from failure? What did you learn from failure? What things will you do differently next time? Failure is our greatest teacher because it teaches us those things that success cannot. We don't fear failure because we fear losing something valuable that we can never recover. We fear failure because we fear it is saying something truthful about us that our reputation can never recover from. We fear the glances, whispers, finger pointing, loss of respect and disdain that come with failure. That's what we fear. Being the subject of ridicule, scorn, slander, and laughter. Somewhere inside of us all is that person who tells us that we cannot achieve our goals, that we are not smart enough, or talented enough, or educated enough, or young enough, or socially connected enough to succeed. The difference between those who go on to success and those who remain mired in mediocrity is what we do with that inner voice and those outer voices. Do we allow those voices to melt us and our dreams down to nothing or do we use those voices as rocket fuel to propel us to success? Failure is just another steppingstone on the pathway to success for we who are bold enough to dream big and work hard.

Failing to Deliver Value: At the core of any business, organization, or relationship is value. The world's most successful businesses are the ones who deliver the most value. "What makes your product or service better than your competitors?"

The first stage of a customer's journey is Awareness. This is the stage where your potential customer is aware that he or she has a problem or need. They begin researching information and actively seeking a product or service that will solve their problem or need. This is the stage where you have the opportunity to make a first impression. Next comes the evaluation stage. This is the stage where they are comparing your product or service to other solutions on the market by doing price comparisons, reading customer reviews, checking out competitors, comparing notes with other buyers, and learning more about the details of your product or service to see if it could be the solution they are looking for. The bar is now set. Can you meet or exceed your potential customer's expectations or will you fall short of delivering them the value product or service you promised, and they are hoping for? One of the most egregious modern day sins you can be guilty of in this age of social media is failing to deliver value. Never before has word traveled so fast to spread the news about something good or something bad. You can no longer afford to get it right the second time. If you don't nail it on your first try your sullied reputation may not be granted a second chance. Do your absolute best to deliver a product, service, or experience that not only meets or exceeds the expectations of you and your customers, but in fact exceeds all expectations. If you do your customers will be singing your praises from every mountain top and social media platform they can find.

Not Having the Right Motivation: In his best-selling 2011 book "Start With Why" author Simon Sinek ask a fundamental question, WHY? Why are some people and organizations more innovative, more influential, and more profitable than others? Why do some command greater loyalty from customers and employees alike? Even among the successful, why are so few able to repeat their success over and over? People like Martin Luther King Jr., Steve Jobs, and the Wright Brothers had little in common, but they all started with WHY. They realized that people won't truly buy into a product, service, movement, or idea until they understand the WHY behind it. If you want to succeed, if you want to find the motivation that inspires you to succeed you too must start with why. Having a great idea may get you going but it won't keep you going without motivation. Chasing your dream is going to come down to how badly you want it which translates into what your deepest reason is for pursuing your dream. That's your why. Why do you want it? For many the reason is money, especially for those who don't have much right now. Though money is a motivator it is not nearly the best motivation. It is at best a means to an end. How many athletes once they turn professional and get that first big paycheck say they are overjoyed to now be able to purchase their mother or parents a home? Even after all the blood, sweat, and tears it took for them to achieve their goal still the strongest motivation for the pursuit of their goal was wanting to reward a mother's love. Whether you succeed or fail, not having a strong why will ultimately leave you unmotivated and unfulfilled. Motivation is most often the difference between you giving up or fighting through to success. Find your WHY and ride it "til the rims come off.

Pitfalls

25 Pieces of Advice That Will Change Your Life

1. Never lose sight of your goals. 2. Nothing happens by accident. 3. Stop doing the same things and expecting different results. 4. Always do the things that matter. 5. Don't procrastinate. 6. Do your homework. 7. Focus less on who you are and more on who you need to be. 8. Stop trying to please everyone. 9. Realize that you can't change people. 10. Time is your most valuable resource. 11. Don't get sucked into other people's drama. 12. Learn from your mistakes. 13. Don't make excuses. 14. Don't blame your mistakes on others. 15. Believe hard work pays off. 16. Don't start until you have a good plan.

17. Don't fear change. 18. Improve yourself to improve your chances. 19. Don't waste time complaining. 20. Eliminate your distractions. 21. Don't believe in luck believe in yourself. 22. The decisions you make equal the life you live. 23. Don't fear failure it's a prerequisite for success. 24. Don't waste time. 25. Whatever you feed will grow.

Steer Clear of Pitfalls

If you want to experience success and freedom in your life there are some pitfalls you must avoid. If you have already fallen victim to them you must extricate yourself from these pitfalls to become successful.

Stay out of debt: Late fees and payday loans are nothing more than money wasted. You can't get out of a hole by digging a deeper hole. Desperate people are more prone to making mistakes and falling prey to bad judgement than people who are financially secure and successful. The payday and collateral loan industry make their living off those who can hardly afford to borrow money from them, especially at such high interest rates. If you are already in debt you obviously cannot afford to pay what you owe let alone with interest added on top of that.

Payday loans are short-term cash loans based on the borrower's personal check held for future deposit or on electronic access to the borrower's bank account. Borrowers write a personal check for the amount borrowed plus the finance charge and receive cash in return. In some cases, borrowers sign over electronic access to their bank accounts to receive and repay payday loans.

Some payday lenders also offer longer-term payday instalment loans and request authorization to electronically withdraw multiple payments from the borrower's bank account, typically due on each pay date. Payday loans range in size from $100 to $1,000, depending on state legal maximums. The average loan term is about two weeks. Loans typically cost 400% annual interest (APR) or more. The finance charge ranges from $15 to $30 to borrow $100. For two-week loans, these finance charges result in interest rates from 390 to 780% APR.

Shorter term loans have even higher APRs and rates are even higher in states that do not cap the maximum cost. For more information on payday loans go to paydayloaninfo.org .

Would someone who is financially secure borrow money knowing they have to pay such outrageous interest rates? Of course not. It is almost impossible to get out of debt by taking on more debt. Once you become a payday loan customer and incur more debt the loan may help you to pay your bills momentarily but repaying the loan and the interest on that loan already guarantees that you will be even further in debt when the next month rolls around. To a desperate person payday loans may look like a solution but really they are just another problem. Trying to get out of debt by getting more in debt is a terrible idea. There is a reason you are in debt and that reason is that you don't have enough money. So, what you need is not a high interest payday loan but another source of income.

Better to take a few dollars and bake some cookies to sell at your job, or take on some home job you can do in your spare time, or use your skills to change your neighbors oil for a small fee, sell items in your garage you aren't using, or find some other (legal) short term income you can use to clear up your debt than create more debt trying to solve the problem. A loan may help you out for a week or two but you'll soon find yourself in the cycle of returning to the payday loan company again and again paying back their loan and sky high interest with money you really can't afford to spare.

Payday loans and other high interest payback scams are not the answer to your problems. Again, the answer is creating more income. Don't wait until the utilities are threatening to turn off your gas or lights, or shut off your phone before you create your little extra cash activity. Create your surplus cash maker ahead of time then stash the money away in a safe place so it will be there when you run into an emergency. Don't say you don't have time to spend earning a little extra cash when you spend idle hours each week on social media or watching your favorite TV shows.

Paying for Storage Is Wasting Money

Don't waste money each month paying for a storage bin for items you haven't used in years. If those items were really that valuable you'd be using them not storing them away somewhere so they can collect dust. The price most people pay for the junk they have stored is more than the value of the items in storage. It cost a lot less to be realistic than it does to be sentimental. Sell those stored items and use the cash to pay down your debts or pay bills or put gas in your car or take a vacation and make new memories rather than try to hold onto old ones. Plus, by selling your stored items and getting rid of your storage space you are getting rid of a monthly bill.

Credit Cards, The Good Bad and Ugly

Credit cards are either a good friend in times of need or your worst financial nightmare. For most people there is no in-between. If you are financially disciplined you don't have to think of credit cards as the devil. It is the undisciplined person who knows the horror of watching their credit card go from a good friend to a nightmare. If you want your credit card to be an asset to you and not a liability there are a few key things you must know. Firstly, only charge what you can afford to pay by the time your bill arrives. That is how to use your credit card wisely. Remember, credit cards should be used as a payment tool, not a revolving debt instrument.

There are times when financing a purchase with a credit card makes sense. Always keep your repayment time short. For instance, think of this scenario. You need to replace your refrigerator that just stopped working. You don't have the money to pay for it right now. But, you know you have a tax return check on the way about three weeks from now. You spot a good sale on a quality fridge. Under these circumstances it makes since to charge it on your credit card and pay it off within a month.

Another scenario that works is, your refrigerator cost $1,500 and your credit card charges you an interest rate of $18. You pay off your balance and interest in 4 months which means the finance fees would cost you $57. That's a reasonable cost to purchase an item that is absolutely needed, especially knowing the money for paying off the debt you incurred to make the purchase is already on its way. Some credit cards don't even charge you a fee if you can pay off your bill within 30 days. But, on the other hand, that same purchase can turn into a horror story if you don't have the money to immediately pay off your debt and have to stretch out your purchase over a period of two years. In that case your repayment would cost you an extra $300. That would not be a wise purchase. Your good deal would suddenly become a bad deal. Many people find themselves in that credit card trap.

The credit card trap is an easy one to step into because when cardholders start out their credit card limit is usually low but it usually rises over time. The bigger your credit limit the greater chance of you overcharging your card by purchasing items you can't really afford. Once you fall into that trap paying down debt is difficult because as your balance grows the interest on your debt compounds and your payments increase. Consequently, you can find yourself in a situation where you can only afford to pay the interest each month while your debt grows larger and larger until you are buried in credit card debt.

Low Credit Scores

If you want to stay out of credit card trouble always be aware of what you are charging on your card, what your balances are, and when your payment is due. Continually having high balances on your credit card account negatively impacts your credit score. It should be no secret that personal finance experts advice credit card holders to keep their credit card balances as close to zero as possible. If you want to maintain a high credit score you should keep your account balance under 30% of your available credit limit. To build a good credit score or keep your credit score up you must make your payments on time. If you are financially undisciplined credit card debt will most likely not be your only problem. You will probably have credit score issues as well.

What happens when you fall behind with your card payments? If you fall behind and have to skip a billing cycle your credit card company will report your delinquency to TransUnion, Equifax and Experian the three major credit reporting bureaus after you are delinquent 60 days and your credit score will drop. Now you have a problem that has gone from being temporary to being more lasting because those negative marks won't fall off your credit reports for a full seven years.

There are remedies if you fall a few months behind with your payments. If you can come up with a lump sum for a payment you can negotiate with the card company to settle your credit card debt for less than the actual balance. Though this may be a solution it is recommended that such a settlement be resorted to only after you have exhausted other measures to eliminate your debt because this type of settlement can seriously damage your credit. Settling your debt for less than the balance owed may also cause you tax problems.

There is a book called "How To Settle Your Debts," by Norman Perlmutter, that discusses how to get out of debt. In the book Perlmutter suggest various debt reduction tactics such as: Asking creditors to reduce your credit cards' interest rates; limiting your spending to only purchasing your basic needs to free up cash to pay down your debt; prioritizing the debts you pay off by interest rates (always pay the debts with the highest-interest balances first); and asking companies to suspend charges while you are in repayment mode. If you can't come to an agreement with your credit card company about payments you can contact the National Foundation for Credit Counseling and work with one of their credit counselors to try and develop a repayment plan the credit company might agree with.

Another avenue you may pursue is to ask your credit card company for help. Though they are under no obligation to accept less than the minimum requested payment sometimes credit card companies will allow you to work out payment arrangements.

Be aware that credit card companies have legal means at their disposal to recover the money you owe them. When you have gone months without paying your creditors can and most likely will sue you in a court of law. If they win a judgment they may be granted the right to garnish your wages or take your nonexempt property and assets.

Finally, no matter what credit problems you are facing it is always a good practice to address them immediately.

Chapter 4: Get Your Methodology Right

We've all heard it said, "Where there is a will there's a way."

True. But how much will? What way? Too many people fall under the mistaken theory if they just stay out of trouble things will take care of themselves. I hate to be the bearer of bad news but in the majority of cases things won't. Without planning and strategy things don't usually work out well. Unfortunately, many people plan more for a weekend getaway than they plan for their entire lives. If you want to live your best life DON'T be one of those people.

Chapter 4, Methodology, talks about the Vision, Purpose, Planning, and Execution it will take for you to put together a winning strategy for your life. A strategy that will allow you to go from feeling like the world is on top of you to being on top of the world. Success is within your grasp and this chapter will give you a step by step strategy for how to get it done.

Vision

We need look no further than the legendary visionary Walt Disney to find someone who had the ability to effectively and passionately communicate a vision. Walt Disney was one of the most influential Americans of the 20th century, especially for the ways in which his films, animation, comic strips, documentaries, songs, business and theme parks impacted American culture.

To his credit Disney understood that he could never be successful working alone. To carry out his vision he knew he needed to inspire and motivate his workers to be as passionate about their work as he was. Disney was a great leader not only because of the grand scale of his vision but because he mastered the art of communicating his futuristic vision to his team.

When Snow White premiered in 1937 it was the first full-length animated musical feature. Fortunately for Disney the movie was a huge success. The revenue earned from the film pulled Disney out of the deep debt the company had fallen into with its prior projects. Disney Studios followed up Snow White with more feature-length films that included hits like

Dumbo, Fantasia, Pinocchio, and Bambi. Disney would go on to produce over 100 feature films.

When we talk about vision it is not limited to just one specific goal or idea. Though they may be clustered under one industry visionaries often have visions that overlap into different areas. Disney was best known for his films but he proved to be an innovator and pioneer in several fields. In 1954, he debuted long running TV shows The Mickey Mouse Club and Wonderful World of Color. In 1955, he amazed the world with his magical utopian theme park Disneyland. Disney had dreamed of doing something special with his life since he was a teenager and his stint in the military just further convinced him that he was destined to do great things. Bold and unique visions are only made real by people who are willing to take risks and work relentlessly hard to bring their vision to fruition. Needless to say Disney was a tireless worker who endured loneliness, some discouraging setbacks, several major disappointments, and often tiptoeing on the brink of disaster before he was able to give life to his complete vision.

No one, and I do mean no one, accomplishes great things by his or herself. So, a big part of building any successful endeavor is finding a partner or contributor to partner with you or support you in your efforts, preferably one who is strong in the areas where you may be weak. Over one weekend in September of 1953, Walt Disney and legendary Disney artist Herb Ryman created the map that would become Disneyland. As Ryman recalled, Walt called him on a Saturday morning and asked him to come to the studio. When Herb arrived, Walt explained that he needed $17 million to build Disneyland. Disney verbalized his vision, Ryman drew it, and Walt's business partner and brother Roy was charged with selling the vision to investors to get the $17 million needed to build Disneyland.

After striking out with bankers, Roy took the drawings to New York, where he used them to pitch the Big Three TV networks. CBS and NBC passed on the project but ABC struck a deal with Roy. In exchange for delivering to them a one-hour, weekly TV program from Disney, ABC agreed to provide the financing for Disneyland. The collaboration between Walt, Roy, and Herb created one of the greatest entertainment destinations in the world. As a nod to the power of vision the map that launched Disneyland sold for

$708,000, the highest price ever paid at auction for any piece of Disney memorabilia.

Obviously, the map was worth every penny. How powerful the vision must have been for Disney to verbalize it to Ryman, then have Ryman be able to put it into the form of a map that Walt Disney and his brother Roy could use to raise the financing needed to build Disneyland. It was a vision so powerful, so tangible that it launched the parks and resorts business that rewarded the Walt Disney Company with $17 billion in revenues in fiscal 2016.

Your vision must be just as powerful. It should be so visually stunning that you can paint a verbal picture of it so real that those who hear it can literally see it before their eyes.

To stay on target with your vision it is important for you to create two documents, a mission statement and a vision statement. Below are Disney's mission statement and vision statement.

Mission Statement

The Walt Disney Company's corporate mission statement: "Using our portfolio of brands to differentiate our content, services and consumer products, we seek to develop the most creative, innovative and profitable entertainment experiences and related products in the world."

Vision Statement

The Walt Disney Company's corporate vision: "Our goal is to be one of the world's leading producers and providers of entertainment and information."

To differentiate between a mission and vision statement think of it this way: Usually a company mission statement speaks about what the business does, and a company vision statement is a document that talks about what a company aspires to be. You can see based on Disney's statements that the Walt Disney Company hit the bullseye on reaching both their statement targets.

Visions and Visionaries

As you have probably discovered not everyone with a vision succeeds. Let's quickly take a look at several visionaries to see how their visions worked out.

In a now-famous commencement address at Stanford University, Steve Jobs said that he left college on nothing more than the overwhelming feeling that he was not going to find his true calling there. Jobs said he "decided to drop out and trust that it would all work out okay." Jobs of course went on to team up with engineering genius Steve Wozniak to create one of the world's first personal computers. The company they created would later give the world such products as the iMac, iPod, iPhone, and iPad. In between the birth of the first iMac and its colorful reincarnation Jobs was kicked out of the company he started, Apple. He then bought and reinvigorated the animated movie giant Pixar. Jobs' triumphant return to Apple years later produced the string of amazing aforementioned products while also revolutionizing the music and telecom industries along the way.

Vision of Software for The World

After dropping out of the prestigious Harvard University, Bill Gates co-founded Microsoft with his partner Paul Allen. After setting out to sell computer programming languages Gates and Microsoft landed right in the computer sweet spot by purchasing a computer operating system that they modified into the computer program called Basic. Next, they created the Windows operating system that now powers nearly 90% of the world's personal computers. Gates spent decades as the World's Richest Person before officially retiring from Microsoft in 2008, with a then net worth of $58 billion which at the time ranked him 3rd on the Forbes' 100 Wealthiest People list.

Vision of A New Kind of Talk Show

She was born in the backwoods of Mississippi. She was raped when she was 9-years old. She was a single teenage mother at the age of 14 who gave birth to a child that died shortly after birth. The odds of anyone becoming successful after getting off to that kind of start in life would seem next to impossible. Somehow Oprah Winfrey beat the odds to become not just a success but a mega success. She landed her first radio job while she was still in high school. After flopping as a news reporter she took a job in daytime talk TV and went from success in the ratings for a Chicago TV show to starting Harpo, and The Oprah Winfrey Show, the Emmy Award winning highest-rated talk show in TV history. Over $1.3 billion later Winfrey sits atop her own entertainment empire.

Vision of A Car for The Masses

After working for another car company and raising a small amount of money from family and friends Henry Ford got his company off to a solid start by negotiating deals with his suppliers to let him purchase parts on credit. Though he did not invent the car or the assembly line, by perfecting the automobile assembly line which allowed Ford Motors to build cars faster and thereby sell them cheaper, Ford became the first man to successfully mass produce automobiles. His introduction of the Model T automobile October 1, 1908 revolutionized transportation and American industry. Ford is responsible for many technical and business innovations as well as a franchise system that put car dealerships throughout most of North America and in major cities on six continents. By 1918, half of all cars in America were Model Ts. Production of the Model T continued through 1927. After 19 years of producing the popular model car by the time Ford finally stopped production of the model T sells of the car had totaled 15,007,034. It is a record that stood for the next 45 years.

Vision of A Better Travel Case

If you've glanced at Instagram recently you'll notice every travel blogger's fondness for Away suitcases. Luggage startup Away has quickly become the go to brand of millennial jet-setters. Founded in 2015 by two former Warby Parker execs, Stephanie Korey and Jennifer Rubio, Away has managed to make a rather ho-hum item an object that is now intensely desired. Celebrity collaborations, limited edition designs and plenty of personalization options has made Away a popular travel piece that is both affordable and practical. With Away, you can charge your electronics on the go, and use its wheels to zip through security lines. After only about five years in operation, these ladies are taking on the travel industry brand giants and winning. Of course, one of Away's major selling points is the battery that comes built into either of its carry-on options. A phone-charging suitcase might seem like a needless luxury, but it's actually very useful. No more jostling for outlets or sitting cross-legged on sticky airport carpets to recharge your mobile devices while waiting for a flight. The battery can charge your iPhone or any device that charges via USB. The suitcase itself takes about eight hours to fully charge, which is why the company recommends plugging it in the night before a trip. According to Forbes magazine when luggage startup Away reached a valuation of $1.4 billion, Korey and Rubio's stake in the fast-growing business gave them an estimated net worth of about $130 million each.

Vision of A Better Internet

Had it not been for a $100,000 check from Sun co-founder Andy Bechtolsheim, search engine founders Sergey Brin and Larry Page's ingenious dorm room project might never have seen the light of day. Like some famous tech entrepreneurs before them aspiring Stanford University Ph.D. students Brin and Page felt confident enough in their new venture to leave college and pursue their dreams. Their company Google was introduced as the Internet was undergoing a major technological shift that clearly showed Brin and Page had built a better mouse trap. Google's success rewrote the rules of business and transformed our culture. Following their billion-dollar IPO in 2004 the two tech innovators were billionaires by the time they turned 30.

Vision of A Sports Concierge Agency

For most sports fans Scott Boras put himself on the map by being the agent who negotiated Alex Rodriguez's two record-smashing baseball contracts. Now he is perhaps the most successful sports agent of all time. Heading up his California-based Scott Boras Corporation, former major leaguer Boras has created an entire concierge of services to cater to his superstar clients. Boras began his career as an agent with only a law degree and an idea of what an agent should be able to provide for his client. Flash forward to find Boras at the pinnacle of his profession, as an agent who has negotiated over $1 billion worth of contracts and endorsement deals for the baseball players he represents. Though potential customers are clamoring for his services Boras has turned down lucrative deals to represent Hollywood actors and mega-stars from other sports to remain fully devoted to his major league baseball clients.

Vision of A Connected World

Mark Zuckerberg's Facebook started off as just a Harvard University social media site. Wisely, Zuckerberg garnered the assistance of friend Dustin Moskovitz who had the resources to spread the site to other schools, including Columbia University, New York University, Stanford, Dartmouth, Cornell, Brown, Yale, and the University of Pennsylvania. Quite the prodigy, Zuckerberg began using computers and writing software in middle school. His father taught him Atari BASIC Programming in the 1990s, and later hired software developer David Newman to tutor him privately. While still in high school Zuckerberg even took a graduate course in the subject at Mercy College near his home. The early success of Facebook, encouraged Zuckerberg, Moskovitz and some friends to move to Palo Alto, California in tech hotbed Silicon Valley where they leased a small house that served as an office. During that summer Zuckerberg met legendary tech investor Peter Thiel, who invested in the Facebook. Zuckerberg and his team had planned to return to Harvard but decided to remain in California to try and turn Facebook into a successful company. Zuckerberg had already turned down offers from major corporations to buy the company by July 21, 2010, when he announced that Facebook had reached the 500 million-user mark. The social media site would reach one billion users by 2012. Zuckerberg took the company public in May 2012. As of November 30, 2018, his estimated net worth was $55 billion. In 2007, at age 23 he became the world's youngest self-made billionaire and as of 2018, he is the only person under 50 on the Forbes ten richest people list.

Purpose

Purpose: the reason for which something is done or created or for which something exists.

At our very core we are all searching for it. Why? Because we all want to live lives that have meaning. No one wants to feel at the end of their life what they did in this world didn't really matter. There are few things more depressing or demoralizing in this world than being stuck on a job that you believe is meaningless. It is incredibly important that entrepreneurs create businesses that serve a purpose. Not only is that important for entrepreneurs, it is equally important for those who will work with and for that entrepreneur. Because again, no one wants to waste their life doing some meaningless job.

The question becomes how do we design jobs and careers that serve a purpose? Not just any old purpose but a purpose that makes the world a better place, or enables people to be better, or communities to be better? How do we design something that serves a greater or higher purpose? That it seems would be the ultimate endeavor, the ultimate business or enterprise.

Think about the products that have truly changed the world. The printing press, the telegraph, the electric light bulb, the telephone, radio, television, the computer, the personal computer, the Internet, the cell phone, Artificial Intelligence, are all inventions that drastically and forever changed the world. They put the world on a higher, greater trajectory than it had ever been on before, a trajectory that it would never turn back from. To take away any of these revolutionary inventions and the innovations they inspired would literally cast us back into the dark ages. Today mass printing books that could be circulated around the world, sending messages through a system of dots and dashes that could be interpreted across a country, sending the human voice through a device in one place that can be heard by a person in another place, sitting next to a box and listening to music and other content broadcasted through it in real time from distant places, all these events and other discoveries that helped humanity take giant leaps into the future more than fulfilled the amazing purposes for which they were created. In order for anything created to have meaning for not only groups of people but to humanity itself it must be something that serves a greater or higher purpose than that which has preceded it. That is a tall order. When you begin to think in those epic terms you open your mind to ideas and discoveries that other entrepreneurs and visionaries have not even dared to dream of.

Purpose. Greater, higher purpose. That is what you should strive for if you truly want success. Reaching higher and farther than you have ever reached before. Doing more, asking more of yourself than you have ever done or asked before. That is what produces success. That is what produces greatness. It all starts with purpose. Where is the purpose in what you are doing? If you don't know, stop, and don't proceed any further until you find that purpose. Because only then will you stop chasing success and enter into that rare orbit where success begins chasing you. To excel greatly at any endeavor, in any field, at any task, you must be driven by purpose. It must be the engine that propels you to those nearly unreachable heights you must ascend to in order to capture massive success.

The compass was one of the most important tools ever invented. It was invented by the Chinese to aid in fortune telling, but in the 11th century A.D. it would become the instrument that would enable explorers to travel around the globe and navigate across vast oceans. Without knowing the reference points that help to identify geographic locations traveling and navigating great distances during that time would have been impossible. Though the inventors of the compass believed its purpose to be for fortune telling its true purpose would emerge when placed in the hands of daring explorers like Christopher Columbus and Amerigo Vespucci. Now that we have those compass inspired innovations like satellites and GPS, the compass may not seem so important, but it was certainly a revolutionary invention that changed the world and served a purpose greater than anyone at the time of its creation could have conceived.

As you set out to start a business, or begin a career, or enter into a relationship, or build something monumental think about the purpose behind what you are doing and dedicate yourself to fulfilling that purpose. Be aware that like the compass you may be underestimating what your invention, creation, or endeavor can achieve. Think of the greatest possibilities and outcomes that can result from you succeeding and the most disastrous and detrimental things that can be the results if you fail. With these outcomes in mind pursue your goals with everything in you knowing how high the stakes are and how great your purpose is.

Purpose will direct your steps as you design the objectives that must be accomplished for you to achieve your goal. Success is not one big leap. It is a series of steps that finally culminate in reaching a destination. Those steps are rarely straight. Success is a game of adjustments and readjustments. You cannot be so rigid with your plans that you don't allow for the inevitable problems that you will have to resolve and as a result the detours you will have to take to stay on course. Reaching success is not so much about how you reached your destination as it is about what you overcame to reach your destination. And, that ability to see your dream through to completion can be attributed to how strongly you believe in your purpose.

Google first announced Google Glass -- an eyeglasses shaped head-mounted display with smartphone capabilities -- to the public in 2012. The announcement began with a statement of principle: "We think technology should work for you -- to be there when you need it and get out of your way when you don't." After two years of disappointing sales, it was clear consumers did not need Google Glass. Google stuck to its principle, and in 2015 discontinued the product's development. Privacy concerns, reported bugs, low battery life, bans from public spaces, and an inability to live up to the hype all stymied public adoption of the technology.

Over the 15 years leading up to 1985, Coca-Cola's flagship cola drink had been losing market share to Pepsi-Cola. To compete, the company changed the drink's formula for the first time in 99 years -- but the move today is considered one of the greatest flops of all time. New Coke was met with public outrage and lasted only a few months. The company reintroduced its older formula, rebranded as Coca-Cola Classic.

Many of the worst product flops in recent memory were caused by otherwise popular brands wandering too far outside of their area of expertise. Colgate Kitchen Entrees may be the best example of such a product failure. When it came to pre-prepared frozen meals, Americans had plenty of options in the 1980s. Perhaps because consumers naturally associated the Colgate name with toothpaste, there was never much of an appetite for pre-made meals bearing the Colgate logo in 1982.

Harley Davidson is one of the most iconic and valuable brands in the world. It is also one of the most masculine brands. The company has not deviated considerably from this manly personality, although it has tried. The company released Legendary Harley-Davidson, a cologne for men, among several other varieties, starting in 1994. Another perfume, Black Fire, hit the market as recently as 2005. All are now discontinued. In the 1990s, the company released a number of other products, including wine coolers and aftershave, which after failing miserably have also become classic cases of brand overextension.

In 1973, auto executive John DeLorean left General Motors to form the DeLorean Motor Company. After years of production delays, the DeLorean DMC-12 was released in January 1981. The car's unique design was poorly received, however, and by 1982 less than half of the 7,000 DeLorean units produced had been sold. The DeLorean is widely recognized due to its use as a converted time machine in the "Back to the Future" series. However, the first of these films was released in 1985, far too late to save the ill-fated brand. DeLorean filed for bankruptcy in 1982.

Before EZ Squirt, ketchup was always varying shades of red. To cater to kids, who were -- and still are -- among ketchup's largest groups of consumers, Heinz began producing purple, green, and blue EZ Squirt ketchup in matching, vibrantly colored squeeze bottles. At first, the colorful ketchup was a huge success. The novelty wore off quickly, however, and not long after its introduction, sales of EZ Squirt began to decline. In January 2006, less than six years after its debut, Heinz halted production of the product.

Ford spent a year aggressively marketing the Edsel -- named after Henry Ford's son -- ahead of its 1957 release. It was to be the "car of the future," made available on dealership lots on what Ford dubbed "E-Day." Despite the hype, the car was a commercial disaster. It was considerably overpriced, disappointingly not futuristic, and generally ugly. Ford ceased the car's production after only two years, losing an estimated $350 million.

Social media site Facebook is one of the biggest corporate success stories in recent memory. Unfortunately, when it comes to social media, for every success story there is at least one flop -- as in the case of Friendster. The site's users suffered through slow page loading times and the company's developers failed to scale up when the number of subscribers spiked. Ultimately, competitors such as Facebook provided a much better user experience. Introduced in 2002, Friendster discontinued its services in mid-2015.

I say all this to say, there have been thousands of products launched because people thought something was a good idea, or it was a copy of another successful product, or it was an attempt to enter a hot market, or it was an attempt to build a better mouse trap, or it was a shameless money grab. All these may be reasons to do something but they are not good reasons, as the preceding product failures have proven. Whether you are putting your heart and soul into creating a product or service there must be a strong purpose behind what you are doing, a purpose that not only drives you to produce your product or service but also drives customers to buy it. Don't dare to take a step until you are crystal clear about what the purpose is behind your product or business, and until you have proof that your customer will completely get behind your purpose with their full support. Purpose is the rocket fuel every entrepreneur needs to reach his or her highest goals.

Planning

Repeat it one more time. Those who fail to plan, plan to fail. It amazes me when people simply dive right into projects without the slightest bit of planning. If you are working without a plan things could go right. Then again, there's an equal chance that things could go very wrong.

What Is the Planning Process?

The planning process details the steps a company takes to develop budgets that guide its future activities. The documents developed may include:

Strategic plans (long-range, high-level company goals)

Tactical plans (shorter-term, specific plans to work toward goals in the strategic plan)

Operating plans (detailed plans for a specific department to implement)

Project plans (plans to implement projects such as launching new products or building a new facility)

How Does the Planning Process Work?

Although the specific steps differ slightly from company to company and depend on which type of plan you're developing, there are general steps that should be taken in order to ensure a good result. The steps in the planning process are:

Step One: Develop Objectives

The first step in the planning process is to determine what you want to accomplish during the planning period. A long-range strategic plan might focus on specific market share achievements five years into the future, while a department-level operating plan might target implementation of a new method of tracking sales orders in the next quarter. These are objectives.

Step Two: Develop Tasks to Meet Those Objectives

The next step is to come up with a list of required tasks that help you meet the objectives you have defined. What do you need to do in terms of sales, marketing, production, distribution, training, and other facets of your company to meet the objectives you have set. It could involve building new techniques that take advantage of new software or technologies. It could involve different processes or procedures you introduce to give you a better chance of attaining your objectives.

Step Three: Determine the Resources You'll Need to Implement Tasks

What resources are you going to need to implement the objectives you have set? Resources can include the people needed to implement the plan, the supplies needed to support those people, the equipment, logistics, and other items needed. Your sales department might need more salespeople, brochures, an advertising campaign, and other resources to reel in your objectives. Determine all the resources you will need to accomplish your tasks on your list.

Step Four: Create A Timeline

Yep, a goal without a deadline is just a pipe dream. There is a time period that every task must be done within, and every objective or goal must be completed in. Don't plan task, objectives, and goals without creating a realistic timeline for each. Your timeline will depend on a number of variables, how much time your employees will be able to spend working on each task, how many employees you can assign to the task, what resources and technology you can apply to task, and other things that take up time. Also, you may need to expand the amount of designated time to a few days or even weeks if there are other time consuming projects occurring simultaneously.

In the garden example, it will only take four hours from start to finish, but with everything else going on, your team will need two weekends to get it done. Therefore, when you build your project management timeline, you will reserve several days for each task. Use milestones to track the progress of projects so you can better determine whether you are ahead, behind, or on target.

Understand How to Establish Objectives:

You Can Set Strategic Objectives

Strategic objectives are long-term organizational goals to help convert your mission statement from a broad vision into specific plans and projects. Your objectives must be measurable, and directly relate to the goals you have set. Strategic objectives must turn the idea or concept you wrote in your mission statement into actionable steps you can use to move you toward your goal. This will take some decision-making on the part of your management team. Consider your company strengths and weaknesses before setting objectives so that your expectations are reasonable and reachable.

You Can Set Operational Objectives?

Operational objectives are daily, weekly or monthly projects you break larger strategic objectives into so they can be implemented effectively. Operational objectives are also called tactical objectives. These objectives are tasks that need to be done to place your company in position to attain its larger goals. As an example, in order to achieve the strategic goal of $100,000 in sales per month you may need to set an operational goal of your salesforce making 100 sales calls per week to generate enough sales to reach your sales target. As with strategic objectives, your operational objectives should be measurable. An important difference between a strategic objective and an operational objective is the time frame set for each. The operational objective is a short-term goal, while strategic objectives are longer-term goals. Strategic objectives are too broad to turn into daily tasks or weekly projects, but operational objectives, are specific and short-term enough to be everyday tasks. As a rule of thumb, strategic objectives only become useful if they can be translated into operational objectives and operational objectives are only effective if they are designed to serve a strategic objective.

Strategy Formulation:

Strategy formulation is a process that an organization uses to choose the best course of action to achieve its goals. It provides a framework that contains the organization's objectives, mission, and purpose into a game plan. A strategy formulation must be forward thinking enough to prepare your workforce for the possible changes that may occur. A strategic plan should include an evaluation of the company's resources, a budget allocation, and an effective plan for maximizing the company's ROI (return on investment). A company should also use the strategic plan to provide its employees with direction and focus. Without a strategic plan a business cannot be proactive, and will find itself instead being reactive, addressing unanticipated pressures as they arise, which leaves your organization with a competitive disadvantage.

Strategy formulation requires a defined set of four steps to be implemented effectively:

1. define the organization.
2. define the strategic mission.

3. define the strategic objectives.
4. define the competitive strategy.

Step 1: Define the Organization

The first step in defining an organization is identifying the company's customers. To be successful your company must have a strong customer base with needs that you are filling. You must identify the qualities of your products or services that are valued by your customers. Is that value based on a product or service that is superior to those of your competition? Are your customers buying your products for your low prices? Do you produce products that meet the image needs of your customers? In essence, why do your customers choose your product or service over your competitors?

Defining your organization can be captured in three words, vision, mission, and values. To define your organization you must ask yourself three important questions:

1. What is your vision? In other words, what do you want your organization to become? Your vision is tied to your purpose. Your purpose is your organization's reason for being. Why does your organization exist? What are you in business to do? The answer to this question is your why. Once you understand what your purpose or your "why" is you can now say of your future, "We will use our purpose to become this, which is your vision.

2. What is your mission? Look at what you are attempting to do and that will tell you what your mission is. Your mission is the what of your organization. If you have a business that teaches various languages your mission may be to make your students fluent in a foreign language within 90 days.

3. What are your values? Having strong values will allow you to maintain focus on your vision and mission. Your values will shape the culture of your organization. Values define how you want your management and employees to interact with each other, customers, and the community. Values must be framed by your ethics and carried out with integrity. Your values will form the foundation for how your employees behave. Your values create a

116

workplace where traits like cooperation, collaboration, and excellence inspire employees to deliver on all the promises made by you and your company.

Step 2: Define the Strategic Mission
Your strategic mission offers a long-range perspective of what the organization is striving for moving forward. The strategic mission provides a guide for the organization to follow in its attempt to establish its goals. The strategic mission identifies your organization's position in the marketplace, vision for the future, and what business it is engaged in.

Step 3: Define the Strategic Objectives
With strategic objectives you are identifying performance targets you must achieve to reach your stated objectives. Your stated objectives may include: the market position you desire to occupy relative to your competitors, the quality of goods and services you hope to produce, the percentage of market share you want to capture, how you endeavor to use technology to your benefit, what level of customer service you aspire to provide, the sales revenue amounts you want to achieve, and timetables for any expansion plans. In order for your strategic objectives to be successful you must communicate it to all of your employees and stakeholders. A good organization uses its strategic objectives and actions to make everyone in the organization aware of their role in the company and how their efforts contribute to meeting the organization's objectives.

Step 4: Define the Competitive Strategy

The competitive strategy defines where your company fits into the marketplace and where each individual unit and department in the organization contributes to its overall success. Every department within the company should understand its role and how they enable the organization to maintain its competitive advantage. A good competitive strategy helps your organization develop proactive responses to potential challenges facing your company by identifying possible obstacles and being prepared to take the appropriate action. A competitive strategy also needs to identify an organization's resources and determine how those resources should be used by each department and division of the company.

Strategy Implementation:

The strategic plan is a roadmap of goals you want the company to pursue. Of course, the strategic plan is only a plan full of objectives and goals. None of which can be accomplished without taking action or implementation. It is action that transforms your strategic plan from a document into a business. A strategic plan addresses the what and why of your company, but it is implementation that addresses the who, where, when, and how. So, both the strategic plan and strategy implementation are critical to success. Sadly, the majority of companies with strategic plans fail to implement them. Fortune Magazine, documented why 9 out of 10 organizations fail to implement their strategic plan:

60% of organizations don't link strategy to their budget.

75% of organizations don't link employee incentives to their strategy.

86% of business owners and managers spend less than one hour per month discussing strategy.

95% of the typical workforce don't understand their organization's strategy.

If you want to get the implementation process right you should understand that there are five key components necessary to support implementation: people, resources, structure, systems, and culture. Each of these components must be in place to successfully implement the plan.

Execution

It's About People

The key to implementing your plan is to make sure you get the right people on the bus. Having the right personnel on your staff must be priority one. The right people with the wrong plan won't work. Neither will the right plan with the wrong people. The plan must be built to take advantage of the skills of your workforce. Once you have in place the right people to implement your plan you can use additional training and hiring to fine tune your employees. Implementation is about the execution of your plan.

Resources

To successfully carry out your plan you need to have enough money to support it. The amount of businesses that have failed due to lack of funds are as plentiful as the stars in the sky. Administrators often underestimate the amount of money needed to successfully implement a plan. Time can bring about a change. Cost changes may have occurred between the time you create your strategic plan and when you actually implement it. Your vendor fees, employee wages, material cost, property leases, transportation cost, and logistics cost, could all be higher now than they were when your cost projections were first drawn up. Do a new cost analyses to make sure cost projections for implementing your plans are still accurate. Once you know that you have the financial resources to secure all the materials, equipment, laborers, consultants, vendors, suppliers, and necessary finances you need to implement your strategy you can move forward without having to be cautious of every step, or having to pick and choose what you can and can't afford.

Organization

Before you move forward with any plan you must first outline how your organization is going to be constructed. How is your management team going to be set up? Is your hierarchy defined so it is clear what everyone's responsibilities are and who reports to whom? Your goal in putting together your company command structure is to create the fewest layers of administration possible so that lines of communication flow unimpeded from the top all the way down to each employee. Once your organizational structure is in place be sure to set up regular reviews so progress can be measured and necessary adjustments can be made to ensure that implementation of your strategy is successful.

Systems

Your management structure includes employees, a facility, equipment, your company hierarchy, strategic plans, procedures, technology, financing, and work documents. Now you must device a system that will compliment all these resources and assist you in attaining your objectives and goals. Your system should include the technology, software, communication systems, training, policies and procedure manuals that will assist your business in being more efficient. Uniquely, you want to create a system that helps your company to be cost effective, well coordinated from department to department, responsive to the needs of both management and customers, simple enough to be learned quickly and duplicated, and is scalable. The system should be able to provide information that will allow you to analyze and measure it in part and in whole. The system should allow you to accurately forecast future results and project what adjustments must be made to take market share and outperform your competition.

Culture

If you are able to implement your plan successfully it will be the result of creating an excellent company culture. You should strive to develop a culture that reinforces your stated values and achieves your mission statement. A healthy, collaborative and productive workplace is the result of good company culture. It is key to foster a sense of corporate responsibility and community awareness within the company that is encouraged by management and supported by your employees. It never hurts to incentivize employees by putting in place a reward system for those who contribute to the success and growth of the company, managers who effectively groom and manage these employees, and those who do volunteer work in the community or create volunteer programs to enrich the community. A good company culture is always team oriented, outcome oriented, detail oriented, people oriented, and supportive of employees, customers, and the mission, goals, and objectives of the company.

Finally, if you want to succeed you must avoid these **7 common reasons strategic plans fail:**

1. **The Plan Or Strategy Cannot Be Measured**: In the words of Peter Drucker, "If you can't measure it, you can't manage it." You must create not only a strategy or plan that can be implemented, but you must also create a method to measure the effectiveness of that plan. You should have a method to measure the plan and know whether it is succeeding or

failing, and specifically which part of it is succeeding or failing. Your owners and managers need to be able to get their hands on this information quickly and be able to understand it thoroughly. Continued success depends on delivering value to customers at profitable margins and tracking your results so that you can measure, manage, and repeat your success.

2. **The Plan Is Too Management Driven:** As the saying goes, "Leaders must lead." This is true. But, the companies that sustain success are ones that empower employees to behave as partners in building that success. Employees must do work that is meaningful and feel that they are recognized for their work. It is up to management to provide employees with the means and tools to succeed greatly, the training to improve their knowledge, the methods to elevate their performance, and a pathway for advancement within the company. Management cannot and should not be the drivers of everything.

3. **The Plan Is Not Ambitious Enough:** If your product is just another one, it means that it is not a better one. Products that enter the market without some kind of clear advantage over its competitors are destined to fail. If you have not designed your product or service to give the consumer better value or to satisfy a consumer niche your plan is not ambitious enough. If you cannot create a product or service that is better, or functions better, or is more valuable, or can add more value for less cost, or is technologically superior don't waste your time and money producing it. Create something better, period.

4. **The Plan Is Not Created For The End User:** Why would anyone create a product or service that does not take into consideration the needs of its end user? Think of products that fall into this category. They are usually overpriced, lacking in functionality, unimaginatively designed, unneeded by the consumer, or hazardous. It is not hard to understand why consumers simply pass over such items for better ones.

Successful entrepreneurs know that it is always about the end user.

5. **The Plan Has Not Been Effectively Communicated**: It is all but impossible to work the plan if you don't understand the plan. When employees, or worse managers, cannot grasp the plan or strategy because of a lack of communication, bad communication, or a failure to communicate it is a recipe for having an uninspired workforce and a company chasing after failure.

6. **The Plan Does Not Encourage Employee Buy-In:** Don't assume your employees are buying into your plan simply because you pay them. There are millions of workers who remain at companies because they need a paycheck and not because they believe in the company's mission. What stake does the employee have in the success of your company and what is their reward for helping the company succeed? Have you intentionally built into your plan a reason for your employees to buy-in? Furthermore, do you make an effort to show employees that you value them by hearing and valuing their feedback?

7. **The Plan Holds No One Accountable:** Being accountable means that your company has built into your plan a way for management and employees to be rewarded for the good they do and corrected the bad. If accountability is a valued part of your program you will find it easier to retain those in leadership who are contributing to the success of the company, as well as promote those who are ready to contribute more by playing a larger role. Accountability also allows your company to weed out those who are not contributing value to the company or are proving to be unsuitable for leadership or making meaningful contributions. Whether you are in the startup phase of your company's life-cycle or in the mature stage of your company's growth you need accountability to be able to understand who is responsible for the results you are getting.

Writing A Business Plan

For those of you who want to take your employment future into your own hands, you now have enough information to start putting together your business plan. When you write your business plan you don't have to stick to the exact business plan outline. You can use the sections that make the most sense for your business and needs. Traditional business plans will use some combination of these nine sections. So, look at this as a starter plan for writing your business plan and you can expand or contract it from here.

Executive summary

The executive summary should briefly tell your reader what your company is and why it will be successful. Include your mission statement, your product or service, and basic information about your company's leadership team, employees, and location. You should also include financial information and your growth plans if you plan to ask for financing.

Company description

Use your company description to provide detailed information about your company. Go into detail about the problems your business solves. Be specific by listing the consumers, organizations, or businesses your company plans to serve. Explain the competitive advantages that will make your business a success. Make mention of any experts you may have on your team? Have you found the perfect location for your business? Your company description is the place to boast about your strengths.

Market analysis

You'll need a good understanding of your industry outlook and target market. Competitive research will show you what other businesses are doing and what their strengths and weaknesses are. In your market research, look for trends and themes. What do your successful competitors do and why does it work? Can you do it better? The market analysis is where you answer these questions.

Organization and management

Tell your reader how your company will be structured and who will run it. Describe the legal structure of your business. State whether you have or intend to incorporate your business as a C or an S corporation, form a general or limited partnership, or if you're a sole proprietor or LLC. Use an organizational chart to lay out who's in charge of what in your company. Show how each person's unique experience will contribute to the success of your venture. Consider including the resumes for key members of your team.

Service or product line

Describe what you sell or what service you offer. Explain how it benefits your customers and what the product lifecycle looks like. Share your plans for intellectual property, like copyright or patent filings. If you're doing research and development for your service or product, use this space to explain it in detail.

Marketing and sales

There are many ways to approach a marketing strategy. Your strategy should evolve and change to fit your unique needs. Use this section to describe how you'll attract and retain customers. You'll also describe how your company will conduct sales. Knowing that you'll have to refer to this section later when you make financial projections, make sure you thoroughly describe your marketing and sales strategies.

Funding request

If you're asking for funding, this is where you'll outline your funding requirements. Your goal is to clearly explain how much funding you'll need over the next five years and what you'll use it for. Specify whether you want to take on debt or offer equity, the terms you'd like applied, and the length of time your request will cover. Give a detailed description of how you'll use your funds. Indicate if you need funds to buy equipment or materials, pay salaries, or cover specific bills until your business is producing sufficient revenue. Always include a description of your future strategic financial plans, like paying off debt or your exit strategy if you are planning on selling your business.

Financial projections

Supplement your funding request with financial projections. Your goal here is to convince the reader that your business is stable and will be a financial success. If your business is already established, include income statements, balance sheets, and cash flow statements for the last three to five years. If you have other collateral you are willing to use to secure a loan, make sure to list it now. Provide a prospective financial outlook for the next five years. Include forecasted income statements, balance sheets, cash flow statements, and capital expenditure budgets. For the first year, be even more specific by using quarterly or even monthly projections. Be sure you clearly explain your projections and match them to your funding requests. If you have graphs and charts you can use to tell the financial story of your business attach them to this section.

Appendix

Use your appendix to provide supporting documents or other materials where requested. The items you might include in this section are credit histories, resumes, product pictures, letters of reference, licenses, permits, or patents, legal documents, and other contracts.

Chapter 5: The Journey

You may have discovered by now that life is not a sprint, It's a Journey. Chapter 5, The Journey, will teach you how to not only survive but thrive through each phase of the journey. Twilight, when you are busy trying to find your way and settle on that special thing that's going to be your life's work and the relationships that will revolve around it. Midnight, when it seems like every force in the universe is coming against you and what you believe. And Morning, when the darkness finally lifts and the road ahead leads straight to massive Success.

Twilight

Ray Kroc was born on October 5, 1902 in Oak Park, Illinois, near Chicago. Kroc's father had made a fortune speculating on land during the 1920s, only to lose everything with the stock market crash in 1929. After spending most of his life in Oak Park, Kroc lied about his age and became a Red Cross ambulance driver at the age of 15 years old during World War I. Interesting enough one of his fellow ambulance drivers was Walt Disney. Fortunately for both men the war ended shortly after they enlisted throwing them back into what was left of the Great Depression. During this period Kroc earned a living by working a variety of jobs like selling paper cups, selling real estate in Florida, and even playing the piano in bands.

As fate would have it after World War II, Kroc found employment as a milkshake machine mixer salesman for Prince Castle the foodservice equipment manufacturer. When sales of the Prince Castle mixer took a dive mainly because of competition from lower-priced Hamilton Beach mixers, Kroc noticed that a restaurant named McDonald's owned by brothers Richard and Maurice McDonald in San Bernardino, California had bought eight of his multi-mixers. In 1954, Kroc decided to pay McDonald's a visit to see why the restaurant was ordering so many mixers. When he arrived and saw lines of customers purchasing food at the restaurant he was fascinated by the concept and design of the small restaurant chain.

Kroc had been in over a thousand food kitchens and believed strongly that the McDonald brothers had the best-run operation he had ever seen. The long lines of customers moved along swiftly with customers placing their orders and receiving their food in mere minutes. The restaurant was clean, the staff well-groomed and they moved around the floor of McDonald's like a precision marching band in a well-trained and obviously well-planned operation that resembled an auto assembly line. This all resulted in customers getting their food fast. At the time roadside hamburger joints had become hangouts for motorcycle gangs and rebellious teens.

Kroc himself had once said, "In my experience, hamburger joints are nothing but jukeboxes, pay phones, smoking rooms, and guys in leather jackets. I wouldn't take my wife to such a place and you wouldn't take your wife either."

But at McDonald's Kroc saw a wholesome environment where families lined up to purchase their meals. This Kroc believed was a vision for the restaurant of the future and a model that could be franchised across the nation. In 1955, Kroc opened the first McDonald's franchised under his partnership with the McDonald brothers. The restaurant was in Des Plaines, Illinois. At the time of his death on January 14, 1984 at 81 years old from heart failure, entrepreneur Ray Kroc had a net worth of $600 million. That's the same as $1.4 billion today after adjusting for inflation. Kroc not only owned McDonald's franchises, he was also the owner of the San Diego Padres, Major League Baseball team from 1974 until he passed away in 1984. Because of his contributions and business innovations Kroc was listed in the Time 100: The Most Important People of the Century list. As of the end of 2018, McDonald's restaurants are found in 120 countries and territories around the world and serve 68 million customers each day. McDonald's operates 37,855 restaurants worldwide, employing more than 210,000 people.

Do You See Problems, Or Opportunities?

Had Kroc not become curious about the large orders from McDonald's restaurant of the milkshake-mixer he was selling, maybe he would have never taken a trip to California and become involved with franchising the now famous fast food chain. No matter who you are or where you are there are scores of opportunities surrounding you. People complain about their lives all the time. But, if most people would take the time to open their eyes to opportunities instead of open their mouths to complain most people would be able to significantly improve their lives. It comes down to how you view the world and what you see when you look at your environment and your circumstances. Do you just see problems or do you see opportunities?

Most people would agree that a headache is a bad thing. Just about everyone who has had one sees headaches as a problem. But, the makers of Tylenol would disagree. Tylenol is a brand name for acetaminophen, a non-aspirin pain reliever developed by McNeil Consumer Products Co., a wholly owned subsidiary of the pharmaceutical company Johnson & Johnson. Before 1975, it had limited sales because it was advertised mostly to physicians, like a prescription drug. Then Johnson & Johnson changed tactics and began an aggressive campaign of selling Tylenol to the public by claiming it relieved pain without causing any of the side-effects sometimes attributed to aspirin. When sales lagged, Johnson & Johnson took a new approach, increasing the pain-relieving content of each tablet to 500 milligrams against the standard aspirin's 325 milligrams and stressing the product's "extra strength." Tylenol sales took off. Its share of the pain-reliever market is believed to be more than three times that of the other leading pain-relief products, Bayer Aspirin, Bufferin, Anacin and Excedrin. Johnson & Johnson is an American conglomerate that has a net worth of $360 billion. It is almost impossible to walk into a pharmacy, drug store, or grocery store anywhere in the world, and not find a Johnson & Johnson product. Tylenol is a big part of that success.

Businesses exist because they solve problems. You want to be wealthy? Find a problem and solve it. You want to be super wealthy? Find a huge problem and solve it. It's time you see the world through new eyes. Stop looking for a way to make money and start looking for problems you can solve. The fastest way to riches is to provide a product or service that solves a problem.

To further drive home the point let's look at some other entrepreneurs who looked at problems as opportunities and created businesses to solve them, profiting in the process.

In 1998, Sara Blakely was getting ready for a party when she realized that her clothing choice of white pants and regular undies was not going to work. Thinking fast Blakely took a pair of scissors and went to work on a pair of control-top pantyhose, and minutes later Spanx was born. The Atlanta-based company now sells underwear, bras, leggings and activewear in over 50 countries, and Blakely has become one of the world's youngest self-made female billionaires. Forbes reports that Blakely turned her initial $5,000 investment in Spanx into a 2018 net worth of $1.11 billion by solving a simple wardrobe problem.

Today, it may seem like a no-brainer but there was a time when streaming movies and media didn't exist. Now Netflix has a market cap of $116.71 billion and bingeing on our favorite shows and movies has become a favorite pastime. What problem does streaming solve? How about no more trips to the video store to pick up expensive video or DVD rentals. The monthly cost of Netflix is the equivalent of a few DVD rentals. Now that we can stream our favorite shows and series right into our home we're not stuck having to view entertainment at any specific time. No more rental late fees. Ah, such freedom. Looking back, it's hard to believe at its peak in 2000, Blockbuster collected $800 million in late fees alone out of customers. Thanks Netflix.

No matter what our status in life universally there are some things we all hate. Dead cell phones would be on that list, along with chords all over the place for charging our electronic devices. In 2011, Meredith Perry set out to fix that problem with his startup uBeam. The technology behind uBeam is a large transmitter that charges mobile devices via high-frequency soundwaves. Though the frequencies cannot be heard by humans the device charges iPads, and other wi-fi devices without you having to lift a finger to plug in your numerous devices. Whether you are at home or Ubeam is provided at your local coffee shop it will wirelessly charge everyone's phone. With early investors like Mark Cuban, uBeam has already attracted $31.7 million in funding to jumpstart a wireless industry that Allied Market Research projects will be worth $37.2 billion by 2022.

In 2017, a Harvard Business Review study confirmed what we have suspected for at least a generation. Only 10 percent of Americans actually enjoy cooking. According to the Bureau of Labor Statistics, the average American spends an average of $3,008 per year eating out. Taking advantage of the pain most people feel in the kitchen the company Blue Apron boxed the complete ingredients along with the instructions needed to cook a wide assortment of meals. To make mealtime even more convenient Blue Apron delivers the fresh package of goodies right to your door. By doing so Blue Apron cuts out grocery shopping, meal planning, as well as the meal prep headaches of cutting and chopping, while saving customers money on food costs. Its obvious Blue Apron is solving a big problem because by the first quarter of 2017, the company had 1.04 million customers and was already raking in $245 million in revenues.

Small businesses are forever fighting the cost of doing business to trim their margins enough to make a profit. With so many people using credit and debit cards to make purchases today having a point-of-sale system to process those card payments is almost a necessity. But such machines can cost between $5,000 to $7,000. Small retail owners who couldn't afford the machines were stuck running "cash only" businesses that lost sells and consequently profits until the advent of the company Square. Square came along and targeted small businesses directly by offering a POS system at a fraction of the cost by using cloud storage and a device you can run on smart devices such as mobile phones, tablets, and laptops. Goodbye cash register and hello iPad at your bakery checkout station. Square is another example of a business that solved a common problem and is being rewarded handsomely for their effort. The company is now worth approximately $12.62 billion.

Seeing problems as opportunities and making the solutions to those problems your life's work can not only bring happiness to a lot of people, it can change your life for the better as well. Being a problem solver and earning profits go hand in hand. The difference between not being successful and being successful may come down to how you see things. So, changing how you see life can bring you out of twilight and into the marvelous light of day.

Midnight

Marvel

The first Marvel Cinematic Universe film was Iron Man in 2008. That film began the first phase of films that culminated with the crossover film The Avengers in 2012. Phase Two for MCU began with the film Iron Man 3 in 2013 and concluded with Ant-Man in 2015. Phase Three began with the film Captain America: Civil War in 2016 and concluded with Spider-Man: Far From Home in 2019. These first three phases in the MCU franchise are collectively known as "The Infinity Saga." And the cash register goes cha-ching!

What does that have to do with anything? About 2 decades ago Marvel was bankrupt and trying to inch its way to profitability. The company had a trunk load of popular comic book properties but hadn't found a way to earn real money with them. What made their floundering sting even more was watching the success their rival DC Comics had turning their iconic characters like Batman and Superman into blockbuster movie franchises. Marvel had attempted to turn its own lineup of superheroes into stars on the silver screen but all they could show for their efforts was the now infamous 1986 flop Howard the Duck. In the late '90s, Marvel struck licensing deals that brought Marvel characters like Spider-Man, the X-Men, and Blade, to theaters in successful films. But Marvel still wasn't making much money.

The company was started in the late 1930s by Martin Goodman, a New York pulp magazine publisher, who decided that comic books could be a profitable investment. Being that it was during the Great Depression it would seem like it was a bad time to start a business, but Goodman correctly believed that during such a grim time people would welcome a form of escapism to take their minds off their circumstances. The first two super-heroes to appear in the first number of Goodman's comic books were the Sub-Mariner, half man-half fish; and the Human Torch, fighting crime in a light-hearted manner. These premiere issues quickly became a success introducing Marvel Comics to the world.

In the late 1980s, Marvel's success attracted the attention of millionaire Ronald Perelman. He purchased Marvel Entertainment Group in 1989 and changed the company's business model to reflect his own business agenda which included taking the company public and selling stock. Perelman purchased a number of other entertainment firms and undertook other risky moves such as creating a comic book collecting bubble by encouraging fans to buy multiple copies of the same issues. In 1993, the bubble burst. In 3 years, Marvel's stock value tumbled from $35.75 per share to just $2.37. Scores of comic book fans quit purchasing Marvel due to the decreasing quality of its product and its increasing price. A group of Marvel's shareholders, led by Carl Icahn, initiated a power struggle with Perelman. One of their aims was to reduce the company's spending to keep the share price from falling even lower. Perelman responded by filing for bankruptcy. The move didn't help him. In 1998, the board and shareholders were so upset that they ousted Perelman and Icahn from the board.

Marvel was in bad shape and bleeding red ink but it continued its struggle to turn its hit comic books into successes on the big screen. Marvel had failed to make good business deals in the past and made some costly tactical errors like selling the rights to some of their biggest and most valuable properties. In the late '90s, when Marvel began to see some success. Comic hero Blade was a hit onscreen, and X-Men was about to see the same kind of success when released to the theaters by Fox. But due to its bad license deals profits from these successes would be measly. Blade made $70 million at the box office, but the profit for Marvel, according to a Slate article, was a measly $25,000. The X-Men and Spider-Man movies were huge hits as well, but Marvel only saw a small percentage of the profits from them too.

In 2003, while sinking into financial oblivion, just when it seemed that Marvel like one of its super-heroes was on its knees about to be obliterated, a talent agent named David Maisel came to Marvel's Isaac Perlmutter with a bold proposal. Produce your own movies under your own banner and reap the lion's share of the profits yourself. Furthermore,

Maisel stated, if you're producing your own movies, why can't the stories cross over with each other, just like they do in your comics?

In theory the idea could be worth hundreds of millions but the problem was going to be convincing Marvel's board of directors to make such a daring pivot and if that hurdle could be crossed the next sizable hurdle would be securing financing. In 2005, another bold move allowed Marvel to hurdle that obstacle as well when they managed to cut a deal with investment firm Merrill Lynch. The details of the deal revealed it to be as risky as a billion dollar winner take all steel-caged match. Marvel used the jewels of its super-hero empire, characters like Thor and Captain America as collateral. If their films failed to make money those superheroes would belong to the Merrill Lynch.

As part of the deal, Merrill Lynch granted Marvel access to a huge stash of cash: $525 million over seven years that it could use to make 10 movies with budgets ranging from $45 million to $180 million. Finally, the tables had turned for Marvel. The company used some of its freshly delivered money to reacquire the rights to characters it had sold over the years, including Iron Man, Black Widow, Thor, and the Hulk. Soon after the deal with Merrill Lynch was finalized, Marvel announced that Iron Man would be its first independent production. In the 1990s, Universal had originally purchased the rights, before they sold it off to Fox, who then passed it on to New Line Cinema. At last, Iron Man was home again and ready to take on the world.

While work on Iron Man was ongoing, Marvel made another gamble that would prove to be one of their smartest of all. Kevin Feige got his start in the film business as an assistant to producer Lauren Shuler Donner (wife of director Richard). Though only 27 years old, Feige was a comic fanatic who in spite of his tender age landed the role of producer on Fox's production of X-Men. He would go on to produce other Marvel films including Spider-Man, Daredevil, and Hulk. After his successes, Feige, in 2007, was brought in as president of Marvel Studios. With the wiz kid Feige at the helm, Marvel continued to soar. Iron Man, with Feige scoring his first credit as producer for the studio, reeled in $585 million.

Marvel's track record over the past near decade has become one of the most staggering turnaround successes in business history. Its release, The Avengers alone made billions, and currently ranks as the third highest grossing film of all time. Iron Man 3 became the second Marvel film to gross over $1 billion. Surprisingly, Guardians Of The Galaxy, a quirky space opera many thought to be a financial gamble, grossed more than $750 million. And, then came Black Panther, which has become not only another Marvel billion plus mega-hit, but one of the highest grossing films of all time.

In August of 2009, The Walt Disney Co. announced it had agreed to purchase comic book and action hero company Marvel Entertainment for about $4 billion. In December 2017, The Walt Disney Company agreed to acquire assets from 21st Century Fox, including 20th Century Fox, for $52.4 billion. The following June, after a counteroffer from Comcast worth $65 billion, Disney increased its offer to $71.3 billion. The transaction officially closed on March 19, 2019. The acquisition would usher in the return of the film rights to Deadpool, and the X-Men and Fantastic Four characters to Marvel Studios.

Midnight too often is the result of bad decisions as Marvel proved. But it can be reversed by good decisions as Marvel also proved. From its darkest days, through continuing to believe in the quality of its properties, making bold bets on the value to be unlocked from them, and using good decision-making to undue their prior bad decisions Marvel has turned their midnight into morning. And there is plenty of evidence to predict that the best of Marvel is still ahead of them.

Apple

When it comes to corporate turnaround stories, there may be none more famous than that of Apple. It's easy to forget now that Apple is one of the most valuable companies in the world, but there was a time when the tech giant was stuck in midnight and teetering on the edge of bankruptcy. Twenty years ago, the media was predicting the death of the company and it was losing $1 billion a year. All that changed when co-founder Steve Jobs returned to the helm of Apple and revived the company by launching a string of revolutionary products like the iMac, iPod, iPhone, iTunes, and iPad. Those investors who scooped up Apple stock when it was selling at bargain-basement prices and held on to it until Apple returned to its place atop the tech world are happy campers.

Midnight is a time of adversity. Adversity does not just happen to companies or people without cause. It is brought on by factors such as decisions, changing times, and an assortment of other variables. There is much for us to learn from the story of Apple, their founding, early success, their failures, almost demise, and their return to glory. If you really want to understand what it takes to not only succeed but sustain that success, by avoiding pitfalls and overcoming adversity, study the following paragraphs about Apple well and you should come away with a Ph.D. in Success-ology.

Apple Computer Company was founded on April 1, 1976, by Steve Jobs, Steve Wozniak, and Ronald Wayne. The company's first product the Apple I, was a personal computer entirely designed and hand-built by Wozniak. The machine was first introduced to the public at the Homebrew Computer Club in Menlo Park, California. The Apple I was sold as a motherboard with CPU, RAM, and basic textual-video chips. The base kit Wozniak built was more for hobbyist and would not be considered as a complete personal computer today. The Apple I went on sale in July 1976 and was market-priced at $666.66 (that would be $2,935 in 2018 dollars, adjusted for inflation).

Apple Computer, Inc. was incorporated on January 3, 1977. Third partner Ronald Wayne was not included in the incorporation because he had left the company selling his share of Apple back to Jobs and Wozniak for $800 just twelve days after having co-founded the company. Wayne's misfortune turned into multimillionaire businessman Mike Markkula's fortune when he struck a deal to provide Apple with his business expertise and $250,000 in funding. Over the next five years Apple's revenue grew steadily, doubling about every four months. Between September of 1977 and September 1980, the company's yearly sales grew from $775,000 to $118 million. That's an astounding average annual growth rate of 533%.

That explosive growth was mainly due to sells of the Apple II, which was also invented by tech wiz Wozniak. The computer was introduced on April 16, 1977, at the first West Coast Computer Faire. The Apple II, differed from its major rivals, the TRS-80 and Commodore PET, because it had character cell-based color graphics and an open architecture. The Apple II hit the jackpot when it was chosen to be the desktop platform for the first popular app of the business world, a spreadsheet program named VisiCalc. VisiCalc created a whole new market for business sells for the Apple II along with giving home users an additional reason to buy the computer. Before VisiCalc, Apple had been running a distant third behind its competitors the Commodore and Tandy but after the boost from VisiCalc the Apple II bolted to the front of the personal computer race. Timing is so important, and functionality is even more important.

By the end of the 1970s, Apple had grown from a few friends building computers in Steve Job's garage to a staff of computer designers and a production line quickly churning out product. For its next act the company introduced the Apple III in May 1980 in an attempt to compete with IBM in the business and corporate computing market.

Good to Great

On December 12, 1980, Apple (ticker symbol "AAPL") went public selling 4.6 million shares at $22 per share (adjusting for stock splits that price would be the equivalent of $.39 as of March 30, 2019). The IPO generated over $100 million. It was the richest IPO since Ford Motor Company's initial public offering in 1956. By the end of the day Apple stock rose to $29 per share instantly creating 300 millionaires, among them were some Apple employees. At the end of its first day of being traded on the stock market Apple's market cap was a whopping $1.778 billion. As important as hitting this financial jackpot was for Apple, a year earlier something possibly even more important for the future of the company had occurred that would take Apple from a good company to a great one.

Jobs and several Apple employees, including computer interface expert Jef Raskin, had paid a visit to Xerox PARC in December 1979 to see a demonstration of the Xerox Alto computer. Xerox was granting Apple engineers three days of access to the PARC facility in return for Apple giving Xerox the option to buy 100,000 shares of Apple at the pre-IPO price of just $10 a share.

It was love at first sight. Upon seeing the mouse driven computer software innovation at PARC, Jobs was immediately convinced that all future computers would be using a graphical user interface (GUI). Upon returning to Apple he began development of a GUI for Apple's new Lisa computer. It would seem that the radically successful young computer company was about to enter a period of even greater glory but by this time there was trouble brewing at Apple. In 1982, after infighting between Jobs and the company's Board of Directors, that centered on Job's cost overruns and volatile management style co-founder Jobs was stripped of his position as head of the team creating the Lisa. Now a captain without a ship Jobs took over Wozniak and Raskin's low-budget computer project, the Macintosh, recreating it with a graphical user interface system that was cheaper and faster than Lisa. In 1983, though Lisa became the first personal computer sold to the public with a GUI, it was a commercial failure mainly due to its high price and the limited software applications available to it. In 1985 Lisa would be repositioned as a high-end Macintosh. Sadly, it was discontinued in its second year.

In 1984, Apple launched the Macintosh, the first personal computer to be sold without a programming language making computers easy to use for the highly populated non-technical people of the world. The Mac's debut was celebrated with a television advertisement entitled "1984" directed by Ridley Scott, costing $1.5 million. The commercial aired during the third quarter of Super Bowl XVIII on January 22, 1984. "1984" is now hailed as a pinnacle moment in Apple's history and was called a "masterpiece" by CNN. It is widely known as one of the greatest TV advertisements of all time by TV Guide and those in the advertisement industry.

The Macintosh sold well out the gate but follow-up sales lagged because of the computer's high price and limited software support. Sales of the Macintosh did pick up with the introduction of the LaserWriter, the first PostScript laser printer sold at a reasonable price, and PageMaker, an early desktop publishing package. The grouping of these three products ignited the desktop publishing market. The Macintosh became a favorite of the desktop publishing industry because of its advanced graphics capabilities and the intuitive Macintosh GUI.

It's Him or Me

In 1985, a power struggle developed between Jobs and CEO John Sculley, who Jobs had hand-picked for the position two years earlier by winning him away from Pepsico with the now famous question, "Do you want to sell sugar water for the rest of your life or come with me and change the world?"

The Apple board of directors had instructed Sculley to "contain" Jobs and control his ability to launch expensive products without market testing them first. Jobs, however, refused to give in to the restraints and tried instead to boot Sculley out of Apple. When Sculley discovered that Jobs was attempting to organize a coup against him he called a board meeting to address the issue. The showdown reached a head when Sculley issued an ultimatum to the Board to side with either him or Jobs to lead Apple forward. The Board of Directors chose Sculley and voted to remove Jobs from his managerial duties. Feeling betrayed by the people hired to run the company he created Jobs resigned from Apple. As Alan Deutschman, author of the book "Change or Die, The Second Coming of Steve Jobs" put it:

"He co-founds Apple Computer when he is 21, and by the time he is 23 he's a millionaire. He becomes legendary. And then, at 30, he has this humiliating defeat."

In his now famous 2005 Stanford commencement speech, Jobs admitted that he, "really didn't know what to do for a few months. I felt that I had let the previous generation of entrepreneurs down, that I had dropped the baton as it was being passed to me."

Jobs went on to say, "I even thought about running away from (Silicon) Valley. But something slowly began to dawn on me. I still loved what I did. The turn of events at Apple had not changed that one bit. And so I decided to start over."

The day after Labor Day, 1985, Jobs dialed up a former colleague and together they launched a new computer company, NeXT. Jobs decision to start NeXT would pay off handsomely later.

1985 turned out to be a very historic year for Apple as Wozniak also disappeared from active employment at Apple to pursue other ventures. He expressed his frustration with how Apple had treated the Apple II division. Wozniak thought they deserved better because while other Apple products had lost money the Apple II had been the product earning money and yet he felt the other products and departments were treated as though they were more important. As he departed Apple, Wozniak assessed the company by saying it had, "been going in the wrong direction for the last five years."

Though he left Apple voicing these grievances, Wozniak did leave the company on good terms. Both now absent, Wozniak and Jobs remained Apple shareholders. Wozniak continues to represent Apple at various events. For his public relations efforts he is said to receive a stipend estimated to be $120,000 per year.

Too High A Price

Without Jobs and Wozniak, the Macintosh product line began to pursue a philosophy that pushed for higher price points for the computer. The "high-right policy" so named for its location on a graph charting price vs. profits was adopted by Apple executives. Whereas Jobs had argued for the company to produce products aimed at the larger segment of the consumer market and a $1,000 price point for the Macintosh (though it is said that he himself always seemed to be running over budget). The post-Jobs Apple saw that Macintosh models selling at higher price points resulted in higher profit margins. They were also convinced their pricing policy showed no negative affect on total sales. To the contrary the consumers gobbled up every increase of power for the machine and price increases as well. Jean-Louis Gassée, was the Apple executive who popularized the mantra "fifty-five or die". The "fifty-five" referred to the 55% profit margins of the Macintosh II.

In 1981, Gassée became Director of European Operations at Apple Computer but he would become famous at Apple for how he changed the history of the company in 1985. It was Gassée who after learning of Steve Jobs' plan to oust CEO John Sculley over the Memorial Day weekend while Sculley was away in China, that preemptively informed the board of directors about Jobs' plan. The failed coup resulted in Jobs eventually resigning from Apple.

As new desktop publishing programs appeared on cheaper PC clones offering some of the same functionality of the Macintosh, Apple started to lose its grip on consumers. With Macintosh prices continuing to rise many of Apple's core customers could no longer afford the high-end products. The change in Apple's fortunes became clear over the 1989 Christmas season which became the first in company history to suffer declining sales. The drop in sells also led to a 20% drop in Apple's stock price. Though Gassée continued to preach higher prices for Apple products and urged the company to maintain its pricing course his words went unheeded and he was forced out of the company in 1990. Apple changed its strategy and introduced three lower cost models, the Macintosh Classic, Macintosh LC, and Macintosh IIsi, all of which were rewarded with significant sales.

Hitting the Mark

In 1991, Apple made another good decision when it introduced the PowerBook, replacing the Macintosh Portable. The design of the PowerBook was truly a shape of things to come. Its handsome figure has been copied by almost all of today's laptops. Apple introduced System 7, a major upgrade to the operating system the same year. It added color to the interface and presented consumers with new networking capabilities. It is still the architectural basis for the Classic Mac OS. The success of PowerBook and other Apple products during this period continued to increase the company's bottom line. The cash register continued to ring for Apple until it lost its way completely and began to produce more misses than hits.

Lost and Losing

Apple executives had come to believe the Apple II series was too expensive to produce. They also thought that it took away sales from the low-end Macintosh. In October 1990, when Apple released the Macintosh LC, they advised their developer technical support staff to recommend developing applications for the Macintosh rather than the Apple II. They also authorized salespersons to steer consumers towards the Macintosh and away from Apple II. As a result, the Apple IIe was discontinued in 1993.

The once high-flying upstart now seemed to be not only lost but losing. The success of Apple's lower-cost consumer models, especially the LC, led to cannibalization of their higher priced machines. In efforts to address this problem management introduced several new brands, selling almost identical machines at different price points while aiming the products at different market segments. The high-end Quadra, the mid-range Centris line, and the consumer price friendly Performa series only confused customers who failed to understand the difference between these models. Apple seemed to be suffering from an identity crises that confused its customers even more with each new and unsuccessful product experiment pushing out an array of consumer products during the 1990s, that included digital cameras, portable CD audio players, speakers, video consoles, the eWorld online service, and even TV appliances. It was clear to everyone that Apple had completely lost its way. In addition to these strategic mistakes Apple also burned through an enormous amount of cash and labor capital with their problem-plagued Newton division. As Apple continued to flounder the company's market share and stock price continued to dive. All these misfires took place under the watch of CEO John Sculley.

Facing more than their share of troubles already Apple made another strategic error. The software company Microsoft continued to gain market share with its Windows operating system by focusing on delivering their software to cheaper personal computers thereby stealing away customers from Apple. Meanwhile, Apple continued to target those customers interested in richly engineered computers boasting higher prices because they delivered higher profit margins. Instead of responding to Microsoft with competing consumer offerings Apple chose to compete by sueing Microsoft for using a GUI similar to the Apple Lisa in the case Apple Computer, Inc. v. Microsoft Corp. Yes, the same GUI system both Apple's Steve Jobs and Microsoft's Bill Gates first saw at Xerox PARC. The lawsuit dragged on for a number of years before it was finally dismissed. Sculley, led Apple through a series of major product flops and missed product release deadlines that severely damaged Apple's reputation before he was released and then replaced as CEO by Michael Spindler.

The Wilderness Days

The top job at Apple turned into a game of musical chairs as Spindler was replaced by Gil Amelio as CEO in 1996. Known for being a corporate turn-around specialist, after taking over at Apple, new CEO Amelio made drastic changes that included extensive layoffs and cost-cutting. But none of these tactics could stop Apple from collapsing. The company had tried in various ways to change their fate. One of those ways was their failed attempts to modernize its Mac OS operating system, first in 1988 with the Pink project, then with Copland in 1994. Finally, they adopted a different strategy in 1997, when Apple purchased NeXT mainly to get its hands on the NeXTSTEP operating system. Yes, the same NeXT owned by Steve Jobs. At the time it was estimated that Apple was weeks away from bankruptcy. The NeXT acquisition was finalized on February 9, 1997. With this move Steve Jobs returned to Apple as an advisor.

Siding with The Dark Side

The stage was set for something momentous when Steve Jobs took the stage at the January 1997 Macworld Expo. But few in the audience were ready for just how momentous the upcoming announcement would be. Apple employees still viewed Microsoft as their mortal enemies, so it was no surprise when they let out a seismic gasp when Jobs announced that Apple would partner with Microsoft to release new versions of Microsoft Office for the Macintosh. It was like Luke Skywalker making a pact to join forces with Darth Vader. But, feelings aside the move was a stroke of genius. Microsoft would benefit from the revenue that would flow their way every time someone purchased a Macintosh that included Microsoft Office software, and the non-voting Apple stock it received. For its angst Apple employees would benefit from the $150 million investment

Microsoft would make in Apple, a financial injection that saved Apple from extinction.

After his tenure produced a three-year record low stock price and almost fatal financial loses, on July 9, 1997, Amelio was ousted by the Apple board of directors and the Steve Jobs was installed as the interim CEO. Immediately, he began restructuring the company's product lines by liberating Apple of all the revenue eating products that fell outside of the company's core competencies. It was during this period that Jobs also uncovered the product design genius of Jonathan Ive. Together this dynamic duo was about to collaboratively build a new Apple that would surpass anything the company had ever achieved.

The Second Coming

On August 15, 1998, Apple introduced a new all-in-one computer reminiscent of the Macintosh 128K. It was called the iMac. The iMac design team was led by Ive, who would later use his design genius to design the iPod and the iPhone. The iMac featured a unique design, with translucent colors, and was a leap forward in technology. The new computer would go on to sale almost 800,000 units in its first five months. Jobs was back and so was Apple.

In his Stanford speech Jobs reflected on the period of his return to Apple. "I didn't see it then, but it turned out that getting fired from Apple was the best thing that could have ever happened to me. The heaviness of being successful was replaced by the lightness of being a beginner again, less sure about everything. It freed me to enter into one of the most creative periods of my life."

"I'm pretty sure none of this would have happened if I hadn't been fired from Apple. It was awful tasting medicine, but I guess the patient needed it. Sometimes life hits you in the head with a brick. Don't lose faith. I'm convinced the only thing that kept me going was that I loved what I did. You've got to find what you love."

Growth Through Mergers and Acquisitions

After ridding Apple of the losers among their product line Jobs sets the company on a new course to fill the product pipeline with new revenue earning goods and services, first not through manufacturing them but through acquisition. Apple uses their purchasing power to create a portfolio of digital production software for professionals and consumers. In 1998, Apple purchased the Key Grip software project, digital video editing software from the company Macromedia. The product was unfinished at the time Apple purchased it but their engineers were able to complete the product customizing it to their own specs. Macromedia had decided to narrow its product focus to web development software and fortunately for Apple "Key Grip" fell outside of that group focus. Apple renamed the product Final Cut Pro before launching it into retail markets in April of 1999. Along with the release of Final Cut Pro, Apple also released iMovie, a consumer video-editing product in October of 1999. The following year Apple bought the German company Astarte developers of DVD authoring technology. After the purchase Apple turned the Astarte digital tool DVDirector into the Profesional-Oriented DVD Studio Pro software. Apple then cleverly used the same technology to create iDVD for the consumer market. By April of 2000 Apple had completely integrated the Astarte products and its engineering team into the company. In July 2001, Apple also acquired Spruce Technologies, to incorporate that company's PC DVD authoring platform into Apple's portfolio of digital video projects.

After landing a solid hit in the DVD and Editing technology product category Apple turned its attention to the music industry. A now defunct company named Casady & Greene was the distributer of a software program called SoundJam MP released in 1998. The program was developed by Bill Kincaid. Apple purchased the program in 2000 and renamed it iTunes. Upon its release it completely revolutionized the way people consumed music. At the time of the purchase, Kincaid, Jeff Robbin and Dave Heller, left Casady & Greene to continue development of the program as Apple employees. At Apple, the developers simplified SoundJam's user interface, added the ability to burn CDs, and removed the program's recording feature and skin support. Apple released iTunes version 1.0 of the program on January 9, 2001, at Macworld, San Francisco. iTunes was originally created to be just a simple music player but over time it was developed into a sophisticated multimedia content manager, hardware synchronization manager and e-commerce platform. The current version of iTunes enables users to manage media content, create playlists, synchronize media content with handheld devices including the iPod, iPhone, and iPad, re-image and update handheld devices, stream Internet radio and purchase music, films, television shows, audiobooks, and applications via the iTunes Store.

Enter the iPod

The first version of iPod, a line of portable media players and multi-purpose pocket computers designed and marketed by Apple Inc. was released on October 23, 2001, about 8 1/2 months after the Macintosh version of iTunes was released. The iPod was phenomenally successful selling over 100 million units within six years. iPod would continue selling for almost two decades but with the popularity of streaming having become the prevalent way to receive music and movies today only the iPod Touch (7th generation) remains in production.

GarageBand and Final Cut Pro

Apple continued their foray into music in 2002, purchasing the company Nothing Real for their advanced digital compositing application Shake. They also purchased the company Emagic to get their music productivity application Logic. The purchase of Emagic made Apple the first computer manufacturer to own a music software company. The acquisition was followed by the development of Apple's consumer-level GarageBand application. The release of iPhoto in the same year completed Apple's iLife suite. Apple's GarageBand, another application using Logic's audio engine, is bundled in iLife, a suite of software which comes included on any new Macintosh computer. On December 8, 2011, the boxed version of Logic Pro was discontinued, along with Logic Express, and Logic Pro is now only available through the Mac App Store. GarageBand is a line of digital audio workstations for macOS and iOS devices that allows users to create music or podcasts. GarageBand is developed and sold by Apple for macOS, and is part of the iLife software suite. Its music and podcast creation system enables users to create multiple tracks with pre-made MIDI keyboards, pre-made loops, an array of various instrumental effects, and voice recordings. By 2007, Apple had registered 800,000 Final Cut Pro users.

iTunes Changes Music

On May 19, 2001, Apple opened its first official Apple retail stores in Virginia and California. On October 23, the same year, Apple debuted the iPod portable digital audio player. In 2003, Apple's iTunes Store was introduced. The service offered online music downloads for $0.99 a song and integration with the iPod. The iTunes Store quickly became the market leader in online music services, with over five billion downloads by June 19, 2008. Two years later, the iTunes Store was the world's largest music retailer.

iPhone and Apple TV

During his keynote speech at the Macworld Expo on January 9, 2007, Jobs announced that Apple Computer, Inc. would thereafter be known as "Apple Inc.", because the company had shifted its emphasis from computers to consumer electronics. This event also saw the announcement of the iPhone and the Apple TV. The company sold 270,000 iPhone units during the first 30 hours of sales, and the device was called "a game changer for the industry." Apple would achieve widespread success with its iPhone, iPod Touch, and iPad products, which forever changed the mobile phone, portable music, and personal computer industries.

The Apple Store

In July 2008, Apple launched the App Store to sell third-party applications for the iPhone and iPod Touch. In less than a month the store sold 60 million applications and was bringing in an average daily revenue of $1 million. By August, Jobs was forecasting that the App Store could become a billion-dollar business for Apple. By October 2008, Apple was the third-largest mobile handset supplier in the world due to the popularity of the iPhone.

After such a magical beginning both Apple and its co-founder Jobs found themselves groping their way through midnight. Would the company survive? Would Jobs be a one hit wonder and end up as just a small footnote in history? After returning to save the company he co-founded and completing the best second act in business, on August 24, 2011, Jobs resigned his position as CEO of Apple. He replaced himself with then Apple Chief Operations Officer, Tim Cook, while becoming Apple's chairman. When Steve Jobs died, October 5, 2011, he left Apple as one of the most valuable companies in the world and cemented his own legacy as one of the greatest entrepreneurs in business history.

Best Buy

Best Buy is the world's largest brick-and-mortar electronics store, but a few years ago, it looked like it might join former competitors like Circuit City in the retail graveyard. In 2010, sales and profits were way down, and a scandal involving the then-CEO in 2012 only made things worse, as Salon reported. Remarkably, the company managed to turn itself around. The new CEO cleaned up disorganized stores, shuttered failing locations, brought in exclusive products, and improved service. Most importantly, the chain integrated the online and in-store experiences making it easy to research products online. Best Buy also staffed stores with employees who were experts in popular brands like Samsung and Apple. The changes worked. Customers returned and by 2016, both profits and the company's stock price were up significantly. Midnight adverted. Midnight does not have to spell the end. Everything broken can be fixed.

Morning

Even though it's closing in on being the next company to reach a $1 trillion market capitalization Amazon continues to grow at the rate of a tech startup. The retailer is dominating the world of e-commerce garnering nearly 50% of digital sales in the United States. Furthermore, brick and mortar companies like Nike and Party City have chosen to sell their products on Amazon's website. In addition to these revenue streams retailers like Best Buy and Kohl's are also partnering with Amazon for a number of in-store ventures. All these income sources make Amazon a financial powerhouse even before you throw the company's money-making cloud computing Web Services division into the mix. Amazon is definitely in the morning stage of its business life cycle.

Amazon

Amazon reported $1.86 billion in net income in the fourth quarter of 2017. While that may have seemed like business as usual for the retail behemoth who seems to be everywhere and in everything, don't forget that it took Amazon more than 14 years, that's 58 quarters, to make as much net profit as it made in that single quarter counting from its May 1997 initial public offering. That's a pretty long midnight.

Amazon reported its first quarterly profit in the fourth quarter of 2001. Though the $5 million gain it reported that quarter was not an earth-shattering amount it did signal that after years and years of losing money the e-commerce seller had finally turned the corner on profits. But, from its beginning earning quarterly profits was not the game that Amazon was playing. It was pursuing an entirely new and different business model. Amazon CEO Jeff Bezos has long maintained that investing in future growth is more important than hitting quarterly earnings targets. So, after centuries of businesses chasing profits maybe we should all rethink how we build our business.

How did Amazon go from the darkest midnight to perhaps the brightest of mornings? When we look at Amazon what do we see? Though the company is best recognized as the world's largest online store it has become much more than that. Amazon now has millions of people perusing its website. So, selling advertising on its website was a no-brainer way to profit off all that attention. Their ad sells are growing to the point of challenging Facebook and Google as an advertising option for businesses. The company's Amazon Studios is rivaling Netflix and HBO in producing award winning original movies and television shows. Amazon is now a hardware maker with a popular line of smart speakers and video streaming devices. Amazon Web Services (AWS) has become the world's biggest provider of cloud-computing services. And, Amazon's acquisition of Whole Foods Market and an increasing flock of cashierless convenience stores now totaling about 487 locations is making the retail monster a player in the grocery business. We won't even get started about Amazon Prime and the company's growing delivery fleet. Amazon has its hands in a lot of pies.

But what was the formula that got them to Morning? In 2000, Amazon launched Marketplace, offering other merchants the option of paying to list their goods on Amazon's digital shelves. After the success of that venture the company offered other companies the opportunity to stock their items in Amazon warehouses for a fee. The genius of that move was that it dramatically increased the selection of product Amazon could offer customers without tying up the company's cash in inventory.

In 2005, Amazon introduced their Prime membership program. The program offers quicker shipping on a selection of Amazon items for an annual fee. As Amazon was expanding their product offerings the Prime program convinced customers to browse the expanding categories of goods to see what else they might like to purchase knowing after their initial Prime membership payment shipping would be free. Prime has now passed more than 100 million paying members making it one of the largest paid membership programs in the world.

By the early 2000s Amazon had already started to reorganize their corporate technology department. One of the company's strong suits is streamlining processes to make them more efficient. The company learned from mastering its own massive consumer websites. Amazon had learned by breaking down their own computing services into basic building blocks of digital storage, processing power, databases, software applications, and infrastructure. In 2006, Amazon offered those services to other companies on a pay-for-what-you-use basis with their Simple Storage Service. As more and more companies began to use the service Amazon was forced to build massive server farms. But, as always seems to be the case with them they found a way to capitalize off it. By using economies of scale Amazon is able to lower prices for their services and build a series of increasingly powerful computing tools.

By 2015, Amazon Web Services, the company's cloud-computing unit had changed the way businesses used technology while raking in billions of dollars per year in profits. AWS is now Amazon's biggest source of revenue. Amazon uses the money AWS brings in to reinvest in new services and expand its retail business.

For all its successes Amazon has had its misses too. The Fire phone flopped bigtime and was quickly discontinued. Amazon's efforts to match eBay in online auctions was a failure as well. Various kinds of payment services and online storefronts also met with disaster. Other attempts at starting businesses outside of their core competencies like a travel booking site crashed and burned too. But, one of the reasons Amazon is enjoying their morning stage of success is because after giving these novelties ample time to prove themselves the company shuts down their losers, cuts their loses and moves on. To stay ahead of the curve it is important to sometimes test uncharted waters to see if you can add new products and services to your existing portfolio. However, when you find these new ventures are not panning out end them quickly rather than continuing to throw good money after bad.

Nvidia

Nvidia, may be the best company that ordinary people have never heard of. Nvidia is experiencing its morning, and Founder and CEO, Jensen Huang, certainly has something special. In 1999, Nvidia invented Graphics Processing Units (GPU) making possible real-time programmable shading, which gives game developers and artists an infinite palette for expression. The company continues to reinforce its position as the gold standard for visual computing. The Silicon Valley giant develops graphics and central processing units across four sectors—gaming, data centers, autos and professional visualization. Lately, it has made strides in artificial intelligence with its deep learning technology. In May, Nvidia researchers developed a system for robots to learn how to perform tasks simply by observing humans. Nvidia is poised to continue its rapid growth. In 2018, its revenue and operating income both increased to $9.71 billion and $3.21 billion, respectively. For fiscal 2019, revenue was $11.72 billion, up 21% from the $9.71 a year earlier. Operating income for fiscal 2019 was $3.80 billion, up 19% from the previous year.

At $100 billion, computer gaming is the world's largest entertainment industry and NVIDIA GeForce is its largest platform. GeForce® GTX GPUs and the GeForce Experience™ application are transforming everyday PCs into powerful gaming machines. Nvidia's, GameWorks™ software allows developers to make games photorealistic and immersive. Don't have any idea what that means? Ask any serious gamer.

What's next for Nvidia? Three converging forces brought about the era of AI: the availability of immense stores of data, the invention of deep learning algorithms, and the intense performance of GPU computing. New internet services, like Google Assistant, have learned speech from sound. Self-driving cars use deep learning to recognize the space the car inhabits to know what to avoid. In healthcare, neural networks trained with millions of medical images can find clues in MRIs that until now could only be found through invasive biopsies. AI will spur a wave of social progress unmatched since the industrial revolution. It's a safe bet Nvidia will be leading the charge. Bright? Yeah, it's morning for these guys.

Hilton

The 100-year-old Hilton was chosen in 2019 as the Best Company to Work For in America. That's sweet validation for Hilton CEO, Chris Nassetta, who took over the reins at Hilton in 2007. He found a company that according to him:

"Had lost our way a bit."

The company was trudging through its midnight stage but Nassetta knew exactly what the problem was.

"We forgot that we are a business of people serving people, and the corporate environment got very disconnected from the front line," said Nassetta.

Under Nassetta's guidance, Hilton launched an all-inclusive program to upgrade "back-of-house" areas used by staff to make them as spiffy as the areas Hilton's guests used. Under orders from Nassetta other Hiltons would follow the lead of the New York Hilton Midtown, which now boast renovated employee spaces that feature better lighting and more comfortable furnishings, an updated cafeteria (that serves most employees for free), Break areas with TVs and even massage chairs for employees on break. Hilton has established a free program enabling employees to earn their GEDs and formed Hilton University where they can enroll in workshops and training. Hilton outperforms when it comes to satisfaction among typically more disenfranchised "line-level" workers, such as cleaning and kitchen staff, according to the Great Place to Work Institute. With Hilton stock up 274% from its IPO price in 2013, the numbers are showing that the employee-first changes are working out for Hilton.

"I am obsessed with taking care of my staff," says Nassetta.

A wise investment that is paying off with better service for Hilton clients. When you are engulfed by midnight, you can't just sit around and wait for things to get better, you must bring about the changes that make them better. In business, Morning is not the result of being passive, it is the result of actively pushing change that changes your entire business landscape for the better.

Chapter 6: People You Meet On The Road To Success

You will meet three kinds of people on the road to success. Deceivers, Believers, and Achievers. Chapter 6: People You Meet On The Road To Success, describes the people you'll meet on your journey to success. It also tells you how not to get fooled by the deceivers, how not to chase away your believers, and how to match the accomplishments of the achievers.

Avoid Deceivers

Charles Ponzi (born Carlo Pietro Giovanni Guglielmo Tebaldo Ponzi; March 3, 1882 – January 18, 1949) was an Italian swindler and con artist in the U.S. and Canada. His aliases include Charles Ponci, Carlo, and Charles P. Bianchi. Born and raised in Italy, he became known in the early 1920s as a swindler in North America for his money-making scheme. He promised clients a 50% profit within 45 days or 100% profit within 90 days, by buying discounted postal reply coupons in other countries and redeeming them at face value in the United States as a form of arbitrage. In reality, Ponzi was paying earlier investors using the investments of later investors. While this type of fraudulent investment scheme was not originally invented by Ponzi, it became so identified with him that it's now referred to as a "Ponzi scheme." His scheme ran for over a year before it collapsed, costing his "investors" a whopping $20 million. Ponzi may have been inspired by the scheme of William F. Miller, a Brooklyn bookkeeper who in 1899 used the same scheme to take in $1 million.

There are billions of good people in this world. Trustworthy people, dependable people, responsible people, honest people, helpful people, and compassionate people, all reside on this planet. Unfortunately, there are also untrustworthy people, undependable people, irresponsible people, dishonest people, unhelpful people, and people who are not compassionate, who all reside on this planet too.

You can't see everyone as bad because everyone is not. But you can't see everyone as good either because everyone is not. While there are some people who would dutifully work beside you to help you make your fortune, there are also people who will pretend they are working alongside you so they can take your fortune. Knowing the difference between deceivers, believers, and achievers is an attribute you must have if you want to gain wealth. It is an especially necessary attribute you must have if you want to keep your wealth.

People work hard to learn their craft because hard work plays a big part in being successful. They will do extensive research on subjects to make sure they have all the accurate information they need to be successful. Yet, when it comes to who they work with or trust they barely ask for references. Someone who we mention often is super investor Warren Buffett. Buffett has made billions of dollars by investing in and buying companies. You best be sure that he does extensive research to find out who the executives and managers are that run those businesses before he decides to make an investment in or purchase those companies. There may not be billions of dollars at stake when you are working with someone or investing your time or money in ventures but whatever amount you have at stake is too much to lose because of carelessness.

There are processes in place to help you get information on businesses, workers, vendors, individuals, anyone and everyone in the world. So, why would you believe someone is good at what they do or even honest just because their Facebook or Instagram profile looks good?

"Managers thinking about accounting issues should never forget one of Abraham Lincoln's favorite riddles: How many legs does a dog have, if you call a tail a leg? The answer: Four, because calling a tail a leg doesn't make it a leg." – Warren Buffet

Just because someone says they are a qualified accountant, good teacher, brilliant scientist, or makes some other claim doesn't make it so. There are many kinds of deceivers to watch out for. People who make promises they can't deliver. People who borrow not intending to pay you back. People who claim to have a skill or talent they really don't have. People who pretend to be honest so they can cheat you or take advantage of you. People who make believe they have your best interest at heart when their real motive is to gain something they want at your expense. Why do I bring up the subject of deception and pause to warn you about deceivers? Because the world is full of them. You can surround yourself with a thousand good people but all it takes is one bad one to ruin your life.

Don't make the critical mistake of thinking it's someone else's job to protect you and your interests. Knowing that there are dishonest people is not a reason to live in fear or walk around in a constant state of paranoia. But it is a good reason to always proceed with caution. Or as the old Russian proverb says:

"Doveryai no proveryai". Translation: Trust, but verify.

It's alright to trust people, even trust that what they are saying is true, but always verify that trust by confirming it through at least three reliable sources before you act upon that information.

Beware of companies that claim they are extremely successful

The collapse of the energy company Enron in December 2001 precipitated what would become the most complex white-collar crime investigation in the FBI's history. The charge against Enron was that the company's top officials for the Houston-based company cheated investors and enriched themselves through complex accounting gimmicks like overvaluing assets to boost cash flow and doctoring earnings statements to make the company more appealing to investors. When the company declared bankruptcy in December 2001, Enron investors lost millions which prompted the FBI and other federal agencies to investigate the company. The Enron fraud was so massive that the case prompted the creation of a multi-agency Enron Task Force, that teamed investigators and analysts from the FBI, the Internal Revenue Service-Criminal Investigation Division, the Securities and Exchange Commission, and prosecutors from the Department of Justice. Agents conducted more than 1,800 interviews and collected more than 3,000 boxes of evidence. In addition to those efforts more than four terabytes of digitized data was collected and more than $164 million was seized by the government. Twenty-two people have been convicted for their actions related to the fraud, including Enron's chief executive officer, their president, chief operating officer, the chief financial officer, the chief accounting officer, and others. Unfortunately, all that happened after the fact.

Why was no one able to verify that Enron was a smoke and mirror hoax before Enron Vice President, Sherron Watkins blew the whistle? Enron was ranked as America's fifth largest company by Fortune magazine in 2002, despite its 2001 bankruptcy filing. Furthermore, on October 16, 2001, Enron announced a third-quarter loss of $618 million. Later, the company revealed that it overstated its earnings dating back to 1997. That's a lot of years getting away with fake accounting. So, who verified that Enron's numbers were correct over all those years? On January 10, 2002, Arthur Andersen LLP, the accounting firm that handled Enron's audits, discloses that its employees had destroyed company documents. So, guess who should have verified that something was very wrong?

Arthur Andersen LLP, was an American holding company founded in 1913, by Arthur E. Andersen and Clarence DeLany as Andersen, DeLany & Co. The firm changed its name to Arthur Andersen & Co. in 1918. It was formerly one of the "Big Five" accounting firms (along with PricewaterhouseCoopers, Deloitte Touche Tohmatsu, Ernst & Young, and KPMG). The firm provided auditing, tax, and consulting services to large corporations. By 2001, Arthur Andersen had become one of the world's largest multinational companies. But, in 2002, the firm voluntarily surrendered its licenses to practice as Certified Public Accountants in the United States after being found guilty of criminal charges relating to the firm's auditing of Enron. In 2005, the Supreme Court of the United States unanimously reversed Arthur Andersen's conviction due to serious errors in the trial judge's instructions to the jury that convicted the firm. The former consultancy and outsourcing practice of Arthur Andersen separated from the firm's accountancy practice and split from Andersen Worldwide in 2000, renaming itself Accenture.

This is a perfect example of why verifying anything through just one or two sources is not verification enough. People have lost millions of dollars investing in companies like Enron. And don't think because a company is large or well known that means there is no need to make sure everything is on the up and up. Even the most reputable company can fall prey to a rogue employee who goes outside the rules or does something illegal. The best way to avoid being taken by the deceivers is to hold everyone to the same high standards. Word of mouth is not good enough. Today, you can take nothing at face value. Trust but verify.

Beware of people who claim to be someone or something they are not

Frank William Abagnale Jr. is an American security consultant known for his background as a former con man, check forger, and impostor. Between the ages of 15 and 21 he became one of the most notorious impostors in history, claiming to have assumed no fewer than eight different identities, including an airline pilot, physician, U.S. Bureau of Prisons agent, and a lawyer. He escaped from police custody twice before he was 21 years old. One of those escapes was made from a plane while it was taxiing for takeoff while another escape was made from a U.S. federal penitentiary. Abagnale served less than five years in prison before starting to work for the federal government. He is currently a consultant and lecturer for the Federal Bureau of Investigation (FBI) academy and field offices. He also runs Abagnale & Associates, a financial fraud consultancy company.

Abagnale's life-story inspired the Academy Award-nominated feature film Catch Me If You Can released in 2002. The movie starred Leonardo DiCaprio as Abagnale and Tom Hanks as the FBI agent pursuing him. It also inspired the Broadway musical Catch Me If You Can, and a TV series called White Collar, which are all based on the book Catch Me If You Can.

Abagnale once decided to impersonate a pilot in order to look more legitimate when cashing checks. He was able to get a pilot's uniform by calling Pan American World Airways (Pan Am) and telling the company he was a pilot working for them who had lost his uniform while getting it cleaned at his hotel. He obtained a new one by using a fake employee ID number. He also forged a Federal Aviation Administration pilot's license. As a teenager, Abagnale noticed that his hair was graying prematurely. He parlayed the gray hair into his pilot impersonation by giving the appearance he was older. He also pretended he had professional credentials that he did not have. Pan Am estimates that between the ages of 16–18, Abagnale flew as a passenger more than 1,000,000 miles on more than 250 flights to 26 countries without paying for a ticket by impersonating an airline employee or "deadheading." By impersonating a company pilot he was able to stay at hotels for free. His expenses for food and lodging were billed to the airline. Wisely, Abagnale did not fly on Pan Am planes, knowing his impersonations could potentially be identified by actual Pan Am pilots or employees. He didn't want to risk being asked for genuine identification or proof of employment or genuine identification by Pan Am. Abagnale says he was often invited by real pilots to take the controls of the plane while it was in-flight. Once he was offered the courtesy of flying a plane while at 30,000 feet.

Abagnale took the controls and quickly enabled the autopilot saying he was, "very much aware that I had been handed custody of 140 lives, my own included... because I couldn't fly a kite".

There are those people who boldly claim to be something they are not and claim they can do what they cannot. The danger with running into one of these people is hiring or worse being conned into sending them money for a product or service they don't supply. The money you stand to lose is probably not as hurting as the humiliation that comes from being duped. I'm sure the people who were fooled by Abagnale were shocked when they discovered how easily they were deceived.

Again, trust but verify. Id's can be faked as can documents like diplomas, but colleges, universities and even certificated programs keep records of those who attended and certainly those who graduated from their institution. Calling the institution and having them verify whether the person in question actually attended and/or graduated from their school, institution or program is easy to do and highly recommended before handing over money or employing anyone.

Beware of people who let you do all the work while they take all the pay

Louis Jay Pearlman was an American record producer and fraudster. He was the manager of successful 1990s boy bands such as Backstreet Boys and NSYNC. In 2006, Pearlman was accused of running one of the largest and longest-running Ponzi schemes in history, leaving more than $300 million in debts. After he was arrested he pleaded guilty to conspiracy, money laundering, and making false statements during a bankruptcy proceeding. Pearlman was convicted and sentenced to up to 25 years in prison in 2008. While serving his sentence in federal custody he died in 2016.

With the exception of the group US5, all of the musical acts that worked with Pearlman sued him in federal court for misrepresentation and fraud. All the cases against Pearlman either have been won by those who brought lawsuits against him or have been settled out of court.

The members of Backstreet Boys were the first to file a lawsuit against Pearlman. They felt that their contract that allowed Pearlman to collect money from them as both a manager and producer was unfair, because Pearlman was also paid as a sixth member of the Backstreet Boys which means he collected one-sixth of the band's income. The band's member Brian Littrell hired a lawyer to determine why the group had received only $300,000 for all of their work while Pearlman and his record label had made millions because of them. The band *NSYNC was having similar money issues with Pearlman, and its members soon followed by suing him as well. In 2002, at the age of 14, Aaron Carter filed a lawsuit that accused Pearlman and his company Trans Continental records of cheating him out of hundreds of thousands of dollars and of racketeering in a deliberate pattern of criminal activity. The suit was settled out of court.

The music industry is notorious for milking millions of dollars out of hard-working entertainers who either failed to completely read their contracts or were far too gullible in believing unscrupulous managers, agents and executives. There is no plausible explanation for your representation suddenly driving expensive cars and buying luxury homes if you are still literally a starving artist. Yes, a record company may be paying for services early in your career that they will bill you for later. But, if you are seeing marketable success from your record sales and public appearances there is no scenario where your managers (the people who are supposedly working for you) should be bathing in material excess while you are still surviving on hot dogs and happy meals. You should always let a lawyer who is familiar with contracts read and explain the contract to you, every word of it, and give you an opinion on what he or she would determine are the positives and negatives of the contract. Make sure the attorney is one you have chosen who is in no way connected to the people you are contemplating signing the contract with. Do the same for all business contracts in any field. The attorney fees will certainly end up being far less expensive than trying to recoup your money after being defrauded. And, if your manager, executive or another party tells you that having your attorney look over the contract is "not necessary" that is definitely a red flag. If this happens. Turn and run immediately and never look back.

Don't trust people simply because others do

Bernard "Bernie" Madoff is a former investment advisor, financier, fraudster, and convicted felon, currently serving a federal prison sentence for offenses related to his massive Ponzi scheme. He is a former non-executive chairman of the NASDAQ stock exchange. Madoff confessed to operating the largest Ponzi scheme in world history and the largest financial fraud in U.S. history. Prosecutors estimated the fraud to be worth $64.8 billion based on the amounts in the accounts of Madoff's 4,800 clients as of November 30, 2008.

Madoff founded a penny stock brokerage in 1960 which eventually grew into Bernard L. Madoff Investment Securities. He served as its chairman until his arrest on December 11, 2008. The firm was one of the top market maker businesses on Wall Street. These businesses bypassed "specialist" firms by directly executing stock market orders over the counter from retail brokers.

At the firm, he employed his brother Peter Madoff as senior managing director and chief compliance officer, Peter's daughter Shana Madoff as the firm's rules and compliance officer and attorney, and his now deceased sons Andrew and Mark. Peter has since been sentenced to 10 years in prison and Mark committed suicide by hanging exactly two years after his father's arrest. Andrew died of lymphoma on September 3, 2014.

On December 10, 2008, Madoff's sons told authorities that their father had confessed to them that the asset management unit of his firm was a massive Ponzi scheme, and quoted him as saying that it was "one big lie." The following day, FBI agents arrested Madoff and charged him with one count of securities fraud. The U.S. Securities and Exchange Commission

(SEC) had previously conducted multiple investigations into his business practices but had not uncovered the massive fraud. On March 12, 2009, Madoff pleaded guilty to 11 federal felonies and admitted to turning his wealth management business into a massive Ponzi scheme. The Madoff investment scandal defrauded thousands of investors of billions of dollars. Madoff said that he began the Ponzi scheme in the early 1990s, but federal investigators believe that the fraud began as early as the mid-1980s and may have even begun as far back as the 1970s. Those charged with recovering the missing money believe that the investment operation may never have been legitimate. On June 29, 2009, Madoff was sentenced to 150 years in prison, the maximum allowed.

According to the SEC indictment against Annette Bongiorno and Joann Crupi, two back office workers who worked for Madoff, they created false trading reports based on the returns that Madoff ordered for each customer. How was it done? When Madoff determined a customer's return, one of the back-office workers would enter a false trade report with a previous date and then enter a false closing trade in the amount required to produce the required profit, according to the indictment. Prosecutors allege that Bongiorno used a computer program specially designed to backdate trades and manipulate account statements. They quote her as writing to a manager in the early 1990s, "I need the ability to give any settlement date I want." In some cases, returns were allegedly determined before the account was even opened.

Frank DiPascali Jr. worked for Madoff for 33 years. He and his team worked on the 17th floor of the Lipstick Building where the scam was carried out, Madoff's brokerage was based on the 19th floor, and the main entrance and conference room for the company was on the 18th floor. On a daily basis DiPascali and Madoff watched the closing price of the S&P 100. After getting the closing prices they picked the best-performing stocks and used them to make bogus baskets of stocks to create false trading records, which Madoff claimed were generated from his supposed "split-strike conversion" strategy, in which he bought blue-chip stocks and took options contracts on them. As part of the scam Madoff and his team frequently pretended they had made their trades at a stock's monthly high or low, which resulted in the high returns that they paraded for the benefit of their customers. On occasion, they slipped up and dated some trades as taking place on weekends and federal holidays, when of course the stock market was closed, and still the scam was never discovered.

Good Lord. How can 4,800 clients not know the man was a fake? How could he falsely claim to have generated over $60 billion in profits and all those clients not know it was all a scam? How did he get all those clients under his wing? How could Madoff have kept all those people and all that money suspended in mid-air for over three decades? Simple, his old clients sold new clients on Madoff being a financial genius. Because one person trusted another person, he or she believed that person when they told them wonderful stories about why they too should trust their investment dollars to Madoff. Then comes the investigation and poof! Billions upon billions up in smoke. DON'T TRUST SOMEONE JUST BECAUSE SOMEONE YOU TRUST DOES. ALWAYS, do your own homework. Trust but verify. As the saying goes, "If it sounds too good to be true it usually is."

Believers

Seek Out Believers, and Only Believers

True believers are willing to invest money, sweat equity, or both into you or your project or business to be a part of the team. If a person is willing to impart some knowledge or wisdom to you based on their expertise or experience, they too should be counted as believers. Surely, an hour of Warren Buffet's undivided time and financial advice would be worth more than a month's salary. Believers are the people you need to build your winning team.

Armas Clifford "Mike" Markkula Jr. is known as an American businessman and investor. He is also famously known as an angel investor for and second CEO of Apple Computer, Inc. It was Markkula who provided the early critical funding and managerial support that got Apple off the ground and kickstarted it into being the business juggernaut it is today. Right when they needed him to be Mike Markkula was a Believer.

Markkula was introduced to Steve Jobs and Steve Wozniak when they were looking for funding to manufacture the Apple II personal computer they had developed. This was after having sold some units of the first version of the computer, the Apple I. With his guidance and funding, Apple went from being a partnership working out of a garage to a corporation on its way to becoming a multi-billion-dollar company.

How did Markkula become a believer? He earned Bachelor of Science and Master of Science degrees in electrical engineering from the University of Southern California (USC). He had made millions on stock options he acquired as a marketing manager for Fairchild Semiconductor and Intel, and at the age of 32 was already retired. So, first of all Markkula had the science and technical background to understand what he was looking at when he looked at Apple.

Regis McKenna, a marketer and man who introduced many of the ideas that are now part of the mainstream in "technology marketing" was an early believer in Apple. Venture capitalist Donald T. "Don" Valentine, known as "The Grandfather of Silicon Valley," and a man who played a key role in the formation of a number of tech industries including semiconductors, personal computers, computer software, digital entertainment and networking, was not so much a believer as he was a conduit for the new company. It was Valentine who after meeting the young, personal hygiene challenged Steve Jobs asked McKenna, "Why did you send me this renegade from the human race?"

Valentine was not interested in funding Apple, but he did mention Jobs' new company Apple to Markkula. On Valentine's introduction Jobs visited Markkula and convinced him that there was a market for the Apple II and personal computers in general. In 1977, Markkula gave Apple the benefit of his business expertise and an investment of $250,000 ($80,000 as an equity investment in the company and $170,000 as a loan) becoming a one-third owner of Apple and the company's employee number 3. Steve Wozniak, designer of the first two Apple computers credits Markkula for the success of Apple more than himself. Markkula used his business reputation and savvy to help Apple secure credit and venture capital. He also introduced the young company to Michael Scott and instilled him as the first president and CEO of Apple.

Showing his continued support of Apple, Markkula took over the positions himself from 1981 to 1983. Markkula promised his wife he would stay at Apple for only four years then retire by 1984. Whether he kept his promise is debatable. Markkula went on to serve as chairman of Apple from 1985 through 1997. Markkula is certainly ingrained as part of Apple history. In addition to being the company's first financial supporter, as chairman he was also the one who approved Jef Raskin's 1979 plan to start designing the machine that became the Macintosh, while preventing Jobs from killing the Macintosh project in favor of his own Lisa computer.

You may run across many people who talk a good game saying positive things about you and your projects but being a Believer involves more than just talk. Again, it involves investing time, money, or both in you and/or your work. Or, at the very least sharing their wisdom or acumen with you as an unpaid consultant to help you along. Where would Apple have gone without Markkula, or without McKenna? Knowing the tenacity of Steve Jobs and the technical genius of Steve Wozniak it's hard to imagine the two upstart entrepreneurs not becoming successful, but the assistance of Markkula and McKenna sure helped Apple reach their destination faster and without having to take what certainly would have been costly detours. Cultivate relationships with Believers, people who are not only interested in investing themselves in you but are also excited about doing so. Avoid those who are only seeking some kind of financial gain from you. Believers are interested in giving you a boost up the ladder of success because they believe in you and what you are doing. Whether they gain anything financially from their support of you to them is irrelevant. Don't waste your time getting tangled up with opportunists, gold-diggers, speculators, con artists, or purveyors of lip-service. Don't sell out and don't settle. It is Believers you need. So, it should be believers you seek. You and the work you champion deserve nothing less.

Believers add value to you

Maverick Carter, is one of the key architects of Team LeBron. Boyhood friends Carter, Lebron James, Rich Paul, Randy Mims, and co. have built one of the most impressive player-driven empires in NBA history. When it comes to power brokers in the world of sports King James is undoubtedly sitting on the throne. But, standing next to that throne most would agree is Carter, the power behind that throne.

They were still in high school when Carter and James began making plans to turn James' phenomenal athleticism and his business aspirations into wealth, power, and influence. For over a decade and a half Carter has sat courtside as Lebron carved out legendary status in the NBA. But, make no mistake, Carter is not just some hanger's on leeching off of his famous friend while contributing nothing of value to the equation. Carter has said that his focus was not simply to build wealth for James but to establish power and influence.

"I thought the most important thing was just establishing a mindset of empowerment," Carter has said in interviews, his intent, "was more or less trying to get LeBron to understand the mindset of empowerment, which he absolutely embraces and lives every day."

Early in life Carter learned some hard lessons. Originally from Atlanta, Georgia, the son of a social worker mother, and a drug dealer father who spent much of Carter's childhood in federal penitentiaries. Carter met LeBron James when his family moved to Akron, Ohio and both teens played basketball at St. Vincent–St. Mary High School in Akron. After he graduated from SVSM, Carter played college basketball at Western Michigan University, before transferring to The University of Akron where his interest turned from basketball to business pursuits.

While still in college, Carter interned with the sports apparel giant Nike. That glimpse of business and marketing magic was all that was needed to set Carter on course toward bigger and better things. Carter left school and worked at Nike as an intern. James was a high school sophomore at the time but was already being touted as the next generationally great basketball player. Carter and James had agreed earlier that Carter would go to whichever shoe company signed James and that he would work to represent James' business interests within the shoe company. When James signed with Nike the plan was set in motion. His years at Nike gave Carter a course in business and marketing that allowed him to bring something valuable to the table when he began serving as James' business manager in 2006. Once the team of Carter, James, Paul and

Mims founded agent and sports-marketing company LRMR the business plans Carter and James nurtured back in high school were off and running. Though the venture didn't go off without some growing pains, Carter was responsible for the theatrics that gave us "The Decision" in 2010, when Lebron announced that he was taking his talents to South Beach, a marketing disaster if ever there was one.

Having learned a lesson from that misstep Carter recovered nicely from his gaffe by putting together a string of successes like arranging a deal between LRMR and Fenway Sports Group that purchased James a partial stake in European football franchise Liverpool F.C., a move that broadened his global brand. Carter was also responsible for developing "The LeBrons," a series of commercials featuring caricatures of LeBron. The duo of Carter and James also founded SpringHill Entertainment, and signed their production company to a collaboration agreement with Warner Bros. The partnership has been fruitful yielding projects such as the Disney XD series Becoming; the Starz series Survivor's Remorse; the NBC game show The Wall; the highly popular sports discussion show "Uninterrupted," and of course the upcoming feature film Space Jam 2.

When Lebron James first chose his friends to help run his brand he became the butt of jokes from industry purest who had seen some athletes lose fortunes by hiring family and friends to head their businesses. One reporter sarcastically commented:

"LeBron hiring his friend to run his business is like when he needs knee surgery, hiring his plumber."

Carter, James, and their team endured the jokes and ridicule hurled at them by unbelievers to build a formidable business model that is now a template for how athletes can parlay their success on the court and field into wealth, power, and influence.

As Carter says, "You have to be in it for the long term, you can't be in it for that one hit."

Team Lebron had its models in Magic Johnson with his Magic Theaters, and partnerships with Starbucks, 24 Hour Fitness, and his minority interests in the Los Angeles Lakers, and Los Angeles Dodgers. Michael

Jordan is another athlete turned mogul with his "Air Jordan" partnership with Nike and his majority ownership of the Charlotte Hornets. Being a part of the hip-hop generation Carter can also use another Carter, a.k.a. Jay Z, as a business model. The famous rapper has gone beyond music to build a business empire so successful it has made him a billionaire.

Maverick Carter, sums up his empowerment model by saying, "The idea is to build businesses instead of just taking money for endorsements."

Carter is now a chief architect of a successful brand. From the very start he was a believer in his friend Lebron James. Not only was he a believer in Lebron, he was also a believer in himself. He put in the time and effort to learn his crafts marketing and management, so when the opportunity presented itself for him to partner with his friend Lebron James he wasn't coming into the partnership empty-handed. He had skills to contribute to making their business successful. A believer contributes something of value to the process. Hangers on, like leeches, don't contribute anything of value to the relationship, they only take. Any celebrity can surround himself or herself with hangers-on that do nothing more than pay them lip service and sponge whatever they can get from staying in the near proximity of someone famous. Hangers-on will never add to your success they will only detract from it. Whether your believers be colleagues, a spouse, friend, family, an investor, partner, or mentor, look to partner with true believers who will add value to you, not deceivers who only subtract from you.

Achievers

Associate with Achievers

It does not matter where they start their climb. It does not matter what the odds are against them. It does not matter how many setbacks they have. It does not matter how many obstacles they have to overcome. It does not matter how much hard work they have to put in. Whatever effort it takes to succeed, achievers have the right stuff to get the job done.

Masai Ujiri is a Nigerian born National Basketball Association executive who will now forever be remembered as the NBA front office executive that brought the very first NBA Championship to Canada's team, The Toronto Raptors. Ujiri a former player who is now, president of basketball operations and general manager of the Toronto Raptors was born in Bournemouth, England, where his parents were students. However, the family moved back to Nigeria when he was two years old, and Ujiri grew up in Zaria, Nigeria.

Ujiri played soccer as a youth before forming an interest in basketball as a 13-year-old while playing with friends on outdoor basketball courts in northern Nigeria. His love of basketball was fed by American sports magazines, basketball movies, and VHS tapes of NBA games or basketball movies. Ujiri also had a favorite basketball player in NBA All-Star, and champion, Hakeem Olajuwon, a fellow Nigerian.

Ujiri's father, a Nigerian hospital administrator and nursing educator, and his mother, a doctor from Kenya, allowed Ujiri to pursue his dream of playing college basketball. Ujiri left Nigeria to play for Nathan Hale High School in Seattle, Washington while living with a Nigerian family. After graduating from the prep school, Ujiri enrolled at Bismarck State College, in North Dakota, where he played basketball for two years. His next stop was Montana State University, Billings. Ujiri transferred to Montana State but left after one semester heading to England to begin his pro basketball career.

Ujiri spent six years bouncing around the professional basketball leagues in Europe. He played in Derby County, England for a year. He played for a second-division team in Belgium. He played for a team in Germany, then it was return trips to England and Belgium, followed by three months in Finland. Ujiri's last stop was in Denmark before he finally called it quits on his professional playing career in 2002.

Having given up the sport as a player Ujiri worked as a youth coach in Nigeria. His big break finally came during an NBA summer league game in Boston, when he met David Thorpe, coach, basketball trainer and NBA analyst. Impressed by Ujiri's passion for the game Thorpe introduced him to some college coaches who might be interested in some of the African players Ujiri was working with. In 2002, while Ujiri was accompanying a young Nigerian player to a draft tryout in Orlando, Florida he impressed

Orlando Magic scouting director Gary Brokaw, who introduced Ujiri to then Magic coach Doc Rivers and the team's General Manager John Gabriel. Taking a chance that it might be a way into an NBA job, Ujiri became an unpaid scout for the Orlando Magic. Determined to prove himself Ujiri payed his own way when he had to and shared rooms with other scouts or players whenever he could to save money.

Ujiri had also drawn praise for having been the director of the NBA's Basketball Without Borders Africa program, which promotes basketball throughout the continent. Hubert Davis's 2016 documentary film "Giants of Africa" profiles the Basketball Without Borders Africa program. He conducts two basketball camps, one for the top 50 players of Nigeria, which is sponsored by Nestle Milo; and another for African big men, which Ujiri sponsors himself with help from Nike.

After roughing it as a scout a young NBA executive working with the Denver Nuggets named Jeff Weltman, introduced Ujiri to former NBA player and then Nuggets general manager Kiki Vandeweghe. Seeing the value in developing some of the overseas talent Vandeweghe hired Ujiri and put him on salary as an international scout. It was the beginning of Masai Ujiri's NBA career. He spent four seasons in Denver before he was hired away by Bryan Colangelo of the Toronto Raptors to become their Director of Global Scouting. Ujiri was promoted to assistant general manager for the Raptors in 2008. The NBA was beginning to take notice of the hard-working Nigerian who was showing a lot of promise as an NBA executive. In 2010, Ujiri returned to the Nuggets accepting a promotion and the position of general manager and executive vice president in charge of basketball operations. In 2013, Ujiri's exceptional work building the Denver Nuggets into a winning team won him an award as the NBA Executive of the Year. Ujiri is the only non-American ever to win the award.

Not giving up on securing the talented executive, following his success with the Nuggets, Ujiri was lured away by the Toronto Raptors again. On May 31, 2013, he signed a 5-year, $15 million deal to become general manager of the Raptors, replacing Colangelo the man who had once hired him. As the new Raptors GM, Ujiri immediately shocked the NBA by trading away Andrea Bargnani one of the team's best players to the New

York Knicks. On September 2, 2016 Ujiri received a vote of approval when the Raptors extended his contract as the team's president. Having gone to the playoffs in 2013, led by the backcourt duo of Kyle Lowry and DeMar DeRozan, the Raptors returned to the playoffs in 2014. The Raptors would go on to win five Division titles and finish the 2017-18 regular season with the best regular season record in the Eastern Conference. In the midst of this success the Raptors had reached the Eastern Conference Finals for the first time in franchise history in 2016, but the team suffered consecutive second round eliminations in 2017 and 2018, and to make it worse both years the franchise was swept out of the playoffs in the minimum four games. All three playoff defeats had come courtesy of Lebron James and his Cleveland Cavaliers.

It was apparent to Ujiri that the Raptors were not going to get over their playoff hump with the team as currently constructed so he chose to make some daring moves after the Raptor's quick exit from the 2018 postseason. Ujiri fired head coach Dwane Casey almost immediately after the playoffs, in spite of Casey having been named NBA Coach of the Year for the regular season. Then Ujiri did something even more shocking. He traded his All-Star guard DeRozan for San Antonio Spurs forward Kawhi Leonard, who was coming off a serious injury, and veteran player Danny Green. Ujiri also acquired Marc Gasol during the 2018-19 season just before the trade deadline. Trading the Raptor's best player and fan-favorite DeRozan was a bold move that could backfire on Ujiri for any number of reasons. Would Leonard be able to perform up to the level he played prior to his injury? Would DeRozan outplay him for his new team the Spurs? Would Leonard reinjure himself? Would the Raptors be treated to another quick exit in spite of the trade?

When the 2019 NBA Championship ended it solidified Ujiri as one of, if not the, top executives in the League. After hitting a spectacular last second shot to knock the Milwaukee Bucks out of the playoffs and send the Raptors to the NBA Championship for the first time ever, Leonard put on one of the most dominant performances in championship history. When the final buzzer sounded the Raptors had won their first title in the history of the franchise, and Kawhi Leonard was holding the NBA Finals MVP trophy.

It doesn't matter where they come from, or what mountains they have to climb, achievers exceed all expectations. They can do more with less. They have the ability to endure the harshest of circumstances and still find a way to excel. And, when given an opportunity to shine, they do, like the sun above. Achievers are bold and when it takes being daring to succeed they are all in. Navigating risks and balancing hard work with great preparation, and solid execution, is a formula that leads high achievers to the heights of massive success. Masai Ujiri has overcome outrageous odds to become one of the most sought-after executives in the NBA. He checks every box for achievers and like other relatively young achievers the best is most assuredly still to come. For you as an entrepreneur or individual chasing success achievers are your models. Ujiri is one template that provides a unique and inspiring example you can use as a model for success. Find yourself a Masai Ujiri to work with, partner with, or be mentored by and you will find yourself merging onto the highway of success.

Build A Better Mousetrap

Many people set out to build a better mousetrap, something totally original, but very few succeed. It takes the courage of a lion and a product or service that borders on absolute perfection. There's a reason the old mousetrap is still popular. When people find something that works and has been working for a long time, they are reluctant to give it up no matter how new and shiny your alternative is. People have grown comfortable with the way things are and unless you are offering something 1000% better you will find yourself fighting an uphill battle that would make even Sisyphus give up. All this being said, it is not impossible to get people to give their loyalty to something new if it is something that solves an ongoing problem or stakes new ground. Ethan Brown faces such a challenge. The man is attempting to make people give up meat for God's sake to eat his products. Holy Cow!

Ethan Brown is the Founder of Beyond Meat, Inc. and serves as its Chief Executive Officer, President and Director since its founding in 2009. Brown holds a BS from Kettering University, BBA from the University Of Massachusetts, BA from Massachusetts, Masters from Michigan State

University, MBA from Columbia University and an MPP from the University of Maryland. I know right!

Beyond Meat is one of the fastest growing food companies in the United States. They offer a portfolio of revolutionary plant-based meats that they build directly from plants. This innovation enables consumers to experience the taste, texture and other sensory attributes of popular animal-based meat products while avoiding some of the negative attributes of meat products and enjoying the nutritional benefits of eating Beyond Meat's plant-based meat products. Beyond Meat isn't thinking in terms of competing against other makers of plant-based meat substitutes like their rivals Impossible Foods or Nestle so much as it is on challenging the entire meat industry. Brown wants to challenge the meat industry directly because it means more potential customers.

When he was on CNBC's "Fast Money: Halftime Report," just seconds after the company's stock began trading on NASDAQ, Brown said: "We really don't focus on the plant-based meat sector as much as we focus on the meat sector itself. That's a $1.4 trillion industry with just incredible diversity and potential globally".

That means the meat market is more than 100 times greater than the plant-based sector. Will meat lovers buy into Beyond Meat enough to invite their plant-based meat products to the dinner table? Investors seem to think so. On July 26, 2019, Beyond Meat's stock price was 234.90 per share. That is pretty exciting considering at its Initial Public Offering (IPO) on May 1, 2019 the stock opened at only $25 per share. In less than three months since its IPO the price per share of Beyond Meat has climbed more than 800%.

Ken Goldman and James Allen of JPMorgan wrote, "Demand has soared for plant-based meat alternatives, and industry sales could exceed $100 billion in the next 15 years, with Beyond Meat claiming a $15 billion piece of the pie".

There have been plenty of meat substitutes on the market for years boasting that their products taste just like meat. But when they hit the taste buds almost all these meat substitutes fall short of satisfying those who crave the juicy deliciousness of meat but want a healthier alternative. At least that was the case before Beyond Meat hit markets. The product has a growing population of followers who believe the company's plant-based products taste, look, and feel just like meat. Beyond Meat's burger patties, ground beef and sausage made with proteins from peas and fava beans are now passing the taste tests all over the globe. The rapid expansion Beyond Meat is seeing in the food sector has its investors and customers excited, but what excites them even more is the way the company's products are opening new markets for itself.

Beyond Meat's products are sold at major grocery chains, including Kroger, Walmart, Target, and Whole Foods. Chains such as Bareburger and TGI Fridays have the Beyond Burger on the menu, and Del Taco serves Beyond Tacos. Dunkin' Brands is expanding its breakfast menu with a trendy new item. The chain will start selling a meatless sausage breakfast sandwich made with Beyond Meat's vegan sausage at 163 locations across Manhattan initially, with plans to roll out the $4.29 sandwich nationally at some point. The two company's have hinted that a national roll-out of the item may be coming soon. If that turns out to be the case Dunkin' has over 9,200 stores in the U.S. alone. Cha-ching! Burger King has just rolled out the plant-based Impossible Whopper, and they are one of many other restaurants and chains lining up to put plant-based products on the menu. The race is on. Why? You do the math.

The taste factor is one part of the equation that has customers salivating for Beyond Meat, health issues and environmental concerns are other factors. The World Health Organization has linked processed meat to cancer, causing many consumers to scratch beef and pork off their menus. And, if you think Beyond Meat is some vegan or vegetarian fad think again. According to the grocery chain Krogers, ninety-three percent of people who purchased Beyond Burgers at their store in the first half of 2018 also bought animal products during the same period. Yep, carnivores are craving Beyond Meat too.

If you're wondering does Beyond Meat have the financial capital to take on the meat world here's a clue for you. The California-startup has received venture funding from Kleiner Perkins Caufield & Byers, Obvious Corporation, Bill Gates, Biz Stone, the Humane Society and Tyson Foods.

Tyson Foods purchased a 5% stake in Beyond Meat in October 2016. It then sold its stake and exited the investment in April 2019, ahead of the company's initial public offering. Beyond Meat had the best first day for an initial public offering in the U.S. for 2019. After its IPO the stock price tripled within three days. Shares of the company have soared over 820% since its initial public offering on May 2, putting Beyond Meat's market capitalization at a whopping $13.85 billion.

Clearly, Ethan Brown and his company Beyond Meat, has built a better mousetrap. How far they can go in terms of their meatless, plant-protein based innovations is anyone's guess. How much the company and industry will grow is also anyone's guess, though future forecasts look good. How profitable Beyond Meat becomes depends on many factors but their financial forecast also looks good. Brown didn't just set out to make a passable copy of something, he set out to change the eating habits of millions upon millions of people. That's one gigantic mousetrap. And, because of his vision, persistence in creating an extraordinarily original and value driven product, and one that answers the needs of a very large segment of the food market, he is changing not only the eating habits of people but their lifestyles as well. Ethan Brown is an achiever with a capital "A".

Find something that's broken and fix it

Achievers are those rarest of people who go left when others go right, stand up when others sit down, go when others stop, speak out when others shut up, and do it at just the right time. They are different but not just for the sake of being different. They march to their own beat, but the tricky thing is that they do it in the midst of a whole lot of other drumbeats and still manage to maintain their own unique stride.

While some apparel retailers attempt to differentiate themselves through having the lowest price or the fastest shipping, Stitch Fix differentiates itself through providing a personalized fashion experience. In each shipment from Stitch Fix is a box containing five clothing and accessory items they've chosen just for you. Those choices are based on information you and millions of others have given them, firstly in an extensive questionnaire you fill out when you sign up, and then in feedback you provide after each shipment. A better mousetrap? Maybe. What's more obvious is that Stitch Fix CEO, Katrina Lake, has found something she thought was broke and she's using a new retail model to fix it, no pun intended.

Stitch Fix sold $730 million worth of clothing in 2016 and $977 million worth in 2017, so the sales trajectory is moving in the right direction, up. One hundred percent of the company's revenue comes directly from their fashion recommendations and making fashion recommendations for their customers is at the very core of Stitch Fix's business. The company now has over 2 million active clients in the United States. They offer more than 700 brands. Less you think the company is all about picking clothes they think you'll like, throwing them in a box, then shipping them to you. You should know that the company also employs more than 80 data scientists, the majority of whom have PhDs in quantitative fields such as math, neuroscience, statistics, and astrophysics. The Stitch Fix business model is a combination of data scientists making use of algorithms, and professional human fashion stylists using the data to help select clothes tailored for the individual customer's preferences.

Lake explains the stitch Fix formula this way, "The part of me that loves data knew it could be used to create a better experience with apparel. After all, fit and taste are just a bunch of attributes: waist, inseam, material, color, weight, durability, and pattern. It's all just data. If you collect enough, you'll get a pretty good picture of what clothes people want."

The company leverages data science to deliver personalization at scale, which goes beyond what traditional brick-and-mortar stores and e-commerce retailers can do. The Stitch Fix customer is one who enjoys having expert fashion stylists do the shopping for them and enjoys the hours they save by letting the company take care of this tedious task.

Like so many new businesses today, especially online businesses, data is key to their ability to create a better and more efficient customer experience. Algorithms are created from customer feedback. When shoppers fill out a profile that includes their fit preferences that's data. When a customer provides details on why they're returning a certain garment, that's data. Stitch Fix uses this data to better understand what its customers want. The company created a Style Shuffle game that asked customers to rate pictures of clothes. From the customer responses Stitch Fix data scientists were able to gather more than a billion ratings to feed into their "recommendations" algorithm. The insight gained allows the company to isolate a shopper's preferences on style. When a customer returns clothes from one of their boxes it gives the company more feedback. The items could have been returned because the customer didn't like the fit, or the fabric, or maybe the price. Stitch Fix learns how to do a better job of pleasing each customer from this information.

During her undergraduate years at Stanford University, in the early 2000s, Katrina Lake's first job was as a consultant at the Parthenon Group, where she worked with retailers and restaurants. Seeing how important both industries were to people, Lake was intrigued these industries still provided basically the same customer experience they had in the 1970s, or even 1950s, even with how technology had changed other industries around the world. After thinking about the retail process Lake thought to herself:

"How would someone buy jeans 10 years down the road? I knew it wouldn't be the traditional model: go to six stores, pull pairs of jeans off the racks, try them all on. And, I didn't think it would resemble today's e-commerce model either, where you have 15 tabs open on your browser while you check product measurements and look for what other shoppers are saying. Then you buy multiple pairs and return the ones that don't fit."

Lake enrolled at Harvard Business School to learn information that would benefit her once she set out on her journey into entrepreneurship then used the two years at Harvard to plan before launching Stitch Fix. She received a term sheet (a nonbinding agreement setting the basic terms and conditions under which an investment will be made) to fund Stitch Fix in February 2011, shipped the first Stitch Fix boxes from her apartment in April, and graduated with her MBA in May.

Katrina Lake saw what she determined to be a problem in the retail apparel industry and created a company whose way of doing business she believes is the answer to that problem. Do customers agree with her? Since shipping its first box in 2011, Stitch Fix's annual revenue has risen to $1.2 billion; is valued at over $2.8 billion and has become that rarest of rare species in Silicon Valley, a young company that is already profitable. Katrina Lake is becoming the Ferrari of achievers one stitch at a time.

Chapter 7: Steppingstones

In Chapter 7: Steppingstones, you will learn about the four levels you must leverage on your way to success and how each can lift you up or trip you up. Vocation, Motivation, Dedication, and Determination are steppingstones for those who know how to use them but tombstones for those who dare to abuse them.

Vocation

The first 60 years of modern computers focused on computing itself, with the last 20 years or so centered on computers as tools for communication. These two "chapters" in computing history have led to entirely new industries and technologies, as well as the fast and furious evolution of computer science as a discipline. Today, it is almost impossible to find an avenue of commerce or professional endeavor that has not been affected by the digital revolution. For professionals in the field, the big questions are: What is the next great chapter in computer science and how can I be a part of it?

As the industry continues to grow and evolve, so will competition for the most satisfying and highest-paying jobs. It is therefore imperative that anyone considering a career in computer science stays up-to-date with current and future industry trends. In this in-depth guide, you'll find insightful information and useful statistics on specific computer science areas that are in-demand now as well as a glimpse into what will be trending in the years ahead. Also included are helpful hints and advice from experts in the field. Planning is the key to professional success, and the earlier potential computer scientists begin that planning, the better.

One of the best sources for career information is the U.S. Department of Labor's Bureau of Labor Statistics (BLS). According to BLS data, 74 percent of new STEM (science, technology, engineering and math) jobs through 2022 will be in computing. That's a pretty general statement, however, and does not apply evenly across the broad landscape of computer science occupations. For example, the BLS predicts that nearly a third of all of those new jobs will be created in the computer science subfield of software development. In fact, the BLS breaks down the computer science field into seven distinct subfields and provides percentage estimates for jobs (in relation to all new STEM jobs) in each as follows:

Nevertheless, no matter what specific area of interest a computer scientist prefers, the job market going forward looks promising when compared to employment statistics across the entire job spectrum. The BLS predicts an 18 percent job growth in computer-related occupations compared to 11 percent for all occupations in total.

Below is a list of specific **Computer Science-related careers that are on the rise** to provide an even clearer picture of the job market that awaits computer science college students upon graduation. Again, these statistics are provided by the BLS and relate to predicted job growth through 2022.

High School Computer Science Teacher, Salary range: $37,230 - $86,720, Computer science teachers prepare lesson plans and practical exercises to instruct students in computing theories as well as the use of computer software applications. High school teachers work closely not only with students but also fellow teachers and school administrators. Employment at public schools requires studies beyond a bachelor's degree: depending on the state, teachers may need post-graduate training resulting in a license or a single subject credential to teach computer science at the secondary level.

Computer Programmer, Salary range: $43,640 - $123,490, Coders use their familiarity with programming languages to transform software designs into computer-readable instructions. For some employers, the level of education matters less than practical skill and specialized knowledge. Programming talent is sought after in a range of industries, including software publishing, health care, and insurance. Programmers work alone or in teams, often communicating electronically with remote colleagues.

Post-Secondary Vocational Education Instructor, Salary range: $27,940 - $85,120, Working in public and private institutions, these educators provide career training at a level above high school, but below bachelor's degree studies. Some occupational education instructors have professional experience in addition to a two-year degree, for example, an A.S. in computer system engineering technology. Qualifications for teachers vary by subject, school, and state.

Network and Computer Systems Administrators, Salary range: $45,270 - $117,150, Network administrators manage communications networks, while system administrators keep an organization's IT infrastructure running smoothly and securely. Sys admins are in charge of equipment ranging from servers to desktop workstations to mobile devices. Admins work with IT managers and staff, computer network architects and other employees. Some companies outsource data storage networks to cloud service providers, but admins are still needed in broad-ranging industries. In addition to computer science, students interested in this occupation can take subjects like computer engineering or electrical engineering, computer networking and systems design.

Post-Secondary Computer Science Teacher, Salary range: $37,190 - $137,810, Post-secondary computer science instructors develop class plans and materials to teach the theoretical and practical applications of this discipline. Additional responsibilities often include research and academic publishing. Most of these teachers work at colleges and universities, with a smaller number employed at community colleges and trade schools. College professors regularly interact with students, teaching assistants, department colleagues and administrators.

Computer & Information Systems Manager, Salary range: $76,420 - $156,560+, Computer science leadership positions range from top-level executives to technical supervisors who oversee day-to-day work in the trenches. Entry-level managers may provide guidance for teams of hardware engineers or software developers, while project managers work with technical and non-technical staff. Chief Technology Officers (CTOs) manage the computing infrastructure for giant corporations. A bachelor's degree can lay the groundwork for managerial ambitions, along with experience. However, students should consider an MBA in information systems to truly stand out from the rest of the applicant field.

Computer Network Architect, Salary range: $53,920 - $145,700, Network engineers and architects create blueprints for data communication networks, and they design patches for existing infrastructure in response to security threats. Network architects analyze usage to predict organizational needs, often working with managers and CTOs. Given the extensive knowledge involved, employers require at least a bachelor's degree and may prefer graduate studies in business information systems.

Database Administrator, Salary range: $43,720 - $120,990, Database administrators (DBAs) manage vast amounts of data collected in different industries, such as banking transactions, retail chains' customer records or medical clinics' patient insurance information. To maintain database performance and security, DBAs rely on their study of information assurance and data warehousing. Some work with management and IT staff to develop new databases. As organizations trend toward â€œbig dataâ€? they may prefer DBAs with a specialized master's degree, according to the BLS.

Social Science Research Assistant, Salary range: $18,250 - $67,780, Research assistants harness their knowledge of computer science and statistics to make sense of huge amounts of information. From surveys or lab projects, they gather, analyze and manage scientific data. They work with social scientists in research and development settings or academic environments, as paid staff rather than student assistants.

Computer & Information Research Scientist, Salary range: $61,300 - $158,800, In fields such as business, medicine and science, computer and information research scientists use computing to analyze and solve problems. They improve on current technologies or develop innovative computer algorithms to address specific needs. Many work for the government, hardware and software design firms, academic institutions or R&D labs, where they team up with other experts in their area of research.

Data Mining Specialist, Salary range: $61,300 - $158,800, Working with massive datasets, these information scientists leverage their academic background in computational statistics. To meet requests from management, they design algorithms and software for data analysis in specific environments. They propose data-supported strategies in areas like public policy, science, business intelligence and medical information management.

Geoscientist, Salary range: $48,890 - $187,199, Geoscience, the study of the earth's physical elements, uses advanced technology like computer modeling, data analysis and digital mapping. Geoscientists depend on specialized software packages as they perform fieldwork and lab research, and computer science grads who also study geology can aim for this profession. Working in industries such as government or oil and gas extraction, these scientists share their research with clients and coworkers.

Computer Support Specialist, Salary range: $29,260 - $86,110M, Support specialists offer high-tech trouble-shooting in a range of different environments, from government agencies to industries like telecommunications and computer manufacturing. User support specialists provide customer service for the public, often from call centers, or work in a company's information technology (IT) department helping other employees. Computer network support specialists focus on issues with data and communications networks.

Web Developer, Salary range: $33,320 - $110,350, Web developers build Internet sites for online retail, enterprise operations, non-profit groups, social media and more. Websites serve as e-business cards for partners and clients and digital storefronts for customers. Using tools such as HTML, XML, JavaScript and Cascading Style Sheets, developers create the code underlying a website, considering visual appearance, site architecture, usability and performance. Web designers work with management, sales, marketing, public relations and other departments.

Systems Software Developer, Salary range: $63,140 - $150,760, Systems software designers generally find employment with computer and electronics manufacturers, working on teams to develop new technology. The products in development include operating systems for uses ranging from computers to smartphones to cars. These developers may also invent a system's interface, such as a graphical user interface that permits a human to control a computer.

Applications Software Developer, Salary range: $55,770 - $143,540, Software developers invent applications targeting specific purposes, from online marketplaces to entertainment apps for mobile devices. Applications range from the small scale to the enormous, as in databases constructed to meet the needs of specific companies. Some developers need not only in-depth familiarity with programming languages but also knowledge of an industry and its operations, for example, financial transactions or health informatics.

Computer Systems Analyst, Salary range: $50,290 - $125,460, Computer systems analysis zeroes in on the information technology (IT) used by a specific organization. Analysts take into account factors such as user requirements, workflow and IT capabilities. After evaluating the existing technical infrastructure, analysts suggest efficiencies and improvements. This occupation requires an understanding of a specific field like banking or health information management. Analysts work with managers and IT departments, and they may also train employees on new systems.

Operations Research Analyst, Salary range: $42,070 - $130,210, Operations research analysts help executives and management solve problems and create data-driven strategies in fields like finance, government and manufacturing logistics. They often work with a multidisciplinary team of industry specialists. Analysts take advantage of quantitative methods, statistical software programs and data modeling packages to monitor an organization's processes and find potential improvements. Many applicants for this specialty have a master's degree in a subject such as computer science.

Market Research Analyst, Salary range: $33,490 - $114,250, Market research analysts use sophisticated statistical methods to advise companies on marketing and business plans. They evaluate data on consumer trends and competitor strategies to devise proposals for introducing and pricing new products. Analysts share ideas with clients and managers, and they may also gather opinions from the public. A computer science degree is common in this data-focused field, and a master's degree is often preferable for higher-level positions.

Information Security Analyst, Salary range: $50,430-$138,780, In a networked world, these professionals play an important role in protecting organizations. They examine existing IT systems and propose security measures, including fixes for vulnerabilities. In industries like finance and cloud computing services, they serve as in-house staff or consultants. Security analysts cooperate with network administrators and computer systems analysts, and they often report directly to CTOs or IT managers. Due to the wide-ranging expertise needed, some employers opt for candidates with graduate degrees.

A.I. AND BEYOND: The Future of Computer Science

The following list of trends in computer science has been compiled after speaking with CS experts in both the academic and business worlds. They represent a broad consensus of opinions and provide a good overview of where the field is potentially headed.

User Interface Design, Human-computer interaction (HCI) professionals and UI median annual salaries come in at an estimated $61,000 per year, according to PayScale.com. However, salaries can increase rather significantly with education and experience. For example, user interface engineers, a step above UI designers, earn a reported $76,000 annually.

Software Development, As you might expect, software engineers and computer programmers are in demand by businesses and other organizations of every type and size, and not just those that fit strictly under the heading of computer technology. The top employers for software developers, however, are tech-focused companies with well-recognized names such as Google, Facebook, Twitter, Apple, Oracle and Microsoft, as well as many that may be less familiar, like Sparc, Kony and Zurple.

Cloud Computing, Although specific statistics regarding remote and cloud computing job opportunities are difficult to come by, a look at the numbers related to computer science and information technology employment may provide a good idea of where cloud computing is heading. National median annual salaries can be expected to fall within the $70,000 to $90,000 range with job growth between 20 and 25 percent over the coming decade, according to the BLS.

Security and Privacy, According to the BLS, salary potential and the job outlook for the computer security field is positive. May 2013 statistics indicate a national median annual salary for information security analysts of $88,590, with some industry sectors (such as finance and insurance) trending higher. Job outlook predictions in the field are strong, with the BLS forecasting 37 percent growth between 2012 and 2022. Computer security and privacy issues arise in every corner of the digital world and cyber attacks are becoming more and more commonplace. As a result, information security professionals can be found just about everywhere. Government at all levels, businesses, and non-profit organizations need expert advice in securing their data resources. Top employers in computer security include Cisco Systems, BAE Systems PLC, Computer Sciences Corporation, Intel, Lockheed Martin, Symantec, Raytheon, Hewlett-Packard and the National Security Administration.

Data Science and Big Data, Given the newness of the field, salary figures specific to data science can be hard to come by. With the current high demand for data science professionals, graduates with a bachelor's degree in data science may attract offers at the upper levels of the computer science field. National median annual salaries for computer scientists are currently in the neighborhood of $80,000 to $90,000. Master's and doctorate degree holders may do even better.

Robotics, the BLS includes robotics engineers under the broader heading of mechanical engineers. From that perspective, one might conclude that job growth for robotics professionals will be sluggish over coming decade with just a 5 percent increase. Other industry experts, however, predict healthier job prospects in the field. Estimated salaries for robotic engineers also fall somewhere between median annual salaries for mechanical engineers and computer scientists ($80,000 to $90,000). Businesses hiring robotics-skilled workers include major manufacturers in the auto and aeronautics industries, as well companies like Dyson, Elbit Systems, Autonomous Solutions, Amazon, 3D Robotics, Bosch and Caterpillar.

Artificial Intelligence, The BLS includes AI professionals under the broader heading of computer and information research scientists, for whom job growth estimates come in at 15 percent between 2012 and 2022, slightly under estimates for computer occupations in general, but substantially higher than those for all occupations. National median annual salary estimates for the same group are encouraging at $102,000 for 2012 significantly better than for all computer occupations combined ($76,270).

Motivation

As leaders, the ideas and stories we read about and hear about shape us. To improve your leadership, take the time to read these important books. You will learn from some of the greatest leaders and thought-leaders on the planet. The knowledge and insight you gain from these books will help you to see valuable truths more clearly and open your mind to new ways of approaching problems and opportunities that will significantly widen your path to success. Being a seeker of knowledge and wisdom is one of the surest ways to grow yourself into the leader you were created to be.

1. "Good to Great" by Jim Collins

Jim Collins is one of the best business authors and researchers of his generation. Collins has written several must read books and "Good to Great" is a great one to start with. By profiling some of the excellent leaders in business history this book shows that great leaders come in many shapes, shades, sexes, and styles. Reading about the qualities and methods of some of the most effective leaders who have ever led companies will give you a ton of beneficial knowledge to help you climb the ladder of success.

2. "Getting Things Done" by David Allen

The world is full of people who are very talented but also very disorganized. David Allen's classic book on organization provides a comprehensive system to keep you focused on priorities and help you organize your life. This book shows you how to not just talk about getting things done but actually get them done.

3. "The Effective Executive" by Peter F. Drucker

Peter Drucker is the Michael Jordan of business management. "The Effective Executive" is a short book that gives clear directions on how to master the tasks that make up management and make decisions more effectively.

4. "Developing The Leader Within You" by John C. Maxwell

Maxwell effectively makes the argument that leadership begins with character and then comes your abilities. Maxwell is one of the all-time great thought leaders who has written several excellent books on leadership and this is one of them. This book is written in the style of a workbook with sections to help you turn its excellent concepts into action.

5. "Mastery" by Robert Greene

This book is about mastering your craft. Whether it is business, art, technology, sports, education, or some other field you wish to excel at "Mastery" will help you do it. In the book, Green recommends that those who want to master something apprentice under masters who can teach them the intricacies of the craft and there by accelerate their growth.

6. Think and Grow Rich by Napoleon Hill

Anyone who has read the bible knows that your thoughts can create your reality. "Think and Grow Rich" puts this powerful concept into a book for those who want to understand the mind-set of those who achieve success. Thoughts create beliefs, beliefs lead to actions, actions lead to habits, and so on and so on. This book helps you focus your thoughts on the right things to achieve.

8. The One Minute Manager by Kenneth Blanchard

You wouldn't think a book you can read in one afternoon could be this helpful but it sure is. This book has spent years at the top of everyone's most prized book list. Not only does this book give you excellent advice on management book, it also gives you actionable plans that work.

9.Lean In by Sheryl Sandberg

Lean In written by Facebook's Chief Operating Officer, Sheryl Sandberg, has become the go to book for women entrepreneurs. The book instructs women on what they can do to excel at leading both males and females. Sandberg, advices those who want to be great leaders to care more about succeeding than being liked. For many women growing up in our culture leadership might not be something they are inherently good at, but it is something they can become great at. Lean In tells them how.

10. Leaders Eat Last by Simon Sinek

Simon Sinek's craft is to help inspire leaders to inspire others. Leaders and managers are finding it hard to inspire and lead millennials and other post-baby-boomers. Sinek, is a thought-leader for leaders who is on a mission to create a new generation of leaders who can motivate and effectively lead this present and future generations.

11. The Art of War by Sun Tzu

This classic was written in China more than two thousand years ago as a book of military strategies. But, everyone from military leaders, to business leaders, to politicians, and beyond have found that the strategies taught by Sun Tzu have proven to be just as effective in their field as in warfare. For centuries this book has excellently taught strategy, tactics and means to achieving success that are invaluable, and you will certainly find it has something valuable to speak to you too.

12. Success Never Smelled So Sweet by Lisa Price

Lisa Price, the founder of Carol's Daughter, tells the story of her life, starting from her childhood days in Brooklyn, New York, to filing for bankruptcy, to the moment her business was created. Price tells how she overcame great odds to become a successful entrepreneur who grossed $2 million dollars annually from home. Price believes that regardless of the challenges we face life will guide each and every one of us until we realize our own inner truth. The book shares the treasured advice Price's mother gave her, as well as recipes for her best-selling products.

Dedication

Believe in Yourself

Failure comes in many forms. One of these forms is when people believe whole heartedly in their dream, or the company they start, or their project, but they fail to believe in themselves. If you invest capital and faith in the thing you are doing but don't invest capital and faith in yourself, you and what you are doing will ultimately fail.

Peter Thiel

He is the co-founder of the pioneering e-commerce payments company PayPal which was sold to eBay in 2002 for $1.5 billion. Thiel also cofounded the CIA-backed big data startup Palantir, which was recently valued at $20 billion. His estimated 10% stake in Palantir makes up two-thirds of his wealth which is valued at $2.5 billion. But before starting PayPal and making successful investments in big name startups like Facebook, Thiel went through a difficult period that only his dedication could pull him through. His early hedge fund, Clarium Capital, lost 90 percent of its $7 billion in assets on the stock market, currencies and oil prices.

Theil is looked up to as one of the sages of Silicon Valley (though he now lives in Los Angeles) for the wisdom he shares with aspiring entrepreneurs like his statement about capitalism and competition where he urges them to seek to establish monopolies:

"All happy companies are different: Each one earns a monopoly by solving a unique problem. All failed companies are the same: They failed to escape competition."

In 1985, Thiel entered Stanford as a freshman. While in college Thiel became captivated by the teachings of the French anthropological philosopher René Girard, who was at the time on Stanford's faculty. Girard has written extensively about a concept he calls "mimetic desire". In essence, it is our unconscious tendency to adopt the aspirations of our neighbors. As Girard would put it, imitation engenders competition, and competition engenders imitation.

After college Thiel would make his living as a hedge fund manager, startup founder, and venture capitalist. These are all positions where having a contrarian viewpoint, one who rejects popular opinion, comes in handy. Resisting the herd mentality that so many are infected by is what has made Thiel successful with not just one venture but several. Thiel believes that Girard's analysis of man's unconscious compulsion to imitate his fellow man, which formed a basis for his own instinct to go against the grain, has played a big role in his success. As Thiel says:

"It's been a powerful way of thinking for all these different contexts I've found myself in over the years."

For all his success at being a maverick you would think Thiel was a natural at it. But, once upon a time Thiel was a follower of the pack. He took the mainstream route when he followed expectations that landed him in Stanford Law School. He then followed the obvious course and took a position as a young transactional lawyer at the prestigious New York firm Sullivan & Cromwell. It was a career move anyone in the pack would applaud. But, Thiel says:

"I think it was the unhappiest period of my whole life. It lasted seven months and three days."

Sometime around Christmas in 1994, Thiel was visiting his family back on the West Coast, when he ran into a friend from college, Reid Hoffman. A few days of exchanging ideas and aspirations with Hoffman helped him to reset his life's compass toward what he wanted to do, not what others wanted him to do. It was time for Thiel to believe in himself, to trust his own instincts.

Early in 1996, Thiel quit his job in New York, packed his things and headed for Menlo Park, California. He then hustled hard enough to raise $1 million from friends and family to start his own hedge fund, Thiel Capital. It was a year later that Thiel, the hedge fund owner, met 21-year-old engineer Luke Nosek, fresh out of the University of Illinois at Urbana-Champaign. Nosek had an idea to launch a web-based calendar, and asked

Thiel for advice on fundraising. To Nosek's surprise, Thiel offered to invest $100,000 from his fund. Both men learned a valuable lesson when the company they had such high hopes for failed.

It is not enough to simply believe in your company, your project, or your cause. When tough times come, and they almost always will, it is your belief in yourself that will guide you through and be the difference between becoming one of those people who quits and one who gets back up and perseveres. It was Thiel maintaining confidence in himself that aloud him to take a chance on another venture when Nosek's friend Max Levchin, another former UIUC student pitched Thiel about his idea for a cryptography-related company called Fieldlink, after laying in wait for Thiel after a lecture he gave at Stanford. Thiel was impressed enough with Levchin's business idea to offer becoming his co-founder. Showing no lack of confidence Levchin and Thiel asked Nosek to join their team as well.

Though the direction they took with Fieldlink changed a few times and it went through several name changes, Fieldlink evolved into PayPal. To build out the company Thiel persuaded Reid Hoffman to become a board member. He brought in David Sacks, a former editor-in-chief of the Stanford Review as Thiel had been a few years earlier, to be chief operating officer. The team Thiel and Levchin assembled at PayPal is now legendary. The group is now commonly referred to as the PayPal mafia with many on them going on to build amazing companies of their own. The group included at least seven individuals who are now valued at more than $1 billion. The lineup included Elon Musk who co-founded Tesla and SpaceX, Reid Hoffman founded LinkedIn, Steve Chen, Chad Hurley, and Jawed Karim founded YouTube, Jeremy Stoppelman and Russell Simmons founded Yelp, David Sacks founded Yammer, and Theil is the co-founder of the data-mining company Palantir. PayPal was sold to eBay in 2002 for $1.5 billion.

Don't think that hardships and setbacks are limited to visiting you just once. Many of those who have gone on to experience great success have had several battles with disaster and disappointment and Thiel is no exception. After his success with PayPal, Thiel dumped $10 million of the money he earned from the company into his hedge fund and relaunched it as Clarium Capital. After bringing in good earnings through mid-2008 when the price of oil soared from about $40 a barrel in 2002 to nearly $140 sending the company's value from $10 million to more than $6 billion as new investors rushed into the hedge fund. But, after going up like a rocket, Clarium which had based much of its investments on oil was devastated in February 2009 when oil prices temporarily fell back to almost $40 once again. As a result of missing their forecast on these events Clarium severely underperform in 2009 and 2010, causing many of their institutional investors to ditch the hedge fund as it lost 90% of its earnings. Now, Clarium has about $200 million under management but only handles the money of a few select investors that include its owner Thiel, friends and family.

After such a public failure again Thiel could have cut his loses and run for cover. But, dedication does not mean that you believe in yourself one day and abandon that belief the next. No matter what the nature of your company, product, service, or project is, never forget that you are your most precious resource. All the things you put your time, effort and capital into may fall flat and crumble to dust but as long as you maintain confidence in yourself and believe in your abilities a rebound from your setback is never far away. Your dedication to making the most of your abilities is what will ultimately win the day.

Along with the success of his data-mining company Palantir, Thiel's venture capital company Founders Fund, has done exceptionally well. Its funds under management have grown from $50 million in 2005, when it closed its first fund, to over $2 billion today with annual returns said to be in the range of 35% to 45%.

Thiel's faith in himself and his dedication to the course he has chosen payed big dividends. He has co-founded a pair of billion-dollar companies. In 2004, he gambled on a 20-year-old Harvard sophomore student who had never even had steady job before. Thiel's $500,000 investment in Mark Zuckerberg's company then known as Thefacebook in exchange for 10.2% of the company has netted Thiel more than $1 billion. He has cashed in some of the stock but retains a $200 million stake and remains on Facebook's board of directors. Whether through his individual investments or his Founders Fund, Thiel has certainly had more financial wins than loses with his investments in companies like LinkedIn; Spotify; Airbnb and a $120 million stake in a rocket-ship company called SpaceX.

In case you think Thiel is just another cold-blooded capitalist who is simply all about the money after launching Founders Fund in 2005, Thiel launched the Thiel Foundation, in 2006. Through this charitable fund he manages to give away about $13 million to $15 million a year. Yep, Dedication pays.

Vera Wang

Find Your Place

We are all endowed with certain gifts and talents. We are all created for a specific purpose. Its only when we unite our gifts with that purpose that we are able to reach our unlimited potential. As long as we spend our time and efforts working outside that place we are destined for, we will find ourselves capped by a ceiling under which we will never be allowed to reach our full potential. When we search until we find our place, that place which we were created to inhabit, with it we will find a passion that drives us forward until our talents blossom and grow beyond all we could hope for or imagine. If Oprah had continued as a news reporter she never would have become the greatest daytime talk show host. New England Patriots coach Bill Belichick was fired from his first head coaching job with the Cleveland Browns by their owner Art Modell. Six Super Bowl Championships later I'm sure the Browns have seen the error of their ways. If Vera Wang had stayed at Vogue she would never have become an iconic fashion designer. You will never find the success and prosperity you are destined for if you don't free yourself from someone else's plans for your life and find that place that fulfills your own purpose.

Vera Ellen Wang was born and raised in New York City. She attended Friends Seminary, a private day school in Manhattan and the oldest continuously coeducational school in New York City. She graduated from The Chapin School, an all-girls independent day school in Manhattan in 1967, then attended the University of Paris. Wang returned to the United States and earned her degree in art history from Sarah Lawrence College.

Wang began to pursue her first dream of being an Olympic figure skater at the age of seven. A promising skater in high school, she trained with pairs partner James Stuart, and even competed at the 1968 U.S. Figure Skating Championships. You can catch a glimpse of her in the January 9, 1968, issue of Sports Illustrated, "Faces in the Crowd." But, after such a promising start Wang knew her figure skating dreams were over when she failed to make the U.S. Olympics team.

It was a very hard reality for Wang to come to grips with, realizing that since she was in her late teens already, she was not going to get any better. That meant that there were things she was going to have to accept. She was not going to make the Olympic team. There were younger skaters than her who would now be given priority over her. Her dream of being a professional skater was over. She gave up the dream and set her sights on moving on to something else.

That something else turned out to be the fashion industry.

Upon graduation from Sarah Lawrence College, Wang was immediately hired to be an editor at Vogue where she became the youngest editor at the magazine. Having spent time in Paris is what pushed Wang into beginning a career in fashion. Upon returning from Paris, she was working as a salesgirl at Yves Saint Laurent to earn some spending money and was discovered there by Vogue fashion director Frances Stein. Stein told Wang once she graduated from Sarah Lawrence, she wanted her to come work at Vogue. A year and a half later Wang took her up on the offer and called Stein. True to her word Stein hired her.

Wang spent the next 15 years rising through the ranks at Vogue. Inevitably, she realized that she had reached another dead end. Once again, she realized her career wasn't going to go any further if she stayed where she was. She wasn't in line to get the editor-in-chief job that she coveted. Yet, she felt she had so much more to give than what she was doing. So, after investing 15 years in a career she was passionate about she left Vogue discouraged. Another dream dead. Wang landed at Ralph Lauren, in 1987, and stayed there 2 years until at the age of 40 she resigned to become an independent bridal wear designer.

With two major setbacks in her life Wang could choose to grumble about the breaks she didn't get or she could pick up the pieces of her dreams and use the disappointments as fuel for finding her own place in the sun, a place without limits where she could fly as high as her aspirations could take her. Yes, Wang would have to reinvent herself again but this time it would be on her own terms.

When Wang opened her own design salon in the Carlyle Hotel in New York City, in 1990, there was no guarantee that selling her now trademark bridal gowns would bring her success. She has since opened bridal boutiques in London, Tokyo, and Sydney, in the process becoming one of the legendary designers of our time. Not stopping with bridal wear Wang has expanded her brand to include her own fragrance, jewelry, eyewear, shoes, and houseware collections.

Chelsea Clinton, Karenna Gore, Ivanka Trump, Campbell Brown, Alicia Keys, Mariah Carey, Victoria Beckham, Sarah Michelle Gellar, Avril Lavigne, Hilary Duff, Khloe Kardashian, and Kim Kardashian, are all celebrities that have worn Vera Wang wedding gowns and her evening wear has been worn by the likes of Michelle Obama.

In 2002, Wang began to enter the home fashion industry with the launch of The Vera Wang China and Crystal Collection. She followed this in 2007, with the release of her diffusion line called Simply Vera, sold exclusively by Kohl's. In 2011, "White by Vera Wang" was launched at David's Bridal. Prices of the bridal gowns ranged from $600 to $1,400 giving brides a more affordable Vera Wang design they could wear. In Spring of 2012, Wang teamed up with Men's Wearhouse to offer two tuxedo styles available in both the retail and rental areas of their stores. In June 2012, she expanded in Australia with the opening of "Vera Wang Bride Sydney" and her first Asian flagship store "Vera Wang Bridal Korea", in Gangnam-gu, Seoul. To cap all these accomplishments Lady Gaga, wore Vera Wang Spring/Summer designs at the 2017 Super Bowl. Forbes chronicled Vera Wang as number 34 on their list of America's Richest Self-Made Women for 2018, with revenues of $630 million.

Though she had some setbacks that could have derailed Vera Wang and put her on a treadmill to nowhere, instead Wang recovered from those heartaches using them as signpost to find her place in this world. As Wang herself says:

"There's an old skater's saying: Don't be afraid of falling. Its 90 percent falling, otherwise, you don't master anything. You might hurt your ass. Or break your ankle. Or crack a rib. It's the same thing in life. There are other places to go. Other things to try. So, don't be afraid of failing. I think not trying is worse than failing. Have the courage to try. Otherwise, what are we here for?"

Success is all about finding your place. You may stumble, you may fall, you may flop around like a child learning to swim, or move forward clumsily like someone groping in the dark. It doesn't matter how you get there or how long it takes you. Find your place. Some of us may bounce around from job to job until we finally find our place. Others will hang onto the comfortable and familiar until we are fired and forced into finding our place. Still others will refuse the conventional route and search high and low until they find that place they know is right for them. No matter what road you travel to get there, when you arrive you know it is the place you were destined to be. You not only know it and feel it, you slide into your place effortlessly because it feels as natural to you as breathing. Though it may be hard work it doesn't feel like work at all. You almost feel guilty for getting paid for something you'd gladly do for free. Don't procrastinate. Don't postpone your destiny. Find your place.

Determination

He had worked many jobs from the time he was no more than a boy. Streetcar conductor, railroad fireman, insurance salesman, secretary, tire salesman, ferry operator, lawyer (he reportedly got into a fistfight with his own client during a court case), even a brief period as a midwife. In 1930, a 40-year-old Colonel Harland David Sanders was operating a service station in Corbin, Kentucky. It was there that he began cooking for hungry travelers who stopped for gas. There was no restaurant for customers to comfortably dine in. Patrons ate from Sanders' own dining table in the station's modest living quarters. It was in these humble surroundings that he invented what he called "home meal replacement". Sanders began selling complete meals to busy, on the go families. He called his meals,

"Sunday Dinner, Seven Days a Week." Out of this determination to succeed at something came his recipe for Colonel Sanders Kentucky Fried Chicken, which led to the famous restaurant today known as KFC. In 1964, at the age of 74, Sanders sold his rights to the franchise for $2 million.

In the words of renown motivational speaker Les Brown, "You've got to be hungry!"

Everyone has dreams of success. Landing a flawless routine that scores you a perfect 10 and wins you an Olympic Gold Medal, Founding a tech firm that turns you into a gazillionaire, knocking down a last second shot in the seventh game to bring your team an NBA Championship, starting a business in your basement or at your kitchen table that becomes a Fortune 500 high flyer, grabbing a microphone and performing in front of sold out arena, after sold out arena, of adoring fans. Everybody dreams but it's the determination you put behind the dream that brings success.

There is a common misconception that the most successful new business ventures come from the minds of the young. The image of a young Mark Zuckerberg, Elon Musk, Sergey Brin, or Larry Page may come to mind whenever someone talks about successful entrepreneurs. The image of the swashbuckling young wiz kid creating a successful company may be burned into our minds but the reality is quite different. Statistics show that the average age of most successful entrepreneurs is 45. In fact, those same stats show that business founders in their 20s are the least likely to build a profitable firm.

Since young people tend to have less responsibilities many believe that the best time to start a business is when you are in your early 20s. That is when people think we are at our most innovative and disruptive. Some people advise would-be entrepreneurs to start companies while they still have lots of time and energy, and fewer responsibilities. The story about the young successful entrepreneur makes for great literature. Hearing how the brilliant young college dropout and his frat buddies struck out on their own and created some sick new app, indispensable software or billion-dollar company inspires us all. But, youth often produces more misses than hits. At least that's what the data says.

Using statistics from the United States Census Bureau for businesses launched in the U.S. between 2007 and 2014, when comparing the age of company founders and measuring their performance markers like sales growth, revenue, number of employees, and the profitability of their "exit" through either an IPO or being acquired.

The reality is that successful entrepreneurs are more likely to be middle-aged. Interestingly, among the fastest growing new businesses in the U.S., the average age of the founder for the first year of the business was 45. On the other hand, founders in their early 20s have the lowest likelihood of building a top-growth firm.

What are these numbers saying? They are saying experience counts. They are saying that those who have been knocked down and encountered obstacles, and opposition, and hardships along the way, and had the fortitude to overcome it are usually better equipped to succeed than those with no battle scars. Determination is a powerful ally. One that is often overlooked for more saleable attributes like salesmanship, intelligence, strategy, networking, and branding.

You can tell people to take a course in Six Sigma, or to get an MBA, or learn the ins and outs of multi-level marketing and people will think you must be pretty smart, but tell them that to succeed in business they are going to need more determination and they look at you like you just emerged from the stone age club in hand. There is an old adage in sports, "I can teach you fundamentals but I can't teach you heart."

You either have the will to win or you don't. 99 out of 100 times it's not what you learn outside of yourself that determines whether you succeed or fail, it's what you have inside of you that will be the deciding factor. Yes, you should educate yourself with as much knowledge as possible to give yourself a better chance to compete at a high level. You should work on perfecting your craft so that you can perform at a high level. You need to thoroughly understand the field that you are in so you can have a good handle on what you need to do to stay ahead of your competitors. But, sooner or later it will come down to how much fight you have in you. When times get tough and the fate of the universe is at stake will you simply roll over and let yourself be pinned, or will you kick and scratch and claw your way off the mat? Determination, is a key ingredient for success.

Here are **10 examples of how Determination helped people overcome adversity** to become successful:

Has everyone written you off as a loser? Albert Einstein never spoke a word for the first three years of his life. Throughout his elementary school years many of his teachers thought he was lazy and wouldn't amount to anything. To say he proved them all wrong is a huge understatement. He struggled for years trying to find good jobs and to have his theories recognized by the scientific community. When he developed his theory of relativity, even the most brilliant minds of his time had to recognize his genius. Now, he is the very symbol of genius.

Do you have to overcome homelessness? Jim Carrey had to drop out of school to support his family when he was only 15. Carrey's father was an unemployed musician which led to the family having to live in a van. But not even being homeless could stop Carrey from achieving his dream of becoming a comedian. He went from having his dad drive him to comedy clubs throughout Toronto, Canada to starring in blockbuster movies. He is now widely recognized as a comedic genius and one of the best comedic actors of all time.

Do you have a learning disability like dyslexia or a mental illness? Entrepreneur Richard Branson was not a good student. Having dyslexia affected his ability to read, write and learn. It also caused him to perform poorly on standardized tests. His teachers mistakenly thought Branson was lazy and stupid. But, he stubbornly refused to allow his disability to get in the way of him being successful. Branson instead adopted a management style that accommodated his dyslexia. He went on to found Virgin Records, Virgin Airlines, and a bevy of other companies. His corporation Virgin Group has a net worth of $7.2 billion dollars and Branson is estimated to be the fourth richest person in the United Kingdom.

Do you have to overcome an environment plagued by crime, drugs, and violence? It's obvious why rapper Curtis Jackson, a.k.a. 50 Cent, so easily fit into his thug persona. His mother had Jackson when she was only 15 years old, and dealt drugs to support her son. She was murdered when he was eight years old. Jackson then was sent to live with his grandmother, and eight aunts and uncles. When he bought a gun at the age of 15, began dealing drugs and dropped out of high school, it seemed Jackson was dangerously following in his mother's footsteps. He found himself in and out of jail and infamously survived being shot nine times. After trying to land a music deal for years Jackson was finally signed to Eminem's label. He never looked back. As the rapper 50 Cent he turned his life around becoming a top-selling hip-hop artist, television producer, and successful entrepreneur.

Have you been diagnosed with a terminal illness? On February 14, 2003, Kris Carr, A 32-year-old photographer, actress, and New Yorker was enjoying life. But, a routine checkup resulted in her doctor diagnosing her with a rare and incurable Stage IV cancer called epithelioid hemangioendothelioma. The cancer was found in Karr's liver and lungs. While many would have accepted the diagnosis as a death penalty, Carr decided to attack her cancer by adopting a "plant-based diet, improving lifestyle practices and learning to live like they really mean it." Furthermore, she turned her experience into a series of successful self-help books and documentaries. She launched her own wellness website at kriscarr.com that is now followed by over 40,000 people. Today, Carr is celebrating nearly two decades of "thriving with cancer," and is revered as one of the most prominent experts on healthy living.

Have you been told repeatedly that you're not good enough? Stephen King's first novel was rejected 30 times and if it weren't for King's wife Tabitha, his first literary success "Carrie" may not have seen the light of day. After being consistently rejected by publishing houses, King gave up on writing and threw the beginning pages of the book into the trash. His wife rescued the manuscript from oblivion and urged King to finish it. Now, King has published 58 novels, written approximately 200 short stories, sold over 350 million copies of his books, and have seen many of his books made into major motion pictures.

Are you fighting to overcome physical handicaps? Complications his mother suffered during labor forced her obstetricians to use two pairs of forceps during her son Sylvester Stallone's birth. Misuse of these instruments accidentally severed a nerve and caused paralysis in parts of Stallone's face. As a result, the lower left side of his face is paralyzed, including parts of his lip, tongue, and chin. The mishap at birth can be credited for giving Stallone his snarling look and slightly slurred speech. Be that as it may the actor has nonetheless parlayed these traits into success as an actor starring in franchise hits like Rambo, Rocky, and Creed.

Are you a victim of abuse? Prior to her mother and sister's success as country singers, Ashley Judd and her family were so poor they often lived without electricity and indoor plumbing. Judd's parents divorced when she was four and Ashley was often left home with her father while her sister and mother toured. Ashley was sexually abused by several men in her life, including a family member. She reported these incidents but no one believed her. By the time she was seven, Judd was suffering with severe depression and later contemplating suicide. Judd attended 13 schools before college. In spite of these horrific events she became a successful actress, starring in films like A Time To Kill, Kiss The Girls, Simon Birch, Where The Heart Is, Divergent, and A Dog's Way Home.

Are academics your weakness? Chris Johnson wanted nothing more than to play professional football, but after a terrible senior year, it seemed impossible. A broken leg ended his last high school fall football season, not to mention he was failing. Without the grades or test scores, he wasn't eligible for NCAA competition, and no school would offer him a scholarship. A career in football was looking bleak until East Carolina University head coach John Thompson offered to help Johnson with his studies. Higher grades led to a NCAA scholarship for Johnson who went on to set records for East Carolina and be drafted in the first round of the NFL Draft by the Tennessee Titans. Johnson ran the fastest time ever run at the NFL combine at that time 4.24 seconds in the 40-yard dash. Some consider Johnson's 2009 NFL season to be one of the best ever by a running back. Overall, he rushed for 2,006 yards and finished the year with 11 consecutive games with at least 100 rushing yards to become one of only seven players in NFL history to be in the 2,000 rushing yards club. He averaged 5.6 yards per carry and 125.4 yards per game to lead the league. On November 5, 2018, Johnson announced his retirement from the NFL after 10 seasons in the league, finishing with 9,651 yards rushing, 2,255 receiving yards, a combined 64 touchdowns, and multiple NFL records.

Had to overcome a dysfunctional upbringing? Rosie Perez is a Brooklyn-born actress has overcome so many personal struggles throughout her life including bullying, homelessness, divorce and a speech impediment. Perez became a ward of the state when her mother took her from an aunt, who had been raising her. She was transferred to a group foster home at age three and lived in foster care in New York and Peekskill until age eight and was still legally considered a ward of the State of New York until age 12. Her mother died of AIDS-related complications in 1999. At 19 years old, Perez started her career in the early 1980s as a dancer on Soul Train. In 1988, when she was 24 years old, Perez was noticed at the dance club Funky Reggae by Spike Lee, who hired her for her first major acting role in his movie, Do the Right Thing. Perez has choreographed music videos by Janet Jackson, Bobby Brown, Diana Ross, LL Cool J and The Boys. She was also choreographer for the Fly Girls on the Fox television comedy In Living Color. The multi-talented Perez is an actress, community activist, talk show host, author, dancer and choreographer.

In the legendary words of the great Jim Valvano, "Don't give up. Don't ever give up!"

Chapter 8: Defending Your Dream

Anyone not prepared to defend his or her dream will never achieve success. For those on a quest to achieve success life is not a picnic, it is a war. To achieve success you will have to fight off various assaults on your dream. In Chapter 8, Defending Your Dream, you will learn the different kinds of defenses (cannons, moats, walls, swords) you must be prepared to use, and you will learn how and when to use them.

Cannons

When the attack is coming from a distance

When the attack is coming from a distance. Operating in the global environment can be risky, especially for companies whose product or service is centered around agriculture or other types of natural resources. Weather patterns are only one example of global environmental threats that can impact a company's resources, projects and profitability. Weather patterns can be extremely different from country to country as can the seasons. Before making plans or settling on a strategy, businesses in the global market need to track and trend weather patterns and access what types of risks they will encounter from weather patterns at various times of the year. Adverse weather can cause delays in shipping, snow days or other bad weather days can cause employee absentees, harsh weather can also lead to more facility repairs. For anyone doing business globally, all these things and other climate related issues need to be taken under consideration.

If you are doing business in other countries or if you are having the majority of your products made in another country, you must consider how the political government in those nations will affect your business and how your business operates. Countries that have an unstable government and are at-risk for a regime change could also put your company at risk of having various laws, policies, tariffs and taxation change overnight. If you are or want to be a global company you should protect yourself by already having in place alternative manufacturers, vendors, and suppliers.

Unlike local businesses multinational companies can't just line up and sell standardized products. Clothing companies must be aware of the style differences that exist from nation to nation. Food companies must be aware of the taste differences and availability of ingredients from nation to nation. Transportation companies must be aware of replacement parts availability and fuel costs. Working out such potential problems in advance will put your company in a position to be profitable and not get blindsided by unexpected costs. Also, these factors might make you consider selling your products in one country or region of that country and not others.

Global companies who wish to operate in other countries must consider where they will draw their labor force from. Are their enough skilled workers within a reasonable distance of your facility? Do those workers have the skills and education they will need to do the work you need done? Will the workforce in other countries happily coexist within your company culture or will you be forced to alter your culture to accommodate a foreign workforce? Think about the work force issues that may arise in a foreign country. Thoroughly examine them and other cultural issues. Some training may be necessary for your workforce as well as your management team to make sure the workforce can work together efficiently and happily. Is there a university nearby that can provide you with an educated and technology smart workforce? Are there enough available workers in the area you wish to operate in or do you need to consider another location? You also need to consider the building of your management team. Will your managers be exported from your own country? Will they be hired in the foreign country you are going to operate in? Or, will your management team be a mixture of foreign and domestic workers working together? For companies to run smoothly communication needs to be good at every level of the business. Be sure you consider any language barriers that may exist.

What are the logistic issues you will face operating in another country? Are there trucking services available to transport your goods to your wholesalers or retailers? Are there rail lines available nearby to transport your goods? Is there an airport nearby with shipping services available to transport your goods out of the country or region? Or, will you have to depend on your products being shipped by waterways? Calculate all the logistics costs before you decide where and how you will operate.

Larger international companies may have a sales advantage that allows them to take advantage of the "economies of scale" but they should still adapt to local preferences in areas where it is smart to do so, especially if it does not compromise your company or brand. Determine where your company, product, or service ranks in the foreign markets you wish to compete compared to your competition. What are your strengths and weaknesses and what are the strengths and weaknesses of your competitors? Which of your competitors if any have an advantage because they are native to the country in which you are competing? Create a strategy to counter that advantage.

Be aware that many emerging-market companies have assets that give them a competitive advantage in their home market. These advantages may include having a local distribution network that would take years for you as a multinational company to build. They most likely will have relationships or subsidies in place with local government officials that are not available to you as a foreign company. Foreign competitors may have also developed distinctive products, goods, and services that appeal specifically to local tastes that you may not be able to produce cost effectively. Whether you are entering a foreign market or are defending your home market against foreign companies take time to examine how defensible your company's market position is against your competitors in a foreign market, or how defensible your company's position is against foreign competitors in your domestic market. The answers you discover will determine if it is feasible for you to compete in a foreign market, and if so what strategies and methods you will need to employ to compete successfully.

Study the case of PepsiCo, who tried to enter the bakery market in Mexico in 1991. A Mexican company named Bimbo met their competition by examining their operation to see where they might have a competitive advantage over the American global giant PepsiCo. As the smaller company Bimbo found that their low-margin sales, and distribution network was the key to defeating their foreign competitor in their own backyard. Aware that the Mexican consumer prefers having fresh baked goods over packaged ones, which is why they shop daily at a neighborhood store, Bimbo saw this trait as a way to create a barrier to entry for foreign competitors. To further take advantage of their customer's preference for freshness Bimbo's managers increased their store deliveries, while lowering their costs by sending delivery trucks to the smaller tiendas stocked with multiple products instead of the single-product deliveries they sent to larger markets. By executing these "cannon" strategies Bimbo's defensive moves worked to perfection. PepsiCo withdrew themselves from competing directly against Bimbo in Mexico and the smaller company has managed to maintain their leading position in each of its major market segments. Bigger does not always have to equal better. By using "cannon" defensive strategies, it is highly possible to not only compete against larger and wealthier competitors but also to defeat them. There are many factors that determine how successfully you will be in competing against foreign or global competitors such as management strategy, logistics, labor proficiency, your company culture, and understanding your market. Any of these factors can determine whether you gain or lose market share, make profits or sustain loses.

Far from being invincible, multinationals or global companies tend to have built-in defects. Rather than creating products that are unique they typically optimize their operations on a global scale by standardizing product characteristics. Though this allows them to maintain the quality of their standardized products and save on production costs mass producing products eliminates the qualities that may make products totally unique, making it all but impossible to customize products to appeal to a specific taste. Multinational companies tend to unify their administrative and management practices so that there is little or no flexibility in the way they operate, which may not blend well with the culture of a foreign workforce. The pricing structure of global companies are usually more rigid rendering them unable to stray too far from their suggested list price in order to compete against lower priced alternatives. Also, global companies that produce products designed for more affluent consumers cannot make these products available at lower prices because such cost cutting will not be profitable for the company, and with higher prices they cannot attract enough buyers in emerging markets.

Furthermore, by lowering prices they run the risk of damaging the reputation of their brand.

When your competitors are coming from afar it is wise for you to use cannon techniques that can effectively work against them before they can move in closer and take your market share. Cannon techniques include concentrating on the advantages you may enjoy by knowing your home market better or being able to more closely customize your products or services to your customer's specific taste. As a smaller company you can take advantage of being more nimble and able to pivot faster and change directions or strategies quicker than your bigger competitors to meet customer needs. Don't be lured into trying to reach every customer. Multinational companies have the manpower and financial resources for such a strategy. You don't. Focus on your local consumers who will appreciate your customizing your products and services to their individual preferences. Also, make use of technology to close the gap between you and larger competitors. Make use of local labor to beat your competition on labor cost and win the appreciation of the communities in which you operate.

Moats

When the attack is from across town

Use a moat when the attack is coming from across town. Companies that operate in the domestic market may face less challenges than those that operate internationally, but there are still numerous factors that can impact the success of your business. Cultural factors are still present, even in the domestic market. The ways you or your competitors use technology can have a major impact on business too. Before you decide on a marketing strategy for your business examine your target market to see what elements make it different from other markets. Look for things that will give you a competitive advantage over your competition. What is a competitive advantage? A competitive advantage is a factor that distinguishes your business from others and makes customers more likely to choose your product or service over the competition. Without a competitive advantage, your business has no unique method of gaining and keeping customers.

You can create an "economic moat" by setting up barriers for your competitors to keep them from easily entering into the market space you occupy. The harder you make it for competitors to compete with you the easier it will be for you to hang on to your share of the market. Your ability to set up hurdles and obstacles that competitors or new companies will have to overcome is another way of investing in and assuring your future profits and maintaining customers.

Competitive advantage is a phrase you need to become very familiar with. IKEA has become a market leader in the furniture industry because of its ability to provide superior product at an affordable rate; backed by a strong customer support system. Speed and time were once an overlooked source of sustained competitive advantage until FedEx and Domino Pizza used these tactics as leverage to become industry pacesetters. AT&T, Google, and Facebook have become market leaders in their various niches because of the superior database management and data processing capabilities they possess. Wal-Mart is probably the most capitalized company in the world mainly as a result of its low pricing strategy that became a strong competitive advantage. Sony and Apple have held their leadership positions by using innovation as a competitive advantage. "Competitive advantage" is a moat you need to use.

You must build a moat that will keep your competition out and keep your customers in. With there being distance between you and your competitor you have some innate advantages that should help you to win the battle for market share and customers. Your moat is built by emphasizing the positives and making your negatives seem miniscule in comparison.

When your competition is across town you can keep your customers happy by giving them reasons not to travel to find what they need. Why should they travel across town when the food is better right here? Why should customers travel across town when the suits are better quality here and the prices are lower? Why should customers travel across town when the parking situation and customer service is better right here? These are advantages you can build like moats around your business to keep the competition at bay.

Build a moat with price. The key to being able to beat your competition on price is to lower your costs. Lower your expenditures. Use an app or program to track your expenditures and be able to eliminate unnecessary expenses and find better deals on others. You can save money on insurance by comparing providers to get the most competitive rate. Then ask your current insurance provider to match that rate. Save money on monthly supplies by letting your vendors know you are price shopping. Look beyond your usual vendors to find better prices. Be aware that discount suppliers like Amazon, BJ's, Costco, Sam's and Wal-Mart can sometimes give you better deals than your vendors these days.

Build a moat by narrowing your business focus. Whereas larger companies can afford to offer a larger variety of products and services, small business owners especially may want to narrow their business focus. The more products or services you offer the more money you will have to spend on inventory and maybe manpower as well. Having to focus on a larger variety of items usually makes you less efficient simply because there are more things for you to concentrate on and try to master. That means you may take a hit in the area of customer service. A food chain that sells hamburgers, hot dogs, and chicken, is going to incur more costs and work less efficiently than a chain that just specializes in making variations of one of these items with various sides. So, narrowing the products you offer allows you to save on inventory cost, perfect the smaller list of offerings, and give better customer service. This small change can give you a big edge over your competitor. Subcontracting out services can allow you to still generate some income for those services without having to pay for the cost of said services. Keep in mind, more projects, without necessarily adding more work for you, equals more revenue. By lowering your expenses through using subcontracting you add to your bottom line.

Build a moat with your excellence. Whether your business is offering products or services excellence always gives you an advantage over your competitors. You don't get rich by selling a hamburger. You get rich by selling a billion hamburgers. Satisfied customers will help you increase your sales by giving you referrals for new customers and coming back repeatedly themselves to make purchases. Having high quality goods and services also allows you to charge higher prices, which equals higher revenue which you can use to build more moats.

Build a moat with unique products or services. Narrowing your focus is a good idea to save on costs but that doesn't mean that you can't add a specialty item or two to differentiate yourself from the competition. If a fast food restaurant sells homemade peach cobbler or sweet potato pies or has an ice box full of old-time sodas it may be something unique your competitor doesn't offer and reason enough for your customers to choose your place instead of their place. Or, maybe you offer a delivery service for your products for customers within a five-mile radius. Another reason for your customers to do business with you instead of drive across town to your competitor. Think of what unique product or service you can add cost effectively to differentiate yourself.

Build a moat with value added products and services. Maybe your customers can benefit from receiving free training when they purchase DIY products or tools from you. Maybe your furniture store not only delivers the same day but also sets up furniture purchased from your store. Perhaps you give your customers a free makeup makeover when they purchase a certain dollar amount of clothing from your store. Maybe you give your landscape customers a free potted plant when they use your service for a year or more. There are thousands of value-added products or services you can offer your customers to keep them loyal to you and not your competitors. Choose a few and test them to see which ones your customers consider game-changers.

If you hope to stay ahead of the competition, you'll need to do some research to see what it is you are staying ahead of. Check out your competitors. Having a competitive advantage means you offer some things your competitors don't. To be able to do that you need to know what it is your competitors do well, and don't do well. Assess your competitors' locations, products, services, prices, and marketing tactics. Finally, compile a list of all the reasons your customers might choose to do business with your competitors over your company, then think of adjustments you may need to make to your business. Don't forget, you may own an Indian-themed restaurant or soul food restaurant located in a mall. This would provide an economic moat, since it is unlikely the mall would want to open multiple restaurants with the same theme in the same area. The same would be true if you are starting a new business and you are able to negotiate a site monopoly on your type of business because you are located in a multi-business site like a strip mall or shopping center. Ask for an exclusive on your type of business. Remember that your competition includes more than same-as businesses. It is good for you to have an informed understanding of what the word competitor means. For example, a Thai restaurant competes with other Thai restaurants, but it also competes with all other restaurants as well. Also, consider using social media analysis tools that allow you to do consumer insight mining to gain this information.

Remember that having detailed customer knowledge is as important as knowledge about your competitors. Gaining in-depth insights about your customer profile allows you to better understand your customer needs, which can help you increase customer retention, and gain new customers. You don't really know your business until you know your customers. You should be able to identify the demographic qualities of your customer base. Is your customer base made up of people from local businesses, or local residents? Are your customers mostly young or old, male or female, married or single? Do they live within a mile of the business or 5 miles? That is one reason businesses ask your zip code at check-out. What is the median income of your customers? Are your customers in some way different from your competitor's customers? Is your service mainly business to business? What type of businesses do you typically sell to? You can gather demographic information through talking to or observing customers, surveys, using a suggestion box, customer complaints, or analyzing customer information. Until you understand your customers, you cannot know why they patronize your business, and knowing that allows you to build moats that are all but unbreachable.

If you want to get detailed analyses about your competitors or customers and you have the capital to spend on it you can hire a company that specializes in providing business information. Professional research companies will research, construct and analyze all the pertinent information you need to gain an accurate knowledge of your target market. This wealth of information makes it easier for you to know what is working in your business and what is not. You can then use this data to build a moat that gives you a clear competitive advantage.

Walls

When the attack is at your front door.

We all see it. A Pizza Hut located right next door to a Domino's Pizza. A Starbucks sitting right across the street from Coffee Bean. Lowe's is down the block from Home Depot. Three gas stations positioned at the same intersection. Why is it that restaurants, gas stations, and competing businesses often open in such close proximity to each other?

It seems more logical for similar businesses to try and locate themselves farther away from one another. But, according to some popular business theories businesses do not increase their chances of success by placing themselves extremely far from one another. In this competitive technological world where companies must fight for their hard earned share of market share it is interesting how game theories such as Hotelling's Model of Spatial Competition, Nash Equilibrium, and Social Optimal Solution play such prominent roles in determining where a business should be placed in relation to their competitors. Before you learn how to construct a wall that protects you against your competitors there are some important principles you need to understand. Let's study these next level principles one by one.

Hotelling's Model of Spatial Competition

Harold Hotelling was an American mathematical statistician as well as an influential economic theorist, known for Hotelling's law, Hotelling's lemma, and Hotelling's rule in economics. He was also known for his Hotelling's T-squared distribution in statistics. Hotelling also developed and named the principal component analysis method that is widely used in finance, statistics and computer science.

One principle that explains why we find similar businesses grouped together instead of being spread apart from each other is explained with a theory known as Hotelling's Model of Spatial Competition. Hotelling analyzes the location of different businesses in a similar market in respect to one another, in his model of spatial competition. According to Hotelling, when competing on location, each business wants to be located at a central point because it is the most strategic point that allows it to be as close to as many customers as possible. Since each business has the same intention they will be in competition with each other for the best location which causes similar businesses to end up in a cluster focused at one specific point. This principle plays out again and again with businesses like gas stations, fast food chains, liquor stores, and other similar businesses.

Let's look at an example of how Hotelling's Model of Spatial Competition plays out in real life. Let's say there are two hardware stores located on a street that stretches from east to west for 10 miles. Both businesses locate their store 4 miles from the end of the street, with store A to the west and store B to the east. By locating their businesses this way store A will gain all the customers from the left of the middle and store B will get customers from the right of the middle. This creates what is known as the socially optimal solution. It minimizes the distance required to reach either one of the stores when driving down the street and both stores gain an equal amount of customers by locating their stores in this position. Inevitably, both businesses will want to attract more customers than its rival. This will cause both businesses to move towards the center of the street. So, eventually, both stores will end up in the middle of the street at the central point, where both businesses can serve 50% of the customers. This explains why similar type businesses have a tendency to converge on the same point (or location).

Socially Optimal Solution

In the example above, the term "socially optimal solution" is used. Socially Optimal Solution, is a state where something is the best solution for all parties. It is what's commonly known as a win-win situation because both parties benefit equally from the "action."

Since, the socially optimal solution is the most ideal plan or strategy for all businesses involved to maximize their benefits, it presents an obvious problem. The problem the socially optimal solution presents is that it is fluid. With profit being the motive both parties will want to gain more customers than its competitor and both parties have the capability to do exactly that. This desire to gain an advantage over the other party will cause each one to find a way to place themselves into a better position. In real life, the Socially Optimal Solution takes place when store A believes by moving 100 feet closer to the middle of the street towards store B, it will potentially allow it to capture some of store B's customers while at the same time retaining its own customers. To counter the move by store A, and get back its customers, store B decides to also move 100 feet closer to the middle of the street. Consequently, both stores end up moving to the middle of the street, thereby achieving what game theorists have coined as the Nash Equilibrium.

Nash Equilibrium

In the example above, once the stores are located at the center point both stores will be unable to benefit from moving away from the central position and will therefore be stuck with being next door neighbors. Since both stores are now neighbors and cannot benefit from relocating, they will have to rely on marketing strategies to gain an advantage over the other store. Differentiating their products, offering promotions, creating publicity, in other words building a wall is now the only way to create a competitive advantage. As you may guess, this is a reason why similar businesses tend to have promotions that are similar to ones offered by their competitors.

In game theory, the Nash equilibrium, named after the mathematician John Forbes Nash Jr., is a proposed solution of a non-cooperative game involving two or more players in which each player is assumed to know the equilibrium strategies of the other players, and no player has anything to gain by changing only their own strategy. In terms of game theory, if each player has chosen a strategy, and no player can benefit by changing strategies while the other players keep theirs unchanged, then the current set of strategy choices and their corresponding payoffs constitutes a Nash equilibrium.

Let's make that a little clearer. Store #1 and store #2, are in Nash equilibrium if Store #1 is making the best decision it can, taking into account Store #2's decision while it's decision remains unchanged, and Store #2 is making the best decision it can, taking into account Store #1's decision while it's decision remains unchanged. Just as in game theory, a group of players are in Nash equilibrium if each one is making the best decision possible, taking into account the decisions of the others in the game as long as the other parties' decisions remain unchanged.

All this being said, it is obvious why it is necessary to build a wall to gain a competitive advantage. Your company and your competitor are at a stalemate. You have both taken advantage of relocating to put yourselves in the absolute best location possible, and the result is that you are now right next door to each other, so you know your competitor is out of relocation moves, and he knows you are out of relocation moves. Building a wall is the only option you have left to differentiate your company from your competitor's. Again, that wall can consist of differentiating your products, offering promotions, creating publicity, or doing some other form of marketing to gain the competitive advantage you need to increase sells and gobble up a larger market share.

With your competitor literally next door every little thing you do better is a way of building that wall for competitive advantage. Having sparkling clean bathrooms for your customers, faster drive-thru windows, better customer service, a menu that also has vegan food offerings, free beverage refills, 24-hour tech support, longer warranties, no hassle product exchanges, more knowledgeable sales people, are all ways of building a wall and differentiating yourself from your competitors. Each item you can add to the list makes your wall stronger, higher, and more impenetrable.

Swords

When the attack is coming from within.

Some attacks on your company are not coming from outside the company but inside the company. So, it's not a long-distance problem solved by cannons, or a midrange problem that calls for moats, nor a close problem where walls are helpful. It is an internal problem, one so up close and personal that the only effective weapon is a sword. These problems take place within the company and must be solved within the company. Here are four such problems:

Start with the 'Why'

Simon Sinek believes that organizations that start with understanding, 'why' they do what they do', are those that most inspire and enjoy success. It's important to understand what purpose your organization stands for; why do you exist? His inspiring TedTalk, How Great Leaders Inspire Action, discusses this very concept.

Innovation

It seems big companies are struggling with innovation and a better innovation process is at the top of the agenda for most CEOs, but the idea of a more innovative culture appears too frightening for many. The problem to be solved is how to become more innovative while still maintaining a sense of control over the organization.

Technology

The rate of technological changes and improvements are happening at such an alarming pace that it presents not only opportunities for companies but also problems. For companies investing in technology today that investment could turn out to be an asset or a liability. Your competitor may choose to wait for the next-generation technology, that will give them an advantage over your company. Alternately, you could choose to wait before investing in technology and suddenly discover that your competitor has used technology to gain a competitive advantage over you. To invest in technology or not to invest in technology is a decision every CEO must now face. Even the best and most well-informed information technologists cannot see far enough into the future to predict which emerging technology will be a perfect fit for your company 3 to 5 years out. Every company that hopes to stay abreast of today's technology must focus on mastering it as soon as possible. But, to stay ahead of the curve companies must also develop a long-term technology that includes being ready to take advantage of unforeseen technology developments.

Technology has changed the way people communicate in the workplace. Smartphones, social media, chat apps, and other tech innovations have elevated communication to a new level. Communication with employees, management, vendors, suppliers, and stakeholders of all kinds is now instantaneous, whether done one to one, or with a group. Technology has given us the option to communicate by email, text, video chat or even video conference. They can also choose to communicate through social networking apps like WhatsApp, Facetime, and Skype, etc. With the advancements in technology, workers don't even have to be physically present at their workplace to work and can still turn in their work in real-time.

With the click of a mouse Cloud technologies have allowed employees to work from anywhere and video conferencing allows employers to coordinate work with their employees no matter where they are working from. Because of this interconnectivity workers and workplaces are no longer tied to one location. Collaborative software and services help leaders and managers communicate with their employees and keep clients updated on their project's progress. Companies interested in being more efficient can invest in facility management software designed to manage assets and equipment, streamline work order processes, and reduce maintenance costs.

Time management is as important in today's workplace as it's ever been. With the apps and technology available today time management has become easy. Such tools have helped companies to optimize the daily work routine and enabled employees to focus on the most important task. Technology has allowed workers to reduce the amount of time spent on daily activities so they can instead spend more time on creativity and being innovative.

With so much important data it is wise for companies to invest in security software that provides end-to-end hardware and software-based data encryption to ensure only authorized parties are able to receive and read data. Technology can also provide fingerprint and facial recognition features that give an added level of security to a company's systems and workplace. Security technology can also be implemented with algorithms to make sure sensitive information is accessible to the right people and protects against malicious hacking.

Diversity

Diversity is a double-edged sword in that it makes it more likely that people won't be in agreement with each other. It is also a way of ensuring your company does not suffer from the kind of narrow mindedness that can paralyze companies. It is a detriment to have a lack of diversity at the leadership level of your company if you plan on doing business with this diverse world. Having a company that works in harmony together is good but not if it comes at the expense of becoming stuck in doing things the same old way over and over infinitum. That kind of stagnation can take a company's bright future and quickly make it the past. A diverse company that can draw from leadership that is male and female, of varying ethnicities, spans several age groups, even comes from differing geographic regions is one that will more than likely have an abundance of fresh and creative ideas whenever they are needed.

Of course, diversity does not just happen by accident. It must be planned, and that plan must be executed. It may be difficult to build a diverse leadership team if your leadership team is not diverse. Thus, step one for building a diverse company is the hiring process, and you must make sure that process is headed by a team that actually understands what diversity means.

At Merck and Co. Inc., a global pharmaceutical manufacturer, management teams undergo training in "unconscious bias", that is what happens when individuals make judgments about people based on gender, race or other factors without even realizing they're doing it. The training makes people aware of this form of bias. The training also emphasizes the importance of modeling inclusive behavior like actively listening, recognizing the significance of various holidays, being aware of cultural or geographic differences, valuing different opinions and perspectives, and encouraging different points of view.

How do you build a diverse company? First of all, do research to supply yourself with national, state and local employment statistics so you can see where you fall within those numbers. Also, look up the statistics for your industry to see how they differ. Armed with these statistics you will know what kind of percentages you should be aiming for. Next, develop a recruiting strategy that supports your organization's diversity goals. Get the company's human resources department, recruiters, and management involved in the recruiting process. Contact organizations that serve the needs of underrepresented segments of the population and inform them about your program to create diversity at your company.

Connect with job posting sites for diversity-focused groups such as the American Association for Affirmative Action, ask your employees for referrals, to reach diverse job seekers. Join diversity groups through social media channels like Twitter or LinkedIn. Remember to register your organization with local job agencies, career centers, universities, community colleges, trade schools, and the U.S. Department of Labor. When contacting these agencies and institutions be sure to supply them with the qualifications you desire from all applicants. Once you begin the process be sure to monitor your recruitment and outreach efforts. When built properly a diverse company can be the sword that defends your company against encroachment from your competitors and gives you a competitive advantage.

"A diverse mix of voices leads to better discussions, decisions, and outcomes for everyone." — Sundar Pichai, CEO of Google

Company Culture

When people talk about specific companies one subject that comes up is company culture. What is company culture? You might say that company culture is the personality of a company. Company culture encompasses a variety of elements, including a company's work environment, mission, values, ethics, goals, expectations, beliefs, behaviors, communication, and even its aspirations. Great companies usually have a good company culture while failing companies more times than not usually have a bad company culture.

In the past having great company culture was just an added plus for perspective employees but today's worker believes it to be as important a selling point as salary and benefits. In the eyes of workers good company culture is what sets the great companies apart as much as traditional benefits did for the companies that employed our grandparents.

When employees feel that their concerns and opinions cannot be heard by top level executives because of the layers of management between them and the CEO it can hurt company morale. When employees feel empowered to contribute more than just their sweat to the success of a company it creates an environment where morale is good. This is the kind of company culture that makes employees feel good about giving their best efforts toward making the company successful. In employee surveys taken to find out the top companies to work for some of the same companies seem to make the list again and again.

Three Examples of Good Company Culture

SquareSpace

One such company is SquareSpace. The tech company is often voted as one of the best places to work in New York City. Its company culture has been described as "flat, open and creative." Flat meaning the organization has very few levels of management between staff and executives. As companies go from being startups to mature companies layers of managers are often added to administrate the growing number of workers and departments. When these layers are added the voice of the common worker is often drowned out. But, SquareSpace has managed to maintain its flat administration model.

When assessing the success of SquareSpace's company culture it is not just how the company is organized that is impressive. The company also offers hefty benefits and perks that include 100% coverage on health insurance premiums, flexible vacations, catered meals, monthly celebrations, relaxation spaces, and an impressive list of guest lecturers, all in a beautiful workspace. With such employee friendly benefits it is no wonder SquareSpace scores high on the list for company culture.

Zappos

Zappos, the online shoe seller, is another company that regularly finishes at the top of the list of companies with excellent company culture. When hiring new employees the company places highest priority on how prospective employees will fit their company culture. Zappos believes promoting a culture where employees are happy will ultimately lead to the company having happy customers. Beginning with a cultural fit interview that is the most telling criteria for whether a candidate is hired, Zappos also tries to ensure employees who get hired are a good fit by offering $2,000 for employees to quit after week one of training if they decide that working at Zappos does not suit them. Management does not make the final decision on which employees get raises. Instead raises are given to workers who pass skill tests and demonstrate that their knowledge and usefulness is increasing. This reward system eliminates rewards that are the result of office politics. The company actually sets aside part of its budget to promote employee team building and culture. Zappos believes when they get the company culture right, great customer service and a great brand happens automatically.

Google

For years now Google has been the gold standard for company culture. They all but invented the many perks and benefits that tech startups have come to be known for. Free meals, employee trips, bonuses, employee parties, gyms, and a dog-friendly environment are only a few of the goodies you get for working in Googleland. Googlers, as they are known are some of the most driven and talented employees to be found anywhere. Even so, as the company grew into a financial behemoth it encountered the same growing pains faced by other large companies. The larger a company gets the more its culture has to adapt to accommodate the growing number of employees and the expanding management structure needed to run its corporate headquarters, many departments, and necessary satellite offices, all challenges Google had to overcome.

The Four Types of Company Culture

Every organization is different, and all of them have a unique culture to organize groups of people. Yet few people know that every organization actually combines a mix of four different types of organizational culture under one leading cultural style, according to research by business professors Robert E. Quinn and Kim S. Cameron at the University of Michigan.

Quinn and Cameron developed the Organizational Culture Assessment Instrument (OCAI), a validated survey method to assess current and preferred organizational cultures. Can this assessment be trusted? The OCAI is based on Quinn and Cameron's Competing Values Framework Model, which has been used by over 12,000 companies worldwide.

The framework explains how the four organizational cultures compete with one another. The four parameters of the framework include internal focus and integration vs. external focus and differentiation, and stability and control vs. flexibility and discretion.

Based on these parameters, the framework breaks organizational cultures into four distinct quadrants or cultural types: The Clan Culture, the Adhocracy Culture, the Market Culture, and the Hierarchy Culture. Quinn and Cameron discovered that flexible organizations are more successful than rigid ones because the best organizations are able to manage the competition between cultures while activating each of the four value sets when needed.

To determine what type of organizational culture you belong to, or as an entrepreneur what kind you want to create for your company, here is a summary of the four types and their specific qualities:

The Clan Culture: This culture is rooted in collaboration. Members share commonalities and see themselves as part of one big family who are active and involved. Leadership takes the form of mentorship, and the organization is bound by commitments and traditions. The main values are rooted in teamwork, communication and consensus. A prominent clan culture is Tom's of Maine, the maker of all-natural hygiene products. To build the brand, founder Tom Chappell focused on building respectful relationships with employees, customers, suppliers and the environment itself.

The Adhocracy Culture: This culture is based on energy and creativity. Employees are encouraged to take risks, and leaders are seen as innovators or entrepreneurs. The organization is held together by experimentation, with an emphasis on individual ingenuity and freedom. The core values are based on change and agility. Facebook can be seen as a prototypical adhocracy organization, based on CEO Mark Zuckerberg's famous admonition to, "Move fast and break things – unless you are breaking stuff, you are not moving fast enough."

The Market Culture: This culture is built upon the dynamics of competition and achieving concrete results. The focus is goal-oriented, with leaders who are tough and demanding. The organization is united by a common goal to succeed and beat all rivals. The main value drivers are market share and profitability. General Electric under ex-CEO Jack Welch is a good example of this culture. Welch vowed that every G.E. business unit must rank first or second in its respective market or face being sold off. Another example of the market culture is software giant Oracle under hard-driving Executive Chairman Larry Ellison.

The Hierarchy Culture: This culture is founded on structure and control. The work environment is formal, with strict institutional procedures in place for guidance. Leadership is based on organized coordination and monitoring, with a culture emphasizing efficiency and predictability. The values include consistency and uniformity. Think of stereotypical large, bureaucratic organizations such as McDonald's, the military, or the Department of Motor Vehicles.

Reasons Why Having A Great Company Culture Matters

Recruitment. Many HR professionals agree that a strong company culture is one of the best ways to attract potential employees. A positive culture gives an organization a competitive advantage. People want to work for companies with a good reputation from previous and current employees. A company with a positive culture will attract the type of talent that is willing to make their next workplace a home, rather than just a stepping-stone on the way to their next employer.

Employee loyalty. Not only do positive cultures help recruitment efforts, they help retain top talent as well. A positive culture fosters a sense of employee loyalty. Employees are much more likely to stay with their current employer when they feel they are treated right and enjoy going to work every day. It's no surprise that job satisfaction is higher at companies with a positive corporate culture. Employers who invest in the well-being of their employees will be rewarded with happy, dedicated employees.

Eight Ways to Build Great Company Culture

1. Be Good to Your Employees

First things first. If you want to build a great company culture the very first thing you must do is treat your employees good. Bad news travels fast. If your employees are being mistreated they will most likely tell just about anyone within earshot. That will put a serious dent in your recruitment process. Employee mistreatment will also ensure you of having a high employee turnover rate. Remember too that good people like to work with good people. So, when you're hiring new employees don't just look at their skill level, screen them for character as well. Job skills can be learned, but it's awful hard to unlearn a bad attitude and bad people skills. Hiring people with bad character can and most likely will sabotage your company's culture. If you want a great company hire the right people, train them right, and then treat them right.

2. Value Good Health

When you put an emphasis on the wellness of your employees it shows that you value them. It takes healthy employees to create a healthy organization. When employees are at their best physically, mentally and emotionally they will do their best work. It benefits your company to spend time and resources on employee wellness. Make it a priority to make sure employees have the resources, on-site tools, and healthcare benefits they need to live a healthy life both at work and at home. Your company and culture will be repaid many times over if you invest in your employee's good health. People appreciate being appreciated.

3. Create Goals That Reflect the Culture Your Company Wants

No one should expect people to display good behavior just because. If a company wants to have a great company culture it must create for its employees a set of goals they should aspire to. Before an organization can have a great corporate culture it must establish clear goals? These goals should uphold the rights of employees, provide a safe place to work for all employees, protect against discrimination, encourage collaboration, give incentives for employees to do community work, and include other statutes that will help to create great company culture. Include employees among the management teams you designate to write the company culture goals. Find a way to communicate these company goals across the entire company and get feedback from all employees. While your core values remain constant, the overall culture of the company needs to be flexible enough to adapt to your diverse workforce and changing times. Once you have a common set of values that are your company's principles, and a common set of standards to measure how those principles are upheld your company culture will thrive.

4. Make Work Meaningful

Above all things the latest generation entering the workforce values doing work that is meaningful. When employees believe that their work serves a purpose they become more engaged. Developing a workplace that produces a product or service that somehow is integral to people living better lives is a major building block for creating a great company culture. Your company's mission statement and core values should announce the company's purpose loud and clear. To create that purpose, understand the "why" of the operation. What and whom does your business serve and why is that special? Always, keep this purpose at the forefront of why you do what you do, and how you do what you do. Management should take every opportunity to communicate to employees that it takes the effort of every worker to attain the company's purpose. Employees should be given specific examples of how their roles positively impact the company and its customers. Building something that is great and lasting is something that stimulates all employees. Even as the company grows and communication becomes more difficult, doing work that is meaningful will remain a rallying point for employees. Success and growth may signal the end of the tight-knit cohesiveness you experienced as a startup but working toward a meaningful purpose will still allow your company culture to unite employees to do their best work.

5. Remember to Lead by example.

Every leader in your company needs to internally and externally reflect the company's values. Remember that your leaders are your company's best ambassadors. Why? Because a company's culture is really formed by how seriously a company's leaders adhere to the principles the company proclaims. When the leaders of a company are the very embodiment of what the company stands for it sends a clear signal that the company culture is not only important but authentic. Have integrity. Be transparent. As the company's leader you set the standard for what your company culture should be, fun, passionate, courageous, smart, ethical, innovative, generous, and possessing all the other traits that make a great company culture. Exemplary leadership is an inspiration to both current employees and future employees.

6. Create A Sense of Unity

Friendly relationships fostered in the workplace are an essential part of a great company culture. If a company wants to have a positive culture it must create opportunities for employees to interact. If employees rarely interact it is all but impossible to grow a strong culture. Leaders can create activities for employees or sanction employees to create activities for their colleagues to participate in during approved times of the workday. Friendly team competitions, video game-a-thons, weekly team meals, movies, in-house concerts, talent nights, inviting prominent guest speakers and other activities can help employees enjoy their work environment as well as their co-workers. Also, after hour activities like excursions to the local watering hole, softball teams, bowling leagues, annual picnics, book clubs, and other fun activities can not only create more teamwork and camaraderie among workers but make their families fans of your company too.

7. Make Sure Your Employees Know You Hear Them

Listening is a vanishing skill. People feel empowered when they know that they are heard. Being a good listener is one way of showing your employees that they matter. If workers think their suggestions, grievances, and observations are not heard it will be almost impossible to build a positive culture. Research shows employees at companies with strong cultures feel that senior leadership listens to them, while employees at companies who are without a strong culture feel they are not heard. Listening is just one more way to show employees they are valued. Employees who feel they have a stake in the success of the company will do more to ensure that company's success. Take the time to ask employees what they do and don't like about the company and their work environment. Then use these suggestions to help create a positive corporate culture and workplace employees will love working in.

8. Give Your Employees the Best Benefits You Can

The best foundation for developing a great company culture is a great benefits package. Here are some items you need to consider including in your company benefits. Paid time off such as sick days, vacation days and maternity leaves. Flexible work schedules, health insurance, life insurance, dental insurance, vision insurance, retirement benefits, long term disability insurance, short term disability insurance, wellness programs, tuition reimbursement, childcare or childcare benefits, gym memberships or discounts, relocation assistance, commuting assistance, telecommuting options, work from home opportunities, and company perks like recreation activities, gourmet cafeterias, and free food and coffee. Everything else being equal, attracting the most capable and dedicated employees can keep you head and shoulders above the competition.

Cannons, Moats, Walls, and Swords, are all elements that can help you develop a defensive strategy that will give your company a competitive advantage over your competitors whether they are operating from a continent away or happen to be right next door.

Chapter 9: Laying The Foundation

Before you build anything great you first have to lay down a foundation. The higher the structure you want to build the deeper your foundation has to be to support it. Chapter 9, Laying The Foundation, discusses how to lay a good foundation for success and illustrates how to lay the deep, deeper, and deepest foundation you can to support your dreams of success.

Start with Why

In his book, "Start with Why: How Great Leaders Inspire Everyone to Take Action, author Simon Sinek makes some great points. By listening to just a few of his quotes one can understand why starting with your WHY gets your business off to the best possible start.

"People don't buy what you do; they buy why you do it. And what you do simply proves what you believe." — Simon Sinek

Great companies don't hire skilled people and motivate them, they hire already motivated people and inspire them. People are either motivated or they are not. Unless you give motivated people something to believe in, something bigger than their job to work toward, they will motivate themselves to find a new job and you'll be stuck with whoever's left. - Simon Sinek

Very few people or companies can clearly articulate WHY they do WHAT they do. By WHY I mean your purpose, cause or belief - WHY does your company exist? WHY do you get out of bed every morning? And WHY should anyone care? – Simon Sinek

Their customers don't just buy Apple products and services because they are innovative and usually of high quality, they buy Apple because they believe in Apple.

Apple Mission and Vision statement:

Apple mission statement: "to bringing the best user experience to its customers through its innovative hardware, software, and services." And in a manifesto dated 2009 Tim Cook specified the vision of Apple as "We believe that we are on the face of the earth to make great products and that's not changing."

Apple's customers truly believe that the company does put their customer's first and tries their best to deliver to them the best customer experience. When looking at Apple products from the design, to the functionality, to value added items like Apps for their products, Apple makes it easy to believe that the company is on the face of the earth to bring their customers great products. That is a pretty strong WHY. If you are creating a new business, bringing your customers a great user experience is a good place to start.

What is your WHY? Why does your company exist? Why do customers need your product or service? The answers to these questions will supply you with the building blocks that form the foundation of your company. Use this information to build a business foundation that is deep, deeper, and the deepest it can be.

Deep

The Product

What is your product? How does it serve the needs of your customer? How is your product different than other products in its category? Have you perfected it? What are its strengths? Are you aware of its weaknesses? What value does your product bring to your customers? How do you plan to market it?

Do you have a viable product? Here are some questions that will help you answer that question. Who are your customers? Where are they? What is the best way of reaching them with your product? What price is your customer willing to pay for your product? Does that price leave enough margin for you to sell your product, pay for marketing it, run your business, pay to make another product, and still have something left over to claim a profit? No matter how good a product is you will never be able to sell it to 100% of your target market. Is your market large enough to capture 10% of your target market and still make a profit? If so, you have a sustainable market.

Marketing

Even if you have a good product or service it still needs to be marketed effectively to sell it effectively. Before you place your product in the sales channel you should do some market research to prove whether there is indeed a market for your product. Your research should be used to pinpoint where your customer base is located. The test should also be used to see where in the market you should position your brand. Should you market your product or service at the economy end of the market, mid-price, or at the high end? Make sure you are positioning your product or service at the right price point and targeting your sales strategy to reach the right segment of the market. These things should be done prior to launching your product. Finding out these valuable marketing insights will help you to make the necessary adjustments to your product, your sales approach, and your marketing plan to improve your chances of success.

It is imperative that you understand how important marketing is in contributing to the success of your venture. It is a mistake to think that creating a good marketing plan and taking the time to design a winning sales process are not an integral part of what it takes for your company to succeed. Becoming a success in business takes more than having a great idea or a good product or service.

Team

Businesses go through stages and each business must grow through several stages to reach maturity. Before your business becomes successful it must survive its infancy. Infancy is the period where you first turn an idea into an actual product or service and begin your attempt to sell it. As you navigate through this period you may reach a point where you can no longer do all the work by yourself. However, you may also be at a juncture where you cannot afford to pay workers to work with you. Yet, at some point building a team of workers is critical to the growth of your business.

If you are a startup business that finds yourself in this predicament here are a few things to remember. Firstly, you don't have to fill every position in the company immediately. It is better to be cautious and pace yourself when making your first hires. Add only the people the business cannot function without and add them only when you absolutely have to. Make sure your initial hires possess the exact skill sets needed for the positions you are hiring them for and be sure to hire people that can work comfortably and collaboratively together. Remember that you are building a great team not just adding a bunch of individuals. Therefore, it is important that you recruit the right people at the right time.

There are many things to consider when evaluating a candidate for hire. Does he or she have job experience relevant to the position you are hiring them for? Does the employee candidate's career history raise any red flags? Do they have the specific skills required for the position you are hiring them for? Do they have any technical skills that will be beneficial? How are their skills in the areas of communication and creativity? What is the candidate's level of emotional intelligence?

To build a winning team you must find individuals who are a good "cultural fit," ones who comfortably align with your company's unique culture and values. Recent studies have found that 84% of recruiters surveyed agree that cultural fit is one of the most important recruitment factors. Though it is tempting to hire someone that possesses an impressive skillset it may be wise to pass on applicants who you don't feel aligns with your company's unique culture.

It may take some time before your business is profitable enough to hire a permanent employee, so here are a few suggestions on how you can add help before adding permanent employees. Hire an Intern. Quality interns are now in fairly high demand, so there may be some competition for them. To attract highly capable interns you should be able to offer them the ability to grow in their chosen career, pay them at least minimum wage as salary and compensation, and offer them the chance to work in a company culture that is fun and welcoming. If you are thinking about hiring free interns be aware that each state has guidelines that companies must follow if they want to hire an intern for free. Be sure to check with the Department of Labor for a list of their specific guidelines. Here are a few that may apply: The internship must consists of training similar to an educational environment. The internship experience must benefit the intern. The intern must not take the place of your regular staff. The intern must be closely supervised. The employer shall not receive an immediate advantage or compensation from the intern's activities. The intern isn't entitled to a job at the conclusion of the internship. Both parties must understand that the intern is not entitled to wages for the time spent in the internship.

Hire a temp: Hiring a temporary employee is another way to get the help you need without hiring a permanent employee. All you'll need to do is contact a temporary staffing agency to ask about hiring a temp. Most of today's temp agencies specialize in specific professions such as medical personnel, computer programmers, law assistants, clerical, etc. Adding to the benefits of hiring a temp is the fact that many temp agencies pay a lot of the costs that business owners normally have to carry when hiring a "full-time" employee. Here are some of the ways you will save money by hiring a temp instead of a full-time employee: You can hire a temp on an as-needed basis, during your busy season or when you need help to complete a large order. You can let the agency know what type of skills you need and it will recruit and screen the applicants for you. Temporary agencies often train their own employees, saving you that expense. You won't be responsible for paying temps health insurance or paid vacation time. The agency pays all federal, state and local taxes. The temp agency also pays the temp's unemployment and workers' compensation insurance.

Hire an independent contractor: Hiring an independent contractor is another way to get experienced help without taking on a permanent employee. Independent contractors are self-employed and therefore save you costs associated with a staff employee. You will be able to find skilled workers like accountants, social media managers, writers, videographers, sound technicians, landscapers, geologists, editors, office assistants, and about any other category of worker you need by hiring an independent contractor. Remember, that an employer is responsible for employees' taxes, insurance, and benefits, but independent contractors are responsible for paying these expenses themselves. They also pay for their own sick days and vacation time.

Offer stock options: Another way of bringing in valuable employees without paying them a salary is to offer them stock options. Options are usually granted on a four-year vesting schedule with a one-year cliff, which means employees won't actually have the option of owning equity in the company if they leave within their first year of working with the company. On a common vesting schedule, only 25% of the options are available to employees after the first year, and the remaining shares typically vest incrementally each month or quarter thereafter.

Stock options are called 'options' for a reason, as stock options don't actually imply ownership in the company, but rather the option to purchase a specified number of shares. If you decide to buy the shares in the future, they'll cost you the 'strike price', which means the price of the proposed stock when the options were granted, which should be significantly lower than the market value of the shares when sold later. If the strike price were not lower than the market price of the company when it goes public the employee would have no reason to buy them in the first place. The ultimate hope is that the value of the company's shares increases significantly over the time the employee works there and he or she can cash in later for a big profit.

If the employee does purchase the shares, they're not actually worth anything until some sort of exit event, like an Initial Public Offering (IPO) or acquisition and the unfortunate reality is that a large percentage of startups fail, at which point the shares are worth nothing. Yes, for the employee who accepts options as compensation instead of salary it is a risk.

Offer equity: When might you want to pay an employee in company Equity instead of paying them a salary? Certain qualities in your employees or partners are hard to come by. If you are a startup, you need all the help you can get. Equity can be a great way to incentivize individuals to make a long-term commitment to the company. These individuals need to be people who add value that goes way beyond that of a regular employee.

If an employee takes equity in a company instead of a salary, or along with a reduced salary, that employee becomes part owner of the company and thereby will have a right to share in the big rewards if that company is successful. That also means, the employee shares the same risks as other company owners. For the sake of all involved the founder should write out the details of the equity agreement in a contract. If the employee wants to be paid more money in the future, it's mutually understood that in exchange for the raise, that employee will be giving back some of the equity.

If a company becomes successful having equity in that company is far more valuable than cash. Employees should be aware that just because they have equity in a company doesn't mean that they are going to become a millionaire. It is best to have reasonable expectations for the future of the company and not believe that the company will be wildly successful before it happens. Remember that great companies are not built overnight.

Finance

Now it's time to remember that horrible truth. Research shows that 95% of new businesses that fail in their first 5 years fail due to lack of capital which is often the result of poor financial management. Don't fool yourself, businesses run on money. Financial decisions you make in regards to long-term funding strategies and how you manage your cash-flow will determine whether your company survives and thrives or crashes and burns. As an entrepreneur building a successful business depends on you developing the skills it takes to use your capital wisely and effectively. In addition to the day to day management of the business finances you must also access if and when the company needs a new injection of cash and how much. Putting together a sound financial strategy will keep your company profitable and increase your chances to take advantage of new opportunities by having ample cash on hand when new opportunities present themselves.

Profit and Loss Statement

Your balance sheet provides information about how much you own and how much you owe. It is a snapshot of your overall financial picture at a moment in time. Your profit and loss report, or income statement, provides information about how much your company has earned or lost during the statement's period. Net profit (or loss) is calculated by subtracting total expenditures such as rent, materials and payroll from total revenue. It is also broken down by categories such as wholesale and retail. A profit and loss statement is important to business finance because it shows whether your company can handle new expenses such as investments in equipment or property. Just because your business shows a net profit on its income statement doesn't mean you'll have the cash you need to pay off loans or buy new equipment. Be aware there are some outgoing expenditures, such as payments on a loan principal that use up available cash without appearing on your profit and loss as expenses.

Finance and Capital Investments

When your business makes purchases of equipment or property that have lasting value, your financial status will become a determining factor in whether your business can afford the expense. It is not uncommon for long-term capital investments to require loans. If that is the route you take to pay for expenses you'll need to consider how much of an expense the principal payments, plus interest will amount to. Your business will need to earn enough to cover these upcoming expenditures. A cash flow "pro forma" is a very helpful tool for business forecasting and planning. You can enter the amounts of anticipated principal and interest and play with other variables to find the best way of making payments. As an example, if you are investing in equipment that will result in reducing labor costs, your pro forma will show how far these savings in labor will go toward meeting payments on the equipment.

When you make capital investment purchases you can use business finance to weigh the pros and cons of different repayment options. You may have a choice between a lower-interest loan with a high monthly payment and a quick repayment period, versus a higher-interest option with lower monthly payments over a longer period of time. If you are the company's Chief Financial Officer, or the executive in charge of finances a lower-interest option is the best option if you have the cash flow to pay for it. But, if the company's cash flow is tight and the equipment upgrade will save you enough money to cover the added interest, choosing the interest and a lower monthly payment is better. These choices are important because lower payments help your cash flow and having good cash flow can put you in position to take advantage of profitable opportunities.

Finance and Working Capital

The financial concern for a business is to always have enough money coming in from sales of goods and services to pay for the daily operation of the business. But many businesses need some kind of funding to cover short-term expenses that sometimes exceed the company's incoming revenue. Some businesses are seasonal and earn the bulk of their revenue over a couple of months which means that revenue must cover the rest of the year during those periods when the company operates at a loss. There are companies that get busier late in the week or later in the month, but they must continue to spend capital to run the business through these slow periods. That capital must come from somewhere.

Be aware when seeking financing that securing working capital is easier than obtaining financing for major purchases and investments. Banks may offer unsecured credit cards and business credit lines you can use to cover business expenses without having to put up your personal collateral or fill out long loan applications that require extensive documentation. Before you jump at using one of these cards or lines of credit consider that unsecured financing interest rates tend to be considerably higher than rates for other business-lending products though those products such as secured term loans are harder to obtain. Because of their high interest rates it's smart to use these loan products only for short-term needs and even then to pay off your balances as soon as possible.

Finance and Retained Earnings

Let's define the word finance. The term "finance" can be used as a noun describing the process of managing your company's money. It is also used as a verb meaning, "to secure capital from an outside source through a loan or investment." Despite this association with borrowing, you can also use business finance to manage the funds you have available from regular business activities, such as sales of products or services or rent on property you own. These retained earnings are an appealing source of operating or investment capital because unlike loans you don't have to pay interest on them. You also don't have to convince a banker or investor that your project is worthwhile, and you don't have to do all the paperwork that is required for a loan application.

Don't think you have to rely exclusively on retained earnings for your short-term cash flow or longer-term investments. By doing so you may lose out on opportunities you could have taken advantage of if you'd had more money available. A lucrative contract may be offered to your business that requires more of a capital outlay than you can make if you have limited available cash. The cost of losing that business can be higher than the interest you would have paid if you had borrowed the money. Another such scenario may be that you own a retail store that you manage on a strict budget, making it impossible for you to buy enough inventory to provide customers with a wide enough selection to compete with your better stocked competitors. So, while primarily working with money from retained earnings may seem like a more disciplined financial strategy it may end up costing you customers and profits in the long run.

It is smart to have backup sources of financing in place so when you need additional cash it's available for you so you can take advantage of opportunities before they disappear. Not having enough cash on hand can cause a number of setbacks for your business like you having to pass up purchasing equipment you need, or not having enough available money when an emergency occurs. If building a successful business is your goal being proficient at managing your finances and making sure your finance department is running properly can make or break your business.

Deeper

Business, like sports, is all about competition. In order for one business to gain market share another business has to lose market share. When a customer says yes to using a service or buying a product from one company that customer is saying no to doing the same with another company. Solidifying your advantage over rival companies or increasing your share of the market is what digging a deeper foundation is all about. Here are some things that if adopted and taken advantage of can give your company a deeper competitive advantage over your competitors. If you want to compete in today's environment you need to know about The Internet of Things (IoT).

The Internet of Things (Io T)

The internet of things, or IoT, is a system of interrelated computing devices, mechanical and digital machines, etc. that are provided with unique identifiers (UIDs) and the ability to transfer data over a network without requiring human-to-human or human-to-computer interaction. A person with a heart monitor implant, a cow with a biochip transponder, an automobile that has built-in sensors to alert the driver when he or she is weaving out of the lane, any natural or man-made object that can be assigned an IP address and is able to transfer data over a network is a part of The Internet of Things (IoT).

Taking advantage of the IoT can help your business to operate more efficiently, better understand your customers, improve the decisions you make, and help you deliver a better customer experience.

What Is The Internet of Things?

Kevin Ashton, co-founder of the Auto-ID Center at MIT, first mentioned the internet of things in a presentation he made to Procter & Gamble (P&G) in 1999. Wanting to bring radio frequency ID (RFID) to the attention of P&G's senior management, Ashton called his presentation "Internet of Things" because it centered on that new technology breakthrough of 1999 called the internet. The year 1999 was also when MIT professor Neil Gershenfeld's book, "When Things Start to Think", appeared. Though the exact term Internet of Things was not used in the book nonetheless it provided a clear picture of where IoT was going.

IoT evolved from the convergence of wireless technologies, microelectromechanical systems (MEMS), microservices and the internet. This convergence bridged the gap between operational technology (OT) and information technology (IT), enabling unstructured machine-generated data to be mined for insights that can then be used to make improvements. Though Ashton's was the first mention of the internet of things, by name, connected devices have been around since the 1970s.

The phrases embedded internet and pervasive computing are essentially referring to connected devices.

The IoT evolved from machine-to-machine (M2M) communication, i.e., machines connecting to each other via a network without human interaction. M2M refers to connecting a device to the cloud, managing it and collecting data. By taking M2M to the next level, IoT added a sensor network of billions of smart devices that connect people, systems and other applications to collect and share data. So, at the foundation of IoT, is M2M which provides the connectivity that enables it.

The internet of things is also a natural extension of SCADA (supervisory control and data acquisition), which is a category of software application for process control. SCADA is the gathering of data in real time from remote locations to control equipment and conditions. SCADA systems include hardware and software components. The hardware gathers and feeds data into a computer that has SCADA software installed. The data is then processed and presented in a timely manner. The evolution of SCADA is such that late-generation SCADA systems developed into first-generation IoT systems. The IoT ecosystem took a giant leap forward in the middle of 2010 when, in part, the government of China said it would make IoT a strategic priority in its five-year plan.

How IoT works

The IoT has forever changed the way we live. Smart buildings can reduce energy costs using sensors that detect how many occupants are in a room. If sensors detect a conference room is full the temperature can be adjusted automatically by the sensor communicating to the thermostat. It can then turn down the air conditioning or heat if everyone in the office has gone home. In a smart city, IoT sensors and devices such as smart streetlights and smart meters can improve traffic flow, conserve energy, monitor and address environmental concerns and improve sanitation. In agriculture, IoT-based smart farming systems can help monitor light, humidity, temperature, automate irrigation systems, monitor crop and cattle yields and predict their growth patterns, and monitor soil moisture of crop fields all by using connected sensors. IoT applications span numerous verticals, including automotive, telecom, medical, energy, construction, and more. Applications of the internet of things, range from consumer IoT and enterprise IoT, to manufacturing and industrial IoT.

An IoT ecosystem consists of web-enabled smart devices that use embedded processors, sensors and communication hardware to collect, send and act on data they acquire from their environments. IoT devices share the sensor data they collect by connecting to an IoT gateway or other edge device where data is either sent to the cloud to be analyzed or analyzed locally. These devices can communicate with other related devices and act on the information they get from one another. The devices are able to do most of this work without human intervention, although people can interact with the devices to set them up, give instructions or access the data. The connectivity, networking and communication protocols used with these web-enabled devices largely depend on the specific IoT applications deployed.

The era of IoT, has ushered in a consumer segment of smart devices that include smart homes equipped with smart thermostats, smart appliances and connected heating, lighting and electronic devices that can all be controlled remotely via computers and smartphones.

Wearable devices with sensors and software can collect and analyze user data, that can analyze a range of health issues and send its findings to other technologies. Public safety has been enhanced by wearable devices that improve the response time of first responders' during emergencies by providing more efficient routes to a location. These devices can also track firefighters' vital signs during life-threatening situations.

Why IoT is important

The internet of things helps people gain control over their lives by working smarter. Besides automating homes IoT has become essential to business. By using IoT your business can access real-time information into how effectively your company systems work. Smart devices can deliver insights into how effectively your machines are performing, supply chains and vendors are operating, and logistics is working. IoT helps companies reduce labor cost by automating processes. It can also cut down on waste and improve service delivery making it less expensive to manufacture and deliver goods. Given the competitive advantages of using IoT it is safe to say it will soon become indispensable to businesses.

The Benefits of IoT

The Internet of Things gives businesses a viable way to improve not only business but business strategies as well. The IoT can positively affect every area of your business by giving you the tools to monitor business processes, enhance employee productivity, improve the customer experience, better integrate and adapt business models, make better business decisions, and generate more revenue, while saving time and money.

The benefits of using IoT are obvious. It allows businesses to access information from anywhere, at any time, on any device. It improves communication between connected electronic devices. Perhaps most important of all, automating tasks helps save time and money by reducing the need for human intervention.

Some IoT security and privacy issues

For all its benefits and capabilities The Internet of Things does have some obvious downsides. It connects billions of devices to the internet and involves the use of billions of data points, all of which need to be secured. Due to its expanded attack surface, IoT security and IoT privacy are major concerns. As the number of connected devices increase and more information is shared between these devices the potential for hackers to steal confidential information increases as well.

By not updating their devices regularly manufacturers, businesses, and individuals leave themselves vulnerable to cybercriminals. One of the most notorious IoT attacks was Mirai, in 2016, when a botnet infiltrated domain name server provider Dyn and took down a host of websites for an extended period of time causing one of the most widely distributed denial-of-service (DDoS) attacks ever. Attackers were able to gain access to the network by exploiting poorly secured IoT devices. Because IoT devices are so closely connected, all a hacker has to do is exploit one vulnerability to manipulate all the data rendering it unusable.

What is the future of IoT?

The IoT is undoubtedly here to stay. So, what does the future hold for IoT and those who use it? Here is some insight that should convince you to jump onboard before the IoT train has completely left the station. Bain & Company expects annual IoT revenue of hardware and software to exceed $450 billion by 2020. McKinsey & Company estimates IoT will have an $11.1 trillion impact by 2025. IHS Markit believes the number of connected IoT devices will increase 12% annually to reach 125 billion by 2030. Gartner assesses that 20.8 billion connected things will be in use by 2020, with spending on IoT devices and services to reach $3.7 trillion in 2018.

To find out how you can connect your business to the IoT here are a few names you need to be familiar with:

Amazon Web Services (AWS) IoT, is a cloud platform for IoT released by Amazon. This framework is designed to enable smart devices to easily connect and securely interact with the AWS cloud and other connected devices.

Microsoft's Azure IoT Suite, is a platform that consists of a set of services that enables users to interact with and receive data from their IoT devices as well as perform various operations over data, such as multidimensional analysis, transformation and aggregation, visualizing those operations in a way that's suitable for business.

Google's Brillo/Weave, is a platform for the rapid implementation of IoT applications. The platform consists of two main backbones: Brillo, an android-based operating system for the development of embedded low power devices; and Weave, IoT-oriented communication protocol that serves as the communication language between the device and the cloud.

ARM Mbed IoT, is a platform to develop apps for the IoT based on ARM microcontrollers. The goal of the ARM Mbed IoT platform is to provide a scalable, connected and secure environment for IoT devices by integrating Mbed tools and services.

The Cloud

If you have not introduced your business to the cloud you are already behind the competition. Research experts Gartner, Inc. says global spending on public cloud services will grow 21.4 percent through 2018 to total $186.4 billion, up from $153.5 billion in 2017. Global spending on the public cloud by businesses is expected to reach $160 billion this year, according to researcher IDC. Spending is forecast to grow 21.9 percent during the next five years, with total investment hitting $277 billion in 2021.

What exactly is The Cloud? The Cloud is a set of services and features that can help a business achieve its goals. Businesses can match their objectives with a cloud service that give employees a more efficient way of reaching those objectives. Based on their goals and the costs of cloud services businesses must decide whether they should house cloud applications in-house, import services from an online provider, or outsource the work to an off-site cloud service provider. The cloud can be confusing to those who have not been trained to handle its complexities. Over the next 10 years fewer and fewer companies will still be housing their own data centers. It would be hard for a company's own IT department to match what Amazon, Microsoft, Google or Oracle can spend on cloud infrastructure. By using these and other cloud providers a company can tap into the shared pool of resources of a cloud ecosystem that can be delivered over the internet.

What Are the Four Types of Cloud Computing?

Cloud computing comes in two key forms: public and private. The public cloud is provided over the network by an external organization that offers services via their own data center infrastructure. Businesses can buy public resources (services) from these providers on-demand then scale them up or down as required.

Unlike the public cloud, the resources in a private cloud are spent on a single enterprise. Private clouds can be managed in-house or by an external partner. While private clouds can give your company the peace of mind of being located on-site they are costly. If your business grows to the point where you need to scale up your private cloud the expense will be much more than if you were using the public cloud.

The hybrid cloud is the third type of cloud computing and it sits between the public and private clouds. Hybrid cloud computing allows firms to combine private IT resources with public cloud provision. As an example, a company might choose to keep some data in the private cloud but shift other demands to the public cloud when business ramps up.

A number of companies choose to draw on a multi-cloud approach to cloud computing, which is the fourth type of cloud computing. This strategy allows businesses to use a host of providers with each specializing in delivering a specific set of services. By utilizing this broad ecosystem of hybrid cloud computing, organizations can spread their risks should a network go down by not having their entire workload housed with one provider. The multi-cloud approach also allows companies to choose providers based on what area of service the provider does best.

Three Layers Of The Cloud

Businesses can use a range of cloud service models. These models represent different levels of the computing stack that companies use to access cloud resources, by browser, app or a computing device. The different layers of cloud computing are easy to remember. Infrastructure as a service (IaaS) is the foundational layer upon which organizations deploy operating systems and applications. Platform as a service (PaaS) is the control layer through which businesses deploy cloud-based infrastructure resources. It is the development environment for application developers. The final stack of these layers is software as a service (SaaS), which is the customer-facing layer of the cloud. Clients can access a range of provider-based applications to handle various company tasks in areas like productivity, human resources, marketing, sales and finance. In addition to these service-models serverless computing is a specialist area where the end-user does not have to have servers to run their code on. In serverless computing, an external provider uses virtual cloud-based machines to provide businesses with cloud services for specific tasks. If you need to look into even more cloud application approaches you should look into containerization, and DevOps.

How Can Cloud Computing Help Your Business

Now that you have been briefed on the basics of cloud computing, the question is how can using its services benefit your company?

Provide Better Customer service

With customers being the most valuable thing a business has, cloud computing allows companies to create valuable apps for their customers, by which they can more easily access any number of services. The cloud can also enable your company to provide better customer support. You can use the cloud to provide 24/7 customer support. In addition to customer service, thanks to the cloud customers can purchase products, goods, and services around the clock. The cloud connects customers and employees by mobile device, laptop or desktop computer to conduct a wide range of business. This allows people worldwide to access the same information and services day or night. The cloud makes it possible for businesses big or small to have access to high-quality, and high-bandwidth services to host videos, or post training and how-to videos. Hosting these videos is now as simple as upgrading your cloud service to provide more bandwidth. Thanks to the cloud smaller companies now have the ability to put out the same high-quality web content as their larger competitors, much to the delight of their customers.

You Can See an Increase in Productivity

Businesses are using the cloud to get greater productivity out of their workplace by using it as a hub to store their communication, data, and processing. With these services being delivered over the web your employees can work 24/7 from anywhere in the world using an internet-connected device. Perhaps one of the best aspects of the cloud is it can be scaled to match your company's growth and upgrades can be as simple as adjusting your cloud service fees. The cloud can link your business to a variety of software options to help you increase efficiencies. Knowing that security is a big concern for most companies cloud service providers are constantly upgrading their security measures to meet security challenges.

Save Money on Your Infrastructure Costs

Adopting a cloud technology strategy can actually lower the costs of starting a business. Many startups today are experimenting with deploying an entirely remote workforce. Infrastructure costs for buildings, desks, chairs, and other costs related to building and running a business are being done away with by the cloud. Some business models have even eliminated costs by utilizing the cloud as their place of business instead of brick and mortar. The average worker now telecommutes 2 days a month. Having employees connect from home using their own devices, while still being able to communicate, interact, and collaborate with coworkers is changing the way business is done and profits are made. Some innovative companies have their employees split time between the office and home. By doing so they can have employees take turns using desks thus saving infrastructure costs. The days of executives guessing how many servers to buy are gone. Like any cloud-based technology, these services scale, so businesses can start with a cheaper cloud package and simply expand the capabilities of these services as the business grows. The wonders of the cloud allow employees to work from home and still have the entire office working right alongside them. From the largest businesses to the smallest, cloud technology is opening up a gamut of new applications and business models of which the possibilities seem endless.

What Is Fulfilment By Amazon?

With the creation of Fulfillment By Amazon a new day in business has certainly dawned. Businesses or individuals who do not have or cannot yet afford their own warehouse can take advantage of this fulfillment service to house, pick, pack, and ship their products. FBA is a service provided by Amazon that allows sellers to be absolutely flexible in how they sell and deliver their products to customers. FBA provides storage, packaging, and shipping assistance to businesses relieving them of that unnecessary burden. The program allows sellers to ship their merchandise to an Amazon fulfillment center, where items are stored in their warehouses until they are sold. Then when an order is placed, Amazon employees physically prepare, package, and ship the product(s) to the buyer.

What Are The Benefits of Using FBA Services

When businesses or sellers sign up for Fulfillment By Amazon they can take advantage of all of the resources and benefits associated with

Amazon and FBA. For a business to have their name associated with Amazon and their products can't hurt. This association is a quality guarantee that most buyers will appreciate, making them more prone to patronize a smaller seller.

Benefit from Subsidized Shipping Fees

Because Amazon has a relationship with the shipping companies sellers using FBA will be able to pay less in shipping costs than if the items were being delivered from another business or individual's account. Another benefit is that sellers can offer free shipping over a certain purchase amount since products sold through FBA are eligible for Amazon Prime and FREE Super Saver Shipping.

FBA Offers Multi-Channel Fulfillment

Amazon can ship and handle not only products being sold through the Amazon marketplace but also inventory that is being sold through multiple channels. All FBA orders are processed in exactly the same way Amazon handles its own merchandise. When someone purchases an item, Amazon picks the item from their inventory, packs the item, and ships it to the buyer. Plus, a seller can feature an item on his or her own website, as well as through the Fulfillment By Amazon service, and have Amazon take care of all the heavy lifting.

What are the FBA Fees?

Amazon charges several kinds of fees to FBA members. For Standard Seller Fees: Amazon takes approximately 15-18% of the product price as a seller's fee when an item is sold. The exact percentage varies depending on the product. Though Amazon may charge 15%, be aware that there are some hidden costs such as refunds that are not fully charged back, which increases the overall charge to the seller. There are also storage fees, pick and pack fees, and weight-handling fees. Amazon charges the seller a fee to store all the items, another fee to pick the items, and a weight-based fee when an order ships. Amazon now offers Global Export, which allows sellers to send their inventory all over the world garnering international sells.

Deepest

Putting the Digital Universe To Work For You

Digital Marketing

The world has changed, and with that change has come changes to the way business is done. Technology has opened a new world of possibilities for entrepreneurs, business owners, and executives worldwide. You can create, sell, and ship products around the globe from the comfort of your own living room using technologies and a web space that makes you appear as impressive as the big boys. By taking advantage of technologies like The Internet of Things, cloud computing, and digital marketing, your company can dig the deepest competitive advantages possible. Here are some of the components you can use:

Search Engine Optimization (SEO)

Search engines search through billions of pieces of content and evaluate thousands of factors to determine which content is most likely to answer a query by someone on the internet. Search engines do their work by discovering and cataloguing all available content on the Internet (web pages, PDFs, images, videos, etc.) by a process known as "crawling and indexing." They then put content in order by how well it matches the query. This process is referred to as "ranking."

What Are "Organic" Search Results?

Organic search results are the ones that are earned through effective SEO, not paid for (i.e. not advertising). Organic results used to be easy to spot. Ads were clearly labeled as such and the remaining results typically took the form of "10 blue links" listed below them. But with the way search has changed, how can we spot organic results today?

Today, search engine results pages, often referred to as "SERPs", are filled with both more advertising and more dynamic organic results formats (called "SERP features") than ever before. Some examples of SERP features are featured snippets (or answer boxes), People Also Ask boxes, image carousels, etc. and new SERP features continue to emerge, driven largely by what people are seeking.

For example, if you search for "Houston weather," you'll see a weather forecast for the city of Houston directly in the SERP instead of a link to a site that might have that forecast. And, if you search for "Houston restaurants," you'll see a "local pack" result made up of Houston restaurants. It's important to remember that search engines make money from advertising. Their goal is to better solve searcher's queries (within SERPs), to keep searchers coming back, and to keep them on the SERPs longer. Some SERP features on Google are organic and can be influenced by SEO. These include featured snippets (a promoted organic result that displays an answer inside a box) and related questions (a.k.a. "People Also Ask" boxes). It's worth noting that there are many other search features that, even though they aren't paid advertising, can't typically be influenced by SEO. These features often have data acquired from proprietary data sources, such as Wikipedia, IMDb, and WebMD.

What Makes SEO so important?

While it is true paid advertising, social media, and other online platforms can generate traffic for websites, the majority of online traffic ending up on websites is driven by search engines.

Organic search results cover more digital real estate, appear more credible to savvy searchers, and receive way more clicks than paid advertisements. For example, of all US searches, it is estimated only 2.8% of people click on paid advertisements. SEO generates 20X more traffic opportunities than PPC on both mobile and desktop. SEO is also one of the only online marketing sources that, when set up correctly, can continue to pay dividends over time. If you provide a solid piece of content that deserves to rank for the right keywords, your traffic can snowball over time, whereas paid advertising needs continuous funding to send traffic to your site.

Search engines are getting smarter, but they still need our help. Optimizing your site will help deliver better information to search engines so that your content can be properly indexed and displayed within search results giving you a better chance of generating traffic to your site. Search engine optimization is more important now than ever. Therefore, it is necessary for every webmaster to understand the true meaning of SEO as well as the potential it creates for your business.

What is SEO?

Search engine optimization or SEO in short, is a set of rules for optimizing your website for search engines. They improve your search engine rankings. It is a great way to increase the quality of your web site by making it user- friendly, faster and easier to navigate. SEO can be considered as a complete framework since the whole process has a number of rules (or guidelines), a number of stages and a set of controls.

In today's competitive market, SEO marketing is more important than ever. Search engines serve millions of users per day looking for answers to their questions or for solutions to their problems. If you have a web site, blog or online store, SEO can help your business grow and meet its business objectives.

Technical SEO

The first stage in the SEO process is called technical SEO. As the name implies, technical SEO has nothing to do with the actual content of a website or with website promotion methods. It refers to the settings you need to configure to make the job of search engine crawlers easier. Usually, once you get your technical SEO correct, you may not have to deal with it again. But, if you have problems with crawling and indexing, it can negatively impact on your rankings.

On-site SEO

Next comes On-Page SEO. On-Page SEO has to do primarily with the content and other elements found on a page. Unlike technical and off-page SEO, the main focus of on-page SEO is to provide search engine crawlers enough signals so that they can understand the meaning and context of your content. Search engines don't read a page like humans so they are looking for signals to figure out what a page is all about. With On-site SEO you are dealing with website structure, including SEO keywords, title optimizations, headings, internal links, image SEO, structured data markup and other techniques that can send the right signals to search engines. If done correctly, on-page SEO will also improve the usability and credibility of your website or blog.

Off-site SEO

The third stage of building a website that ranks higher in the SERPs, is Off-Page SEO. Off-site SEO is generally known as link building but promoting a website involves much more than building links. When a user types a search query, search engine algorithms look into their index and try to find the best pages to satisfy the intent of the user. Pages that are good candidates appear at the first positions of the search results. One of the factors that determines the position a webpage shows up in the results, is the number of incoming links (backlinks) it has. Backlinks signal that the site is trusted. Depending on where the links are coming, they can greatly affect your site's ranking position. If the links are coming from well-known and trusted sites, your ranking will be positively affected. On the other hand, if they are paid links, links in article directories, link farms, or a result of exchanging links, your ranking will be negatively affected. Getting links this way, is a violation of Google guidelines and most likely will also result in a Google Penalty.

So, what can you do to get more links the right way? Actually, your focus should not be link building. Your primary focus should be how to create good quality content for your web site because good content will get you natural links which in turn will give you high rankings and traffic. People who try to buy links or get them the easy way may have temporary success but they will soon see their website disappear from the top search pages after the next Google update.

For websites wanting to rank high in search results good content is still the most important success factor. With this in mind, realize that SEO cannot help your site if it does not have good content. The best of both worlds is creating a website or blog that has great content and great SEO.

To sum it up, search engine optimization (SEO) is a way to optimize your website so that search engines will understand it better and give you higher rankings. If you put together try to SEO a website with not very good content your chances of succeeding (in the long term) are minimal. On the other hand, a website with good content can do well with or without SEO. Good SEO will just give the web site an extra boost.

Social Media Marketing

The days of plastering your message all over a billboard, newspaper, magazine, or broadcasting it over radio or television are fading into the distance. With the advent of the Internet and all that entails there are many exciting new marketing avenues to explore. Social Media Marketing is not only the hot spot for reaching prospective customers, it is probably the best spot to find millennials and the more recent generations. If you want to capture your audience through social media marketing it is important that you know some important performance indicators so you will know how to measure your marketing success. The most important of these indicators are called Key Performance Indicators (KPIs).

A **Key Performance Indicator** is a measurable value that demonstrates how effectively a company is achieving key business objectives. Organizations use KPIs at multiple levels to evaluate their success at reaching targets. High-level KPIs may focus on the overall performance of the business, while low-level KPIs may focus on processes in departments such as sales, marketing, HR, support and others. Here are some social media KPIs that you should know:

Frequency: Number of posts published

Traffic Generation: Referrals or quality visits from social media channels

Audience Growth: New followers and fans

Reach: Paid and Organic (or Earned/Owned) reach and impressions

Engagement: Interactions, video views, comments, shares

Lead Generation: Leads generated from social media campaigns or channels

Lead Nurturing: Visits from prospects in the nurturing funnel stage from social

Customer Acquisition: New customers closed attributed to social media campaigns

Customer Retention: Number of engaged members in your private Facebook Group

Customer Support: Inquiries and tickets resolved through social channels

Here are the most popular social media sites that you can use for your social media marketing campaigns. **Top 20 Social Media Sites by Monthly Users (2019).**

1. Facebook – 2.32 Billion
2. YouTube – 1.9 Billion
3. Whatsapp – 1.6 Billion
4. Messenger – 1.3 Billion
5. WeChat – 1.01 Billion
6. Instagram – 1 Billion
7. QQ – 807 Million
8. Qzone – 532 Million
9. Tik Tok – 500 Million
10. Sina Weibo – 462 Million
11. Tumblr – 437 Million
12. Reddit – 330 Million
13. Twitter – 330 Million
14. LinkedIn – 303 Million
15. Douban – 300 Million
16. Baidu Tieba – 300 Million
17. Snapchat – 287 Million
18. Viber – 260 Million
19. Pinterest – 250 Million
20. Discord – 250 Million

Even with a fantastic social media marketing plan still you must not forget that SEO, and good marketing alone can't build you a great company. To build the deepest competitive advantage there is a key area you absolutely must establish excellence in if you want to have a great company.

A Great Company achieves excellence by having great employees

Great Companies Have Great People

It may sound obvious, but finding great people is harder than you may think. People come and people go. Having a company full of great people means that you not only have to hire great people but you also have to keep them. So how do Great Companies find the great people they need and retain them?

Locating the People You Need

Today the easiest way to locate prospective employees is by using online job sites or job boards. Be aware that when you post job listings on online job boards, they tend to quickly get pushed down the ranks and disappear from view within a matter of days. However, a few sites like, Indeed, let you sponsor your job postings so they stand out from the crowd and appear at the top (and bottom) of search result pages for as long as you'd like. The longer your job posting is viewed the better chance you'll get quality job seekers to choose from. The more quality people you attract the faster you can fill your roster with top-notch applicants.

A great company workforce is usually a diverse workforce. By extending your search outside your own company and usual channels you will increase your chances of finding diverse candidates. Crowdsourcing is another source that enables you to hear about experts from other experts outside of your internal network. Using crowdsourcing allows your company to finding top talent and achieve greater company diversity. Also, remember it's not about finding the most people, it's about finding the best people for your company and its culture.

Don't overlook colleges and universities. Volunteering to speak at colleges for individual classes and building strong relationships with the professors who teach courses within your industry is highly recommended. I'd recommend small businesses form strong relationships with their local colleges and universities. You can cover your bases by using professional recruiting sites like ZipRecruiter or LinkedIn, but don't neglect to focus on homegrown talent right in your own backyard. By collaborating with colleges and universities you can essentially let them do the recruiting for you. Make full use of your collegiate connections by asking professors to recommend top-tier candidates for hiring.

Make an effort to word your job advertisement properly. To many companies use overly masculine language. By sending out such signals it's not surprising when job advertisements get a poor response from women. By inadvertently aiming your ad towards a male audience you are missing out on half the qualified candidates. If you make your listing more gender neutral, you'll appeal to candidates who may have otherwise overlooked your post. Don't just list the obvious candidate requirements, salary, and benefits information. Go the extra step and talk about your company culture.

While you are on the lookout for great employees you should realize that nearly 50% of job seekers search for better job opportunities through their mobile phones. Therefore, in this digital age having a mobile-friendly hiring process is one of the best methods to attract potential candidates. Optimize your business website or app for mobile phones so possible candidates can instantly learn about, evaluate, and accept your job offers. Mobile optimization is the surest way to find the best employees for your business today.

Retain Your Great Employees

One way to retain great employees once you find them is to give your employees the opportunity to learn and grow professionally. Your managers should look for ways to match their employees' skills and passions with the organization's needs. Of course, this requires them to notice what individual employees are good at doing in order to promote their strengths. Managers should also find out what their employees are interested in learning or accomplishing, to help those with excellent potential advance their careers. Structure your workplace, policies, procedures, and processes to ensure that employees are working with people they respect for the work they do and how they contribute to great company culture.

Create a Culture of Trust.

Never forget that employees in Great Companies trust the people they work for because they are treated with fairness, respect, and honesty. Trust is a powerful retention tool and you should honor that fact. Your employees may not always agree with the decisions your management makes but as long as they trust that these decisions are legal, ethical, and ultimately in their best interest they will be on board for the success of the company.

Lastly, great companies allow their employees to make mistakes, in order to figure things out, perfect their skills, and solve problems. They also reward and celebrate successes while encouraging their employees to stretch themselves and their capabilities. For employees that want to excel challenging work is a motivational tool for retaining their services.

Chapter 10: Elevation

Success is not the end of the journey. It is great to be successful, but the ultimate success happens when you reach your full potential. Chapter 10, Elevation, leads you through the growth it will take to reach your full potential. Reaching the high, higher, and highest levels of success is possible but ascending to these heights can be as dangerous as it is exhilarating. As is often said, "No Risk, No reward." Elevation is about going up. Gravity will always try to pull you down. But, becoming successful is about trying and trying until you break free of that resistance and ascend to the heights you were created to reach.

High

No one knows what success is for you, except you. For some people success means money. For others its peace of mind. Still some more people believe that success equates to how much power one has. So, again, only you can define what success is for you. Whatever you define as success still one thing remains true, you will never reach it without effort, and without taking chances. When you take a chance you run the risk of failing. If you have a fear of failure you will never elevate yourself to the high, higher, and highest places you were created to go. It is up to you to live up to your potential. No one can do it for you. Now, if you are ready to soar open your mind and let's build you a rocket to the stars. Let's begin with the parts you will need.

Set Your Goal

Don't take a step until you have defined what your ultimate destination is. Would you go to an airport and buy a ticket to anywhere? No. When you go to the airport and buy a ticket it is because you want to go to a specific place. Once you know where you are going you can take the next steps to determine what you need to pack, begin to map out how you are going to get to the airport, see what plane you have to take, what gate the plane leaves from, where you are going to eat, and a number of other important steps. None of this happens until you decide what your destination is. Setting a goal is setting a destination for your life. Once you do this you can begin to map out the steps you must take to get to that destination.

Until you set a goal and begin to pursue it you are just drifting aimlessly through life. Once you set your goal be sure to write it down. When you write it down it solidifies the goal in your mind and at that point it becomes real. Write it out in as much detail as you can. Along the way you will have to make some adjustments to stay on course and that's alright. However, before you can adjust anything you must first have something to adjust. Writing down your goal is step one.

Set Specific Goals

When you set goals those goals should be clear and specific. If goals are vague or too general they will not provide you with enough direction to set good objectives. You will need to reach specific objectives to reach your goal. Your goal should define exactly where you plan to end up and your objectives should mark the individual milestones you will need to accomplish to get there. Once you set these goals and objectives your path should be as easy to follow as connecting the dots.

Set Goals You Can Measure

As the great Peter Drucker said, "If you can't measure it, you can't manage it." When you set your goals make them precise. Write down the precise date you intend to reach your goal, and the dates you will need to achieve each of your objectives. Write out a monthly budget and how you expect the money and resources to be allocated. Write down who is responsible for doing what and when they should complete doing it. If you don't set actual dates and place time limits on things how can you hope to be efficient? Employees need to know how and when an objective has to be reached? Without these timetables you can't coordinate your efforts or measure success. If you can't measure it, you can't manage it, or instruct people on whether they are doing a good job or not, or tell them how to do it better. You cannot manage ambiguity or people who just get things done whenever.

Set Goals That Are Meaningful

Set goals that will lead you to the things you want to accomplish. What sense does it make to set goals that lead you away from where you want to end up? All your objectives should point directly to your goals, and all your goals should lead you directly to where you want to end up. By keeping your goals and objectives in alignment it will help you to remain focused and stay on point. If your goals are not relevant to what you are trying to accomplish they are nothing more than a waste of time. Once you set these goals be consistent in following through with them. Remember, everything matters. If you follow through on the big things but overlook the small details, you are setting yourself up for failure. If you want to succeed set goals that are meaningful and do things that are meaningful.

Set Goals That Can Be Attained

I've heard people say, "Set goals that are beyond your reach if you want to achieve great things." While this may sound good, it may lead people to achieving more stress than greatness. Set goals that you can attain with hard work. They may take time, and money, and resources, and determination, and perseverance, but you know you can reach goals that are attainable, so it keeps you motivated to keep trying. Once you reach these goals you can always set bigger and higher goals. But, don't set ridiculous goals that discourage you before you can even get a chance to see what you are capable of. That will only demoralize you and kill your confidence. Your goals should be attainable but challenging.

Determining What Your Goal Should Be

For many people reading the preceding paragraph may only cause confusion because they don't have a clue what their goal should be. Let me make this easy for you. Do what you LOVE. If you have a passion for something there is a reason for that. It is generally because you have a gift or talent for it. You may have to grow or nurture that talent, but it is there. Some people get thrown off course because they feel that they do not have the ability to do something professionally. Let's say they have a passion for playing basketball but not the ability to play it at a professional level. Still, there are plenty of jobs that go along with basketball. There are players, coaches, announcers, scouts, analysts, journalists, marketing reps, general managers, statisticians, cheerleaders, security, ushers, and dozens of other jobs connected with the running of professional basketball teams. So, if basketball is your love there are plenty of jobs to choose from other than being on the court. No matter what your passion is there is a way to make a living from it. Do your research, lay out your strategy, put in the work, market it, promote it, and turn your passion and gift into a goal and career.

Only Massive Action Will Do

If you want to accomplish the incredible you must do the improbable. Big goals require big actions. Only massive action will achieve the goal and lifestyle you desire. Doing the ordinary will not achieve the extraordinary. People who go into business and expect to work less have no idea what it takes to succeed. If your competition is giving 100% effort how do you expect to beat them with 75% effort? If your competition is using a water hose, you must use a firehose. If they use a shovel you better break out the skip loader. It takes massive action to overcome and outdo your competitors and you best plan for nothing less. With good planning and preparation you can work smarter but that does not mean you won't have to work hard. If you want to succeed let me say it again, only massive action will do.

Prepare to Win

Champions prepare themselves to win. They don't prepare themselves just enough to finish second, third, or fourth. One of the first things you need to do before you begin your journey on the road to success is determine what training, education, or experience you will need in order to achieve your goal. Then figure out when you will need it. All you know is what you know. If your competitor knows more than you, that's a problem. If your competitor is better trained than you, that's a problem. If your competitor has more experience than you, that's a problem. Any area of expertise that allows your competitor to have an advantage over you becomes a problem for you. That is why making sure you are the best trained, best educated, and strategically sound player in your field is the only way to go. When you do that you are preparing to win. Great preparation will absolutely help you win the day.

Make A Plan of Action

First you write your goal, or if necessary, goals. Then you write the objectives needed to reach your goals. Then write out your plan of action. Your plan of action are all the things you need to do and steps you need to take to reach your objectives. Sometimes people get so focused on the outcome that they forget to plan out all the steps they need to take along the way. Once you write out the individual steps you need to take you now have a plan of action that can serve as your map to guide you day by day. Use this map to determine how well, or not so well, you are doing as you chase your goal. Each time you complete one of the steps cross it off your list. By using this plan of action checklist you can monitor your progress. You will especially find this helpful and encouraging if you are pursuing a goal that is difficult or long-term.

Talk It, Walk It, Live It

Success is not a slogan. It's a lifestyle. Successful people talk success. They walk success. And, they live success. If you want to be successful you must do the same thing. Successful people don't talk in 'ifs' and maybes. They don't behave as though what they are aiming to accomplish will not happen. They don't live as though the world is too tough or too scary for them. Learning to talk, walk, and live success is all a part of attaining it. People want to do business with confident people, not people who are unsure of themselves. People want to do business with people who dress like success, drive their success, live a successful lifestyle, and yes, talk success. Talk success. Know your numbers, production costs, breakeven points, identifying your market segments. Walk success. Be the living embodiment of your company. Promote, market, and stand behind the quality of your company, its products, and services. Live it. Successful people treat others with respect, they shoulder their fair share of community responsibilities, and share their success through philanthropy. Your company will rise only as high as you can fly with it. Don't let your limitations be your company's limitations. Be the excellence you strive for with your company. When it comes to elevation aim high and strive with all your might to reach that high mark.

Higher

261

After you have reached a high level of performance by upping your personal game it's time to take things to a higher level by lifting your company to a higher level. When asked which companies people are clamoring to work for the list usually includes names like Google, Netflix, Facebook, Zappos, and Microsoft. The list is a result of the strong interest these companies place on building a great work environment and perk rich employee culture. These companies and others like them pour millions of dollars into creating the ultimate workplace for their employees and the result is a strong internal company culture to go along with their highly respected brand recognition.

Without Vision Nothing Happens

Having a clear vision for your company is step one for rallying your employees around the company cause. A clearly defined and compelling vision should be a rallying cry for not only your employees but your customers as well. It should be something that makes your customers want to support you. Your vision is your identity. It tells customers what you value. Your vision is a big part of that higher mark you want your employees to reach. Once you establish your vision you must then communicate it to your employees. It should appear on your website, print and broadcast media content, be proclaimed in meetings, and conveyed in the company's promotions and advertisements.

Higher Performance Levels Begin with Great Leadership

Great companies are not the result of leaders who are indecisive. Neither are they usually the result of merciless tyrants who drive their employees to the point of collapse. Great companies are the result of leaders that make good decisions even when they are under extraordinary pressure to do so. Guiding an organization to profitability and longevity is not for the faint of heart. Great leadership and great companies go hand in hand. These leaders know how to build strong relationships with their employees while at the same time holding them accountable to the highest standards. Without doubt, great companies begin with great leadership.

Legendary former GE, leader and CEO, Jack Welch says great leaders have 5 Traits.

1. Positive Energy

Leaders neither exhibit a lack of energy nor negative energy; they have an inbuilt positive energy. Positive energy drives someone forward through good times and bad. Positive energy enables an individual whether working alone or managing a team to see the future they want to create and to keep going until they break through the barriers and create it.

2. The Ability to Energize Others

Positive energy is infectious. It not only rubs off on the team, but it becomes part of who they are. Team members see and feel the leader's energy. It attracts them and they want to copy that powerful trait. A positively charged team accomplishes goals, works through problems, and develops its own energy. That energy drives them all forward and keeps them wanting to succeed.

3. Edge

Welch uses this word to define the leader who can make difficult decisions. Decisions are based on knowledge, experience and, quite often, gut. Leaders give decisive answers – a definite "Yes" or a definite "No". They do not waffle or wander off topic because a problem is complicated or has support from both sides of the argument. Leaders have authority and responsibility. That is not always an easy position to be in. Hire the right people, fire the wrong people, support the right project or cancel the wrong one. Leaders know they must make decisions, so they set about learning enough to be able to make the right decision more often than the wrong decision or no decision at all.

4. The Talent to Execute

Leaders get things done. They learn, they consider, they decide, and they implement. Decisions without follow-through are not decisions, they are just conversation. Leaders get things done and they earn a track record for getting things done. The net result is that others want to follow them – and get more things done.

5. Passion

Leaders care deeply about themselves, their team, their goals, the organization as a whole, the market they are in and the markets they want to get into. They also care deeply about their customer base. People who are passionate about these things become driven. They have to succeed. That passion, just like positive energy fuels the team and the team's actions as a whole.

Make Customer Service A Priority

As you do all these things to take your business to a higher level don't neglect the item that belongs at the top of your list of priorities. If you don't provide your customers with excellent service none of the other things may matter. Your customer base is responsible for your success. Be sure to pay attention to customer concerns and handle concerns quickly and fairly. It is also important to understand customers so you can anticipate and fulfill their needs. Customers that feel appreciated and cared for will stick with you and continue to utilize your services. Whatever else you do make customer service a priority.

Reward Your Employees

A whopping 39% of people feel under-appreciated at work, and 77% say they would work harder if they got more recognition. Consider Netflix's approach to people-focused HR, which is one that routinely evaluates its employees by their accomplishments and abilities, rather than number of hours worked or other formulaic HR rules. Good companies offer a flexible vacation and family leave policy that rewards employees for their hard work. Such generous benefits fuel the desire in employees to work hard and continue achieving at a high level. Hire the right people, with the right attitude, skill, and work ethic, then reward them for their excellence.

As a business leader don't be reluctant to establish a good incentive structure because you think it might be too expensive. Rewarding excellence doesn't have to be cost prohibitive. Remember, monetary incentives are just one method of motivating employees for their success in the workplace. Offering flexible work schedules, hosting social events, and providing more career development opportunities are other great ways to reward hard-working employees. Don't overlook the impact of a simple compliment or other daily encouragements. Praising the hard work of employee's goes a long way in fostering a sense of company loyalty.

Focus on Your Strengths

Know who you are. Each business has a unique identity and strengths that make them who they are. When businesses forget who they are or fail to play to their strengths it usually causes problems. Good companies focus on their main strength then use seamless execution to make sure they get their products or services into the hands of their customers. Don't make the mistake of chasing new opportunities or expanding your product line at the expense of your primary product or service. It is delivering that favorite product or service, with great customer service that makes your company special in the eyes of customers. It is hard to carve out a consumer niche so don't lose it.

Be Willing to Take Risks

Whole Foods Market, is an example of a company that took a big risk and saw that risk pay off. Today, you can go to just about any major city and find a market selling natural foods. In fact, most grocery store chains now have whole sections devoted to natural and organic lines. But back in the 1970s, that wasn't the case. When co-founders Renee Lawson Hardy, John Mackey, Craig Weller, and Mark Skiles opened their business the chances of them failing were pretty high. Still they left already-successful grocery store businesses to invest in a supermarket devoted exclusively to natural foods. As we can all attest Whole Foods became a highly successful supermarket. After years of success the chain was purchased by Amazon.

Most successful businesses have founders that were passionate enough about their business to take the risks of starting it and growing it. Though starting a business is ripe with dangers, nonetheless taking risks can lead to great success. Business owners must be courageous enough to take advantage of opportunities, cultural changes, and advances in technology to grab their share of the market. But, taking risk does not mean that you should be reckless. Before you take risk be smart enough to take the precautions that come with diligent planning. Risks should be backed up by the good research, training and preparation that will minimize the chances of failure.

Take Advantage of Technology

As a business owner you should be fully aware of the developments in technology. Be willing to embrace and take advantage of those technologies that can help your company reach its goals. Look for technologies that give you operational efficiency or allow you to reach more consumers with your products or services. You can find new technologies that make it possible for you to improve your company's HR department, sales department, finance department, marketing department, management and every other facet of your business. Technologies like cloud computing, artificial intelligence, robotics, and software of every kind now make it possible to increase profits and efficiency with minimal expense to your company. The opportunity to optimize your business by using your website to keep the doors of your business open 24 hours, to using social media to increase brand awareness, to using cloud computing and the Internet of Things to increase business productivity, technology has made it possible to capture a host of opportunities that once may have been out of reach.

Ethics is More Than A Motto

Today, many employees are motivated to work for companies that believe in the same values they do. Ethics is something that should be shared by both your company and your employees. As one of the world's most recognizable companies Google's code of conduct, "Don't be evil," reflects what the company stands for, namely, hiring great people, building strong products, and respecting their users. Promoting and working to attain these high standards places Google on the list of favorite places to work. As a leader you should know that ethics pays off not just for customers but also for the companies that practice it. Research shows 75% of Millennials would take a pay cut to work for a responsible company, especially if it contributes to social and environmental issues. Companies that perform ethically and contribute to the welfare of the community through outreach, volunteer work, and donations to worthy causes are repaid by the brand loyalty of their customers.

Highest

Elevate Your Company with Philanthropy

There is no business without customers. The businesses who soar beyond high, and higher, to reach the highest levels of success are ones who not only build successful business models, but also forge lasting relationships with the communities they operate in. Philanthropy is one way to show appreciation for the success customers have helped you achieve. Companies that encourage their employees to serve their communities and even incentivize them for doing so often build stronger company cultures as a result of that philanthropy. When you as a business become an integral part of your community through philanthropy or philanthropic works you become more than just a business to the people whose lives you impact. If you are ready to become a catalyst for success in your community and as such be rewarded with their undying loyalty, here are some areas of philanthropy that you can adopt to impact your company and the communities you serve.

Have Holiday Food Drives

Holiday food drives are an easy way to get your company and employees involved in philanthropic activities and at the same time create team-building activities. The food drive can be turned into a friendly competition between the different departments in your company who can compete to see who brings in the most canned goods and food items. You can advertise for months in advance of the holiday season for businesses and individuals in the area to commit to donating food and other items for the drive then donate food packages to needy families for the holidays.

You can also have food drives periodically throughout the year. Putting food on the table for those less fortunate can give your employees a sense of pride. Contact local food banks for a list of suggested foods items and check with them to see what they need the most. Have your employees donate non-perishable items. Organizations like feeding America and No Kid Hungry can provide you with ideas for ways your employees can use their talents to raise money. Even something as simple as having a bake sale can raise funds to help your community.

Have Your Company Sponsor A Youth Sports Team

As a company you can sponsor a local amateur sports team. You can even do it by themes if you want by sponsoring a girls team, or a special needs team, or a team in an impoverished area, or a senior team, or teams in any number of other categories. Sponsoring youth teams has a direct positive impact on the lives of the participants and if you encourage your workforce it can have a positive effect on them as well. You can allow your employees to leave work a little early on game days to support the team with their families. Employees can also support local leagues by participating as referees, assistant coaches, grounds crew, scorekeepers, or as volunteers in the concession stand. Don't forget to take plenty of pictures of the events and your volunteers to display on your social media pages and around the office.

Use Crowd Funding to Support Local Creators

By using Kickstarter or other crowd funding platforms your company can provide local projects that benefit the community with backing. By supporting local projects and creators your company can encourage growth and innovation in the community helping it to thrive. Your employees can even provide mentorship to creators to help them turn these start-up programs into micro businesses that can employ local residents. Employees can start their own Kickstarter projects such as neighborhood gardens etc. to benefit the community.

Rally Your Employees to Build A House

A significant philanthropic activity your employees can participate in is building houses. When your company's staff is responsible for providing some needy family or individual with a place they can call home it is an uplifting experience that creates a unique bond among your employees that enhances the way they interact in the workplace. You can work with organizations like Habitat for Humanity or local construction companies. The volunteer hours your company donates will leave employees with a valuable memory that results in providing a priceless life-changing gift to someone special.

Have Your Company Adopt A Local School

Before kids return to school you can contact a local school board and ask to be matched with a school that can use corporate support. Your employees can also volunteer time tutoring students or assisting the school with fundraising activities. Your company can raise funds for a back-to-school drive to provide backpacks and school supplies for children unable to afford these necessities. You can sponsor a job fair for students to learn about different careers or provide internships at your company to give students learning opportunities. Adopting a school is a cool way to give back to the community.

Let Employees Mentor Students

Big Brothers-Big Sisters offers a workplace mentoring program where local students learn through one-on-one mentorships with your employees. The program provides valuable learning opportunities for students without your employees having to leave the office. Your employees can give students they are mentoring valuable work experience and teach them communication skills while bonding over lunch.

Have A Clothing Drive

Your employees can have a clothing drive for organizations like Dress for Success, that gather donations of work apparel for women in need so they can go on work interviews and find employment. They can collect clothing donations and call for the Salvation Army to pick them up. Or, even run a clothing drive and have people in need show up at an appointed location like a church or homeless shelter to receive clothing. You can set out a bin for new or gently-used clothing and encourage employees to donate used clothes or new items if they choose.

Give Animal Lovers their Chance for Philanthropy

Most companies are full of pet lovers. Supporting your local animal shelter and rescue organization would be a philanthropic project most employees would enjoy. You can put a bin out to collect new and gently-used pet items, blankets, collars, leashes, toys, water bowls, grooming tools, and other items for pets and donate them. Have employees volunteer a day at the animal shelter or rescue shelter. Get in touch with the local pet shelter or rescue organization and find out their needs, then have a drive to supply those items.

Run to Help Charities

Your company can host a "fun run" or walk-a-thon to raise money for a good cause. Having your employees run or walk together as a company to raise money for or support a nonprofit builds great team spirit as well as supports health and fitness.

Use Givinga to Set Up A Charity Program for Your Company

Givinga helps companies add charitable giving to their list of benefits. Givinga's workplace giving software allows employees to create their own personal giving accounts, choose the charities they want to support, easily request a matching gift from your company, and raise funds from family and friends. Employees can add their own funds to Flexible Giving Accounts and link together with other employees around shared causes, so working at your company doesn't just pay the bills, it makes an impact on the community and empowers employees to be influencers of that impact.

Your customers don't care if you are the smartest person in the room. How does your presence benefit their community? The more visible you are doing good things in the communities you serve, the more those communities will feel a loyalty to your company, your products, and services. As the saying goes, "People don't care how much you know, until they know how much you care."

Chapter 11: Becoming The Ultimate You

"Here's to the crazy ones. The misfits. The rebels. The troublemakers. The round pegs in the square holes. The ones who see things differently. They're not fond of rules. And they have no respect for the status quo. You can quote them, disagree with them, glorify or vilify them. About the only thing you can't do is ignore them. Because they change things. They push the human race forward. And while some may see them as the crazy ones, we see genius. Because the people, who are crazy enough to think they can change the world, are the ones who do." **– Steve Jobs**

There is you. The one you see every day when you look in the mirror. The you that you wake up with each morning and go to bed with every night. That is the you that you see walking and hear talking. It is the you that you go to work with and spend weekends with, laugh, cry, experience joy and pain with. You know that you well. There is also another you. One you may rarely glimpse though that you is always present too. Always looking over the proceedings, waiting to be summoned to the rescue, or called upon to take over or lead the way when you need him or her most. That you, is the Ultimate you. The you that you want to be so badly but can't find the right technique, or routine, or energy, or courage, or formula to be at all times. No matter how much you desire to keep that you engaged, that you seems to elude you. So, how do you do it? How do you become the ultimate you, once and for all, permanently?

Here are the ingredients, the characteristics you need to become and remain the ultimate you, the conqueror, the champion, the leader, the warrior, the winner:

Have A Passion to Compete – Wherever the arena is, the business world, the athletic field, the concert stage, the classroom, the laboratory, or any number of other places or settings, the ability to compete at a high level, at all times, is the main ingredient that separates those who do from those who don't, those who can from those who can't, those who will from those who won't. Life is about competition. In the wild it is obvious that the law of survival is always in play. Those animals that win the struggle to survive live to fight another day but those who lose the struggle become dinner. There is no pat on the back or friend there to say,

"Nice try, you'll get them next time." The wild is a place where it's kill or be killed, eat or be eaten, live or die. But the world for the human species is much more subtle.

We do not think of ourselves as being in a life or death situation, or our environment as being a jungle, but the reality is that the two scenarios are more closely related than we may think. The lazy, or careless, or weakest, or least competitive caribou do not survive. The lazy, careless, or weakest, or least competitive lion goes hungry. The lazy, or careless, or weakest, or least competitive employee does not get promoted. The lazy, careless, weakest, or least competitive executive does not reach the top of his or her profession. The lazy, careless, weakest, least competitive student does not end up the valedictorian. This pattern repeats itself in every area of life.

Do you think Steve Jobs did not have a passion to make Apple the best? Do you think astronaut Neil Armstrong didn't want to be the first man on the moon? Do you think everyone at the top was driven to finish closer to the bottom? Don't let those modest speeches fool you. Champions love to compete.

There are only so many executive positions to go around. Only so many promotions, only so many jobs, only so many starting positions on teams, only so much room at the top of the class, only so many good husbands and wives, only so much of the best of anything to go around, and if we want it, you, I, and everyone else must compete for it, and keep on competing at the highest level, because the moment we stop competing at the highest level is the moment we are replaced by that other person who is competing at the highest level. We may not want it to be that way but that's the way it is. The ones who have a passion to compete, that hunger to be the best, to never lose, never surrender, never be outdone, never succumb to defeat, are the ones who will continue to excel because they ARE their Ultimate selves more often than the rest of us.

Fixate on The Details - The devil is indeed in the detail. Again, look at the legends of any profession and you will find people totally obsessed with getting the details right. Legendary Green Bay Packer football coach Vince Lombardi rode one specific play "The Packer Power Sweep" to 5 NFL

Championships in the 1960s, and that included winning the first two Super Bowls ever played. Lombardi would have his team practice the sweep again and again and again until they perfected the running of it. Then Lombardi built his entire office around the running of the sweep which other teams found almost impossible to stop.

That same fixation with details is found in this era's greatest NFL football coach Bill Belichick with his 6 Super Bowl titles and was found with former coach Phil Jackson with his "Triangle Offense" and 11 NBA titles. You think former General Electric Chairman and CEO, Jack Welch wasn't fixated on the details when he told the company that they would be number 1 or 2 in every industry they competed in or sell that business? Welch led GE to improve from a market value of $14 billion to $410 billion? Do you think 14-time World Championship Gold Medalist, Simone Biles, wasn't fixated on the details while scoring perfect 10s and being the first gymnast to ever land a triple double during a floor exercise, and a double-double dismount from the balance beam in competition? Successful people know that mastering the details is the most important part of mastering the task. People who rise to being their ultimate selves definitely do "sweat the Details."

Work Relentlessly to Improve – If you are not your worst critic, you are not your ultimate self. People with a championship mindset are perpetually trying to improve themselves. No matter how well they do they are never satisfied. They are always striving to do even better the next time. It does not matter how the other person does because they are only competing against themselves to be the best they can possibly be. To become the ultimate you, you must believe that there is always another level. Even when you finish on top there is still some flaw to fix, some miniscule correction to be made. Just because you are the best does not mean you have reached your best. Continue to strive for perfection and you will find that there is more in you, and more for you to accomplish.

Even if you are already successful how can you improve?

Wake up early. Most people are most productive in the early hours. Again, research shows that our brains work most effectively during the first 2-4 hours after we wake up. **Keep Learning.** Successful people are always searching for ways to learn something new. They read books, watch documentaries, watch how-to-videos, read articles, listen to podcasts, talk to other smart people, find websites with good information. By continually learning new things you keep your brain sharp. **Stay Active.** The more active your body is, the more active your brain is. Make sure that you are exercising regularly. Exercise means better blood flow and better blood flow means more oxygen to the brain. A high percentage of successful people have personal trainers, go to the gym regularly, run, bike, swim, box, practice martial arts, hike, walk, on a regular basis to keep fit, and so should you. **Get Mentally Tough.** No matter how talented, skillful, or determined you are there will still be obstacles to face. Too often people think that ability alone will take them to the top and keep them there. But, giving up when things get too tough is one of the main reasons people fail. A big part of success is the mental toughness it takes to persevere long enough to succeed. When people possess mental toughness they see obstacles as opportunities.

Perhaps no one in history was more mentally tough than Abraham Lincoln. In 1832, he ran for the Illinois state legislature and was defeated. In 1833, he started a business that failed. In 1835, his girlfriend died. In 1836, he had a nervous breakdown. In 1838, he was defeated for Speaker of the Illinois House. In 1843, he ran for congress and was defeated. He was elected to Congress in 1846 and lost his bid for reelection in 1848. In 1849, he was rejected for the position of land officer. In 1854, he ran for the U.S. Senate and was defeated. In 1856, he was defeated in his nomination for Vice President. In 1858, he ran for a U.S. Senate seat and was defeated again. After all those setbacks Abraham Lincoln was elected President of the United States in 1860, and became one of the nation's greatest presidents, and perhaps the glue that held the nation together through its bloody civil war.

Be Disciplined

If you cannot discipline yourself the battle is lost already. Having not only the willpower but also the discipline to do what needs to be done is a good start. Keeping yourself on task, avoiding procrastination, not allowing yourself to be distracted, managing your time well, maintaining control over your emotions, never getting too high or too low, will keep you performing at a high level. It is not surprising that many high-achievers rise early each day long before the sun is up. That takes discipline. High achievers also hold themselves accountable for what they accomplish or don't accomplish each day because they know when all is said and done the only person who can stop you from succeeding is you. Take it from successful people, self-discipline is a powerful tool.

Small disciplines repeated with consistency every day lead to great achievements gained slowly over time. -John C. Maxwell

Success is a matter of understanding and religiously practicing specific, simple habits that always lead to success. -Robert J. Ringer

Mastering others is strength. Mastering yourself is true power. -Lao Tzu

Hold yourself responsible for a higher standard than anybody else expects of you. Never excuse yourself. Never pity yourself. Be a hard master to yourself and be lenient to everybody else. -Henry Ward Beecher

Discipline is the bridge between goals and accomplishment. -Jim Rohn

How many talented people have come ever so close to success but failed because they were not disciplined enough to follow through on implementing their plans? How many people achieved success then lost it all because their lack of discipline caused them to make some horrible mistake? Of all the traits people associate with success, self-discipline is probably the most underrated, and the most important.

Be Proactive

"It's cool to be a nerd. There's a general understanding that smartphones didn't come from jocks. The digital age was foreseen by a group of short-sleeved, buttoned-down, white-shirted guys and their female equivalents designing the very stuff that's now ubiquitous." – J.J. Abrams

Successful people don't wait for life to happen to them. They have a plan for what they want to accomplish. They set goals and then objectives that will lead them to those goals. The ability to act upon your dreams and work them through to completion is what separates the achievers from those who simply dream. Nothing good will happen for you until you make something happen. Some people put more effort into reading about other people's success than they put into trying to be successful themselves. Don't just wish, plan. Don't just think, act. Don't just hope, believe. Don't just start, finish.

As William Johnsen said, "If it is to be, it is up to me."

Your destiny really is in your hands. People who blame others for everything that goes wrong in their lives are usually the kind of people who refuse to take responsibility for their own lives. If you fear you may be one of these people I suggest you read William Ernest Henley's excellent poem "Invictus" for inspiration.

Out of the night that covers me,
Black as the Pit from pole to pole,
I thank whatever gods may be
For my unconquerable soul.

In the fell clutch of circumstance
I have not winced nor cried aloud.
Under the bludgeonings of chance
My head is bloody, but unbowed.

Beyond this place of wrath and tears
Looms but the Horror of the shade,
And yet the menace of the years
Finds, and shall find, me unafraid.

It matters not how straight the gate,
How charged with punishments the scroll,
I am the master of my fate:
I am the captain of my soul.

Yes, you are the master of your fate, and the captain of your soul; and as such it is you that must be proactive and take charge of your life. It is you who must take action to do what must be done to bring all your dreams and goals out of the realm of possibility and into the realm of reality. One thing is certain, you will never succeed at anything until you take action.

Success comes from knowing that you did your best to become the best that you are capable of becoming. –John Wooden

Maintain A Positive Attitude

As the saying goes, "It's not what happens to you that matters, but how you respond to it."

You don't find successful people running around grumbling and complaining about what went wrong. While others are whining about it the successful people are already off somewhere trying to fix it. Successful people maintain a positive attitude. They understand that sometimes things don't work out for the best. But that doesn't stop them from continuing to work toward their goals. Airplanes experience the most turbulence when taking off and landing. And, guess what? So will you. As you begin your ascent toward success you will run into a lot of adversity. How you handle that adversity will determine whether you continue to rise and eventually break free of that adversity, that turbulence, or whether you come crashing back to earth. Even if you break free of adversity and fly off into the clear blue skies of success it doesn't mean you will never have to face adversity again. Adversity is always out there waiting and every now and then you will encounter it. If you have a winning plan with a good strategy stay the course.

You may have to climb to a higher elevation, or go off course by a mile or so, to get around the turbulence before you can get back on course. Stay with it and you will arrive at your destination. Then be ready for some turbulence before you reach your destination. Success may be your destination but it will not make you immune to adversity. As you are reaching your destination some friends will attack you, turbulence. Family members may lie on you, turbulence. People from your past may try to pull you back into the mud, turbulence. Those who once were your advisors may reject you once you stop letting them direct your course, turbulence. You have to get through all that turbulence in order to land safely at your destination, a.k.a. your destiny. Don't run from it. Welcome it. As you overcome the adversity it will help shape you into who you were created to be. Like the file and sandpaper that shapes the wood into furniture, adversity has its purpose. Don't heap turbulence on top of turbulence by having a bad attitude. Through it all maintain a positive attitude. Good, bad, or indifferent, it was all meant to be. Stay positive, work hard, work smart, don't quit, and you will arrive at your appointed destination.

"A pessimist sees the difficulty in every opportunity; the optimist sees the opportunity in every difficulty." -Sir Winston Churchill

Make "No" A Part of Your Process

The surest way to fail is to try and please everybody. You can't do everything. You can't be everywhere. You can't be everything to everybody. If you are going to be successful, saying "no" is a part of the process.

"If you don't know what your purpose is, someone will be glad to use you for theirs." -Miles Monroe

All roads may have led to Rome, but all roads will not lead you to your destination. Your destiny is designed to lead you to a specific place at a specific time. If you arrive early it won't happen. If you arrive late it won't happen. You must be in the right place at the right time to arrive at your destiny. Repeatedly saying "yes" to everything can delay you from being in that right place when the right opportunity presents itself. Timing is so important.

Ryan Graves was born in San Diego, California where he was an avid surfer who grew up competing for his high school surf team at Horizon Christian Academy before going on to graduate from Miami University in Oxford, Ohio. He was just 26 years old when he spotted a tweet from Travis Kalanick, who was searching on Twitter for employees to join him with his new startup business. Graves replied back to Kalanick by tweeting "hire me." The company Kalanick was launching is now known as Uber. Graves was Uber's first hire and has officially joined the Forbes Billionaire list along with Uber cofounder Garrett Camp. The stock options Graves received for being employee #1 and later CEO of Uber according to Forbes has given him a net worth of about $1.4 billion. You could say Graves just happened to be on Twitter at the right time. The fact remains Graves could have said "yes" to some other venture and not been available when that life changing Tweet came through. But, he was there to respond, and as a result Graves is now one of the world's youngest billionaires.

You may have some opportunities come along that are hard to turn down. Still, not every opportunity is meant for you. You might also experiment with different ideas to see what works for you. Keep in mind, anything that leads you away from your ultimate goal is not a good opportunity. It's a liability. It takes a laser-like focus to stay on track when other possibilities are flying about. Whether your goal is to become a top executive for a Fortune 500 company or to start your own company, you must keep your eyes on the prize if you want to succeed. Don't allow yourself to be distracted whether the distractions be good opportunities or bad ones. At the end of the day, you only have so many resources. If you don't learn to say no, you'll find yourself spread too thin with your time and money. It does not do you any good to be overextended. Too few resources spread across too many projects isn't scalable. For those who are pursuing success "No" is a valuable tool. Use it wisely and often.

"The successful warrior is the average man, with laser-like focus." – Bruce Lee

Load Up On Knowledge

Time to discuss the thing that will most likely have the greatest impact on whether you succeed greatly or fail miserably... KNOWLEDGE.

As author Marshall Goldsmith says, "What got you here won't get you there".

The road to ruin is strewn with the lives and careers of those who believed they had what it takes to succeed only to find out they were not up to the task. Many of these people could have achieved success had they only did what was necessary to grow into a person with capabilities to overcome the obstacles standing in the way of success. Instead they took on obstacles for which they were ill equipped to handle and the predictable result was failure.

Just because you have enough knowledge, skill or talent to get to point A does not mean you have what it takes to get to point B. Again, what got you here won't get you there. Would an aspiring heart surgeon become an accomplished heart surgeon without first going through medical training? Could a sculpture turn out fine works of art without learning carving, casting, and other shaping techniques. Is it possible for an amateur to become a professional athlete without first learning the fundamentals of the sport and then repetitively practicing them to the point of perfection? Every career, job, field, or endeavor has its own set of skills and techniques that must be learned before one can consistently do them at a high level. It may not be necessary to learn how to do every task perfectly but in every field there are certain task you must master if you want to have any chance of being successful.

A person who is not interested in learning will not achieve much in this world. Those who attain the greatest success are more often than not people who devour information about their field then work intensely to apply what they have learned. It is this process of learning and working until they are experts in their field that allows them to meet and overcome the obstacles that stop others. These are the ones who master their field and succeed at the highest level. Sure, the Magic Johnsons, Larry Birds, Michael Jordans, Lebron James', and Kevin Durants of the world have been blessed with enormous talent. But talent alone does not guarantee success. When we examine the career of any one of these NBA players we find they were not only great players but also some of the most knowledgeable, hardest working, and fundamentally sound players as well?

It is not enough to want to achieve great things and pursue success. To attain success, especially lasting success you must love the process. The process of acquiring knowledge enough to become an expert in your field, training and working at it long enough and hard enough to master your craft, then using that wealth of knowledge to refine your skills until you become one of the preeminent persons in your field.

Many people chasing success fell into the "Work harder not smarter" trap. They wrongly interpreted this to mean that you should work smart and not hard. That is nonsense. What person has achieved greatness in their field without working hard? In the tech field do you think Bill Gates, Steve Jobs, Michael Dell, and Mark Cuban didn't work hard. In the field of investing do you think Warren Buffett, George Soros, Peter Lynch, and Carl Icahn don't work hard? In entertainment do you think Leonardo DiCaprio, Beyonce, Denzel Washington, Bradley Cooper, and Jay Z don't work hard? These people work extremely hard. That's why they are at the top of their profession. If you are able to put that ability to work insanely hard with also working smart, you'll have something very special.

We are living in a time of infinite possibilities. There are a million ways to make a million in today's world if that's your goal. Hopefully, you see success as more than just dollars and cents. If you don't at the moment I hope you will by the time you complete reading this book. Now, back on the subject of knowledge, there are many avenues you can take to acquire the knowledge you'll need to succeed. Books, CDs, DVDs, Podcasts, videos, seminars, classes, workshops, mentoring, life coaches, the internet, and dozens of other media sources can provide you with the information you'll need to move forward in your career or endeavor, or even elevate your skills to the highest level possible. You must be diligent in seeking out the knowledge and information that can help you ascend to the highest levels and become the ultimate you. Don't try to cheat the process by simply sitting at home Googling information. Google and YouTube are fantastic resources but they are only resources to help you find the information you need. They are not a final destinations in your quest for knowledge.

When he was a young man it was reading the book, "The Intelligent Investor" by Benjamin Graham that inspired the soon-to-be "Oracle of Omaha" Warren Buffett to become the legendary investor and business icon he has become. Buffett was fortunate enough to have also become a student of Graham's at Columbia University in the 1950s. It was Graham's books and teaching that led Buffett to form his own investment philosophies and strategies that have now resulted in him being one of the richest and most successful people in the world.

Today, more than ever, the world is a competitive place. A place where any field or endeavor you choose to pursue will attract scores of people who are trying to achieve the same kind of success you are. Don't give those competitors the advantage of being more equipped than you, being more knowledgeable than you, working harder than you, or pursuing their goals with more passion than you. There are some variables that you cannot control. Like having millions to invest in your business. But how equipped you are mentally, physically, emotionally, and spiritually you can control. How knowledgeable you are you can control. How hard you work is within your control. How passionate you are about what you do is something you can control. All these factors are under your control. Don't let laziness, apathy, fear, ignorance, or indifference be the hinderance that stops you from achieving success. Stuff your mental data base with the abundance of knowledge it needs to help you succeed. When it comes to success the more knowledge you have the better. Be strategic about what parts of that knowledge you use but don't ever think having it won't serve you well. Better to have knowledge and not need it, than need knowledge and not have it.

Stock Your Bookshelf with Knowledge

Knowledge is power. If you don't know that fact you're already far behind in the race for success. If you want to improve your chances of being successful 1000% here are the books you must read NOW!

Without Their Permission: How the 21st Century Will Be Made, Not Managed by Alexis Ohanian: Co-founder of one of the world's most popular online communities, Reddit, Alexis Ohanian has a lot to say about the power of information and community. Further, he has much wisdom in launching and operating tech startups. Ohanian shares his life story in this engaging and inspiring read, of creating Reddit in his dorm room, cashing out for millions, and going on to start many more successful ventures. This book will convince young entrepreneurs that the era of being meek, following the rules, and asking permission is over.

Decisive by Chip Heath and Dan Heath: Decisive is a decision-making guide thoroughly researched and brilliantly presented by Chip and Dan Heath. The authors argue that humans are prone to faulty decision making, due to the nature of our brains. This book will teach you how to eliminate biases and irrational thoughts from your process. With the tools in this book, you can make smarter decisions and get better results in all areas of your life.

What Got You Here Won't Get You There: How Successful People Become Even More Successful by Marshall Goldsmith and Mark Reiter: In this book, Marshall Goldsmith and Mark Reiter look at how to avoid stagnation and reach the next level of success. The book points out some habits and ways of thinking that have a surprising impact on growth. For example, speaking when angry, poor listening skills, and making negative comments can all keep you stuck. On the other hand, cultivating a habit of gratitude and positivity will help you move forward.

Deep Work by Cal Newport: Deep Work gives new insight into how people produce their best work. The author asserts that many people work at the shallow end of focus, with social media and cultural changes to blame. Because of our distracting environment, it is nearly impossible to concentrate on anything. Deep Work helps people rediscover a deep state of focus and concentrate on things that matter. The book will inspire you to eliminate unnecessary distractions and work smarter.

Crushing It: How Great Entrepreneurs Build Their Businesses and Influence and How You Can Too by Gary Vaynerchuk: The stability and longevity of any business depend on the ability of its owner to adapt to changes in the business world. As the world shifts gears to the digital space, entrepreneurs must also move their marketing to digital platforms. Gary Vaynerchuk explains the best way to do that. With an entertaining yet straightforward style – the king of motivational quotes – Gary Vaynerchuk breaks down existing social media platforms. He shows how each one can be used to market your business. The book also includes voices from successful entrepreneurs to show how each platform helped them increase profits.

The Secret to Success by Eric Thomas: When you want to succeed as bad as you want to breathe by Eric Thomas: If you think success is out of reach for you, Eric Thomas wants to prove you wrong. In this inspiring story, Thomas recounts his story of dropping out of high school, becoming homeless, and overcoming challenges to build a successful career and personal life. The book speaks directly to young people facing adversity in their lives. It emphasizes the importance of surrounding yourself with people who motivate you to be better and maintaining a positive mindset.

Lean In: Women, Work, and the Will to Lead by Sheryl Sandberg: In Lean In, Sheryl Sandberg reignited the conversation around women in the workplace. Sandberg is chief operating officer of Facebook and coauthor of Option B with Adam Grant. In 2010, she gave an electrifying TED talk in which she described how women unintentionally hold themselves back in their careers. Her talk, which has been viewed more than six million times, encouraged women to "sit at the table," seek challenges, take risks, and pursue their goals with gusto. Lean In continues that conversation, combining personal anecdotes, hard data, and compelling research to change the conversation from what women can't do to what they can. Sandberg provides practical advice on negotiation techniques, mentorship, and building a satisfying career. She describes specific steps women can take to combine professional achievement with personal fulfillment, and demonstrates how men can benefit by supporting women both in the workplace and at home. Written with humor and wisdom, Lean In is a revelatory, inspiring call to action and a blueprint for individual growth that will empower women around the world to achieve their full potential.

Outliers: The Story of Success by Malcolm Gladwell: Malcolm Gladwell aims to cut through the myths of success by looking at not only traits but origin and environment of the highly successful. He handpicks high achievers and explains how their culture, background, and other factors made them who they are today. Gladwell uses the stories in this book to illustrate how the availability of opportunity is a large contributing factor to many people's success. He also dispels the myth of natural talent by citing those considered to be geniuses in their fields. In most cases, 10,000 hours of practice led them to mastery.

Zero to One by Peter Thiel and Blake Masters: Many businesses come up quickly in today's world, then crumble just as quickly. Among other factors, this is due to a lack of originality and creativity in solving problems. In this book, Thiel takes on the trend of starting businesses that already exist and tears down the copycat mentality. He challenges the reader to focus on innovation. Thiel calls for a mind shift that looks to the future needs of the world. He explains the power and advantage that monopolies hold compared to companies that compete for market share. For those looking for the next big idea, this is the book to read.

Start With Why by Simon Sinek: Start With Why, presented by Simon Sinek, is among the best leadership books to illustrate a new theory of success. Sinek compares successful people and ties them to a common motivation as the driver behind their excellent leadership. Sinek argues the drive that steered leaders like Steve Jobs and the Wright brothers was not profit. It was their ability to answer the question, "Why?" He demonstrates how defining the underlying motivation can inspire an organization to achieve great heights. Whether you want to inspire or be inspired, this book provides many stories and examples about great leaders and why they were so influential.

The One Thing: The Surprisingly Simple Truth Behind Extraordinary Results by Gary Keller: Gary Keller has the answers as to why most time management and productivity systems fail. He argues against multitasking and helps you narrow your focus to one thing that will move you closer to your goals. This book is full of eye-opening realities that will explain why you aren't getting the results you want in your business and personal life. The One Thing will help you eliminate the habits keeping you from success, and create maximum impact.

The Freaks Shall Inherit the Earth: Entrepreneurship for Weirdos, Misfits and World Dominators by Chris Brogan: Chris Brogan rejects the idea that there is only one route to success. Instead, he will show you how your unique character and even your odd traits can lead to a successful business. The book highlights ways of turning your passion into a viable business without conforming to expectations. There are more possibilities now than ever before, with the tools of the digital age at our disposal. If you are thinking of starting a business and feel undecided, this book is what you need.

Idea to Execution: How to Optimize, Automate and Outsource Everything in Your Business by Ari Meisel and Nick Sonnenberg: This book proves you do not need a big budget or staff to start pursuing your dreams. Ari Meisel and Nick Sonnenberg tell the story of how they turned an idea into a functioning business in just 24 hours — without spending any money. Meisel and Sonnenberg reveal the strategies of outsourcing, automating, and optimizing to launch and operate a business with maximum efficiency. Whether you're starting out or looking for ways to simplify your business, this is one of the best entrepreneur books to get you started quickly.

Shoe Dog: A Memoir by the Creator of Nike by Phil Knight: This is a fascinating account from Phil Knight, the co-founder of Nike, of his life and the birth of one of the biggest shoe companies in the world. Many books have been written about Nike, but in Shoe Dog, you get to hear directly from the man responsible for its success. Phil Knight pours his heart out in this emotionally-charged account, and the results are inspiring.

The 80/20 Principle: The Secret to Achieving More with Less by Richard Koch: Richard Koch demonstrates in this book that 80 percent of your output depends on 20 percent of the effort that you put in it. The 80/20 Principle explains how to determine where you spend your time and energy for maximum results. It can also help you identify the 20 percent of customers that contribute to 80 percent of your profits. By focusing on quality over quantity, The 80/20 Principle has the potential to skyrocket your productivity in all areas of life. Not only can you stop chasing after customers that won't help your business, but you can stop wasting time on activities that don't get results.

Rich Dad Poor Dad: What The Rich Teach Their Kids About Money That the Poor and Middle Class Do Not! By Robert T. Kiyosaki: Kiyosaki uses the stories of two influential figures in his early life to illustrate how some people create wealth, and others remain poor. In this classic business book, he pinpoints the thought patterns and beliefs that get in the way of financial success. These include lack of knowledge about investments, and the idea that employment is the only way to earn a living. Kiyosaki encourages parents to expose their children to the business world at a young age, as opposed to emphasizing school. He also looks at untapped opportunities in real estate investing while providing a guide on how to start and own businesses. Rich Dad Poor Dad is on many lists of top ten business books because it covers fundamentals of creating wealth that everyone can learn from. Regardless of your profession or age, Rich Dad Poor Dad can help you improve your financial status.

The Wake Up Call: Financial Inspiration Learned from 4:44 + A Step by Step Guide on How to Implement Each Financial Principle by Ash Cash: The Wake Up Call, is a book designed to teach African-Americans how to manage money more effectively and how to build generational wealth. Jay-Z's 4:44 is the blueprint to bridging the wealth gap & solving economic inequalities for African-Americans! Through deciphering all of the financial concepts delivered within the album, readers will be taught about: • How to Build Credit to Use as Leverage • How to Spend Money Wisely • Cooperative Economics and How to Start a Business • Creating Multiple Streams of Income • How to Invest Money in Order For it To Grow • How to Pass Down Wealth to the Next Generation and more.

Think and Grow Rich by Napoleon Hill: Think and Grow Rich is one of the best business books of all time. Napoleon Hill interviewed and studied the big names in business in Depression-era America. His resulting book, initially published in 1937, is a look at the mindset of those who succeeded in achieving great wealth. The driving force behind success, according to Hill, is a strong desire and passion. This is one of the earliest books in the self-improvement genre. Although short on actionable advice, Think and Grow Rich will motivate you to set lofty goals and work hard every day to achieve them.

Faster Than Normal: Turbocharge Your Focus, Productivity, and Success with the Secrets of the ADHD Brain by Peter Shankman: Having a hyperactive brain is often seen as a disadvantage since attention deficit makes it very difficult to focus and be productive. In this book, Peter Shankman reveals the hidden advantages of the ADHD brain, and how to use them for good in life and business. Shankman describes how he achieved success in his life and career not in spite of, but because of his ADHD brain. The book continuously calls ADHD a gift — if you or someone close to you has an ADHD diagnosis, this book is a must-read. It will not only inspire you but provide practical ways to unleash the potential of a fast-moving brain. Since many entrepreneurs suffer from distracted minds, Faster Than Normal is high on my list of self-improvement and great business books.

Influence: The Psychology of Persuasion by Robert B. Cialdini: After 35 years of research, Robert B. Cialdini produced this simple, yet complete study on what makes people change their behavior. The book outlines the weapons of influence and teaches readers not only to use them but to guard against them. Concepts and practices employed in marketing are explained in depth, with examples and stories to illustrate effectiveness. Learning to use ideas like scarcity, social proof, and reciprocity will help you succeed in your marketing.

Built to Last: Successful Habits of Visionary Companies by Jim Collins and Jerry I. Porras: Built to Last is an impeccably researched business book that is bound to open your mind to new astounding ideas about companies. By comparing visionary companies, Collins and Porras portray that the same ideas won't guarantee you success unless you possess specific characteristics. The astounding yet scary part is that there is no right or wrong – all that matters is your purpose, passion, vision, and values. Built to Last is full of detailed examples that are meticulously organized to form a framework of real-world concepts. This book serves as a blueprint that can be easily applied by entrepreneurs and managers. This is one of the best leadership books you can read to help you accelerate towards your dreams.

How to Win Friends and Influence People by Dale Carnegie: One of the fundamental keys to business and sales is the ability to network and build relationships. This bestselling business book promises to instill the communication and persuasion skills it takes to succeed. Instrumental to people who are socially awkward, this book offers tips on developing listening skills and starting conversations. But ultimately, the book is aimed at helping business people succeed in sales. That's why this self-help classic also has a place on the shelf of must-read business books. Although originally published in 1936, much of the advice in this book is timeless.

WHY SHOULD WHITE GUYS HAVE ALL THE FUN?: HOW REGINALD LEWIS CREATED A BILLION-DOLLAR BUSINESS EMPIRE by Reginald F. Lewis: Reginald F. Lewis' first successful venture was his $22.5 million-leveraged buyout of McCall Pattern Co., where he sold it for $65 million in 1987, and made an astounding 90 to 1 return on his original investment. He re-branded the corporation as TLC Beatrice International Inc. As the CEO and chairman, Lewis increased the company's worth in rapid time, and with revenues of $1.5 billion, TLC Beatrice made it to the Fortune 500. It was also the first company on the Black Enterprise List of Top 100 African-American owned businesses. This book written by Lewis details how all of this happened. It will inspire many bosses for generations to come.

Never Split the Difference: Negotiating As If Your Life Depended On It by Chris Voss and Tahl Raz: This is an easy-to-read and engaging book that will put you in a better position for negotiating in any situation. Voss invites you into his head and shares the techniques he used during his career as an FBI agent. This book is a must read for those who need a competitive edge during high-stakes business negotiations.

The Art Of War by Sun Tzu: The Art of War is an ancient Chinese military treatise attributed to Sun Tzu a high-ranking military general, strategist and tactician, and it was believed to have been compiled during the late Spring and Autumn period or early Warring States period. The text is composed of 13 chapters, each of which is devoted to one aspect of warfare. It is commonly known to be the definitive work on military strategy and tactics of its time. It has been the most famous and influential of China's Seven Military Classics, and for the last two thousand years it remained the most important military treatise in Asia, where even the common people knew it by name. It has had an influence on Eastern and Western military thinking, business tactics, legal strategy and beyond.

Shut Up and Listen! by Tilman Fertitta: For entrepreneurs ready to reach the next level of success, small business owner turned multibillionaire Tilman Fertitta shares the commonsense principles that have rocketed his worldwide hospitality empire to the top. Fertitta, also known as the Billion Dollar Buyer, started his hospitality empire thirty years ago with just one restaurant. He knows the challenges that business owners face, as well as the common pitfalls that cause them to go under. Over the years he's stayed true to the principles that helped him scale his business to what is believed to be the largest single-shareholder company in America, with over $4 billion in revenue, including hundreds of restaurants (Landry's Seafood, Bubba Gump Shrimp Company, Morton's Steakhouse, Mastro's, The Chart House, Rainforest Café, and over forty more restaurant concepts) and five Golden Nugget Casinos. He's also sole owner of the

NBA's Houston Rockets. In Shut Up and Listen!, he shares the key insights that made it all possible.

The Ride of a Lifetime By Robert Iger: The CEO of Disney, one of Time's most influential people of 2019, shares the ideas and values he embraced to reinvent one of the most beloved companies in the world and inspire the people who bring the magic to life. Robert Iger became CEO of The Walt Disney Company in 2005, during a difficult time. Competition was more intense than ever and technology was changing faster than at any time in the company's history. His vision came down to three clear ideas: Recommit to the concept that quality matters, embrace technology instead of fighting it, and think bigger—think global—and turn Disney into a stronger brand in international markets. Twelve years later, Disney is the largest, most respected media company in the world, counting Pixar, Marvel, Lucasfilm, and 21st Century Fox among its properties. Its value is nearly five times what it was when Iger took over, and he is recognized as one of the most innovative and successful CEOs of our era. In The Ride of a Lifetime, Robert Iger shares the lessons he's learned while running Disney and leading its 200,000 employees, and he explores the principles that are necessary for true leadership.

Invest In Yourself

To become the ultimate you will take becoming more than you are today. That is why investing in yourself is not an option, it's a must. There are so many ways of investing in yourself. You can invest in improving your health, increasing your knowledge, learning a new skill, picking up another language, or any other number of things to enhance your abilities. Here are a few suggested areas of improving for you to consider.

Create Multiple Streams of Income

The cost of living is always spiraling up so that one income is not really adequate anymore. Anyone who wants to have a high standard of living should focus on creating multiple income streams. The surest way to wealth is to earn passive income. When you are dependent on one income you are only one disaster away from financial ruin. Having multiple streams of income not only allows you to afford a better lifestyle but it puts you a few steps closer to being financially independent. To get started you can choose a few things that sound interesting to you and try them out. You might choose a few things that require some work like writing an e-book and a few things that require no work like buying dividend-yielding stocks.

Whether it is purchasing rental property, or flipping houses, acquiring something that can bring in income is an excellent way to open the passive income pipeline. Another avenue is to use a rental service like Airbnb. If you live in a desirable place like a big city, or even a cozy suburb, there's a good chance someone would pay to stay in your home a few days. Airbnb connects people with space to rent to people looking for a place to stay. If you happen to live near a college campus, a famous golf course, football stadium, sports arena, or other venues where major sporting events are held you can rent your home out to people attending those events through a service called Rent Like a Champion. You get to set the price and availability of your rental. Most spaces are rented from Friday evening to Sunday afternoon, and the average take for a host is about $1,100 per weekend. And, if you are concerned about damages, the company provides up to $1,000,000 in insurance coverage which acts as your primary insurance policy during the time your home is being rented out. That policy covers liability, structural damage, and damage to items and property. Best of all you are paid via direct deposit 5 to 6 business days after your guests check out. Rent Like A Champion currently has listings in 25 cities in the United States.

Write a blog and link it to a store site like Amazon to earn money from affiliate marketing. Or, create a website and use Google Adsense to monetize your site. Google Adsense pays to post ads on your website or blog. There are two ways to make money with internet ads; (CPM) which stands for cost-per-impressions (the M stands for mille "Latin for thousand") that give you money for every 1,000 page views; and pay-per-clicks (PPC) which provide you with money when a visitor to your site clicks on a displayed ad. There are companies that will pay you in one of these two ways for allowing them to place ads on your website or blog if your site produces sufficient traffic. However, if you go this route be aware that only 4% of professional bloggers make over $10,000 a month from their site, while 9% of professional bloggers make between $1000-$9999 a month, 7% make $500-$999 a month, 17% make $100-$499, 25% make $10-$99 a month, 28% make under $10, and 10% make no money at all.

Build an E-commerce Store

If you are feeling more adventuresome you can try selling stuff on your site by using sales platforms like Shopify. It is a great way to make money by selling things you make or re-selling items you purchase. Shopify makes it easy to build an online store with ready-made templates, so you don't spend time designing your store. They also provide tools to help you create coupons, promotions, process payments, and handle product returns. You can also share your store on sites like Google Shopping, eBay, Facebook, and even price comparison sites like Bizrate, Nextag, and PriceGrabber. Shopify remains the platform of choice for drop shippers.

Buy A Business

If you have a good chunk of available cash you might also consider buying an existing business. Purchasing the right brick and mortar business can be a good investment. Be aware that a physical business has much more overhead and other moving parts than an online business. So, do your research before you invest in a business. There may be an obvious reason the owner is selling the business.

Find A Business Coach or Mentor

The goal is to get astronomically better as quickly as possible. Anything that accelerates your growth is a good thing. If you can find a good coach or mentor who can use his or her experience to share some valuable insights and knowledge with you it can speed up the time it takes to become competent at your craft. Being able to skip some of the trial and error and avoid some mistakes that are a natural consequence of growth can help you master your craft in half the time it would take you on your own.

A business coach or mentor can also provide emotional support and encouragement during those times you may get discouraged. Having an experienced eye to look at things and help you determine what's working and what's not, and what you may need to do differently can be extremely valuable to you. Turning your dream into a reality is never easy but being able to lean on an experienced coach or mentor can certainly guide you through some rough waters. Hiring a coach or mentor will most likely cost you some cash but the knowledge and cost savings you can gain from having this person on your team should be well worth it. If you are ready to invest in yourself by taking on a coach or mentor, you'll be surprised how many experts are willing to share their knowledge and experience with you.

Invest in Investing

At the ripe age of 88, he is still known as the Oracle of Omaha. Warren Buffett is the greatest investor who ever lived and has rode his investments to become the third richest person in the world with an estimated net worth that stands at $87.3 billion according to the Bloomberg Billionaires Index. Buffett announced July 1, 2019 that he will donate $3.6 billion in Berkshire Hathaway shares to five groups including the Bill & Melinda Gates Foundation. Buffett is regarded as one of the most generous philanthropists in the world, having donated more than $46 billion since 2000. Buffett, the CEO of Berkshire Hathaway began building his wealth by investing in the stock market at the tender age of 11.

It has always amazed me how many people have no interest in using the stock market as a tool for building wealth. Yes, it does cost money to invest. But, how many people have come across a lump sum of money and dispensed it without so much as glancing at investing as a wealth strategy?

Here is the **Dow Jones Industrial Average (DJIA) stock market index for the years 1998-2018.** Notice the extreme gains over that time period. That my friends means a lot of wealth was created by the market over this short amount of time.

Year Avg. Closing Price Year Open   Year High   Year Low Year Close Annual % Change

2018	25,046.86	24,824.01	26,828.39	21,792.20
	23,327.46	-5.63%		
2017	21,750.20	19,881.76	24,837.51	19,732.40
	24,719.22	25.08%		
2016	17,927.11	17,148.94	19,974.62	15,660.18
	19,762.60	13.42%		
2015	17,587.03	17,832.99	18,312.39	15,666.44
	17,425.03	-2.23%		
2014	16,777.69	16,441.35	18,053.71	15,372.80
	17,823.07	7.52%		
2013	15,009.52	13,412.55	16,576.66	13,328.85
	16,576.66	26.50%		
2012	12,966.44	12,397.38	13,610.15	12,101.46
	13,104.14	7.26%		
2011	11,957.57	11,670.75	12,810.54	10,655.30
	12,217.56	5.53%		
2010	10,668.58	10,583.96	11,585.38	9,686.48
	11,577.51	11.02%		
2009	8,885.65	9,034.69	10,548.51	6,547.05
	10,428.05	18.82%		
2008	11,244.06	13,043.96	13,058.20	7,552.29
	8,776.39	-33.84%		
2007	13,178.26	12,474.52	14,164.53	12,050.41
	13,264.82	6.43%		
2006	11,409.78	10,847.41	12,510.57	10,667.39
	12,463.15	16.29%		
2005	10,546.66	10,729.43	10,940.55	10,012.36
	10,717.50	-0.61%		

Year				
2004	10,315.51	10,409.85	10,854.54	9,749.99
	10,783.01	3.15%		
2003	9,006.64	8,607.52	10,453.92	7,524.06
	10,453.92	25.32%		
2002	9,214.85	10,073.40	10,635.25	7,286.27
	8,341.63	-16.76%		
2001	10,199.29	10,646.15	11,337.92	8,235.81
	10,021.57	-7.10%		
2000	10,729.38	11,357.51	11,722.98	9,796.03
	10,787.99	-6.17%		
1999	10,481.56	9,184.27	11,497.12	9,120.67
	11,497.12	25.22%		
1998	8,630.76	7,965.00	9,374.27	7,539.07
	9,181.43	16.10%		

When the topic is investing who better to take a few investment tips from than Mr. Buffett. If you are thinking of getting involved with buying stocks here are some of Buffett's choice investment tips.

Invest in what you know

"Never invest in a business you cannot understand." – Warren Buffett

One of the common ways to make an avoidable mistake is investing in stocks that are overly complex. Most people have an extensive knowledge in only a small range of subjects. That means we probably have a reasonable knowledge of companies in the particular markets that cover those subjects and the best companies in those industries. That being said, it is usually a mistake to participate in buying stocks in industries we have little or no direct experience in.

If you cannot get a reasonable understanding of how a company makes money and determine what are the main drivers that impact its industry, within 10 minutes, you should avoid gambling your money on it. Of the

10,000+ publicly-traded firms there may be only a few hundred companies that meet this criteria.

Buy Quality Businesses

"It's far better to buy a wonderful company at a fair price than a fair company at a wonderful price." – Warren Buffett

While saying "no" to complicated businesses and industries is fairly straightforward, identifying high quality businesses is much more challenging.

Over the past 50 years Warren Buffett's investment philosophy has evolved from buying discounted stocks and holding them until their stock price rises to focusing almost exclusively on buying high quality companies that present long-term opportunities for continued growth.

With troubled companies one problem is usually followed by another. Troubled companies usually earn low returns, eroding your initial investment value. Buffett says that one of the most important financial ratios he uses to gauge business quality is return on invested capital. Companies that earn high returns on the capital tied up in them have the potential to compound their earnings faster than businesses with lower returns. As a result, companies that earn high returns have an intrinsic value that rises over time.

"Time is the friend of the wonderful business, the enemy of the mediocre." – Warren Buffett

Buy a stock to hold it forever

"If you aren't thinking about owning a stock for ten years, don't even think about owning it for ten minutes." – Warren Buffett

Buffett is famous for his buy-and-hold mentality. Many of the stocks in his portfolio have been held onto by Buffett for decades. After purchasing a high quality business at a reasonable price, another of Buffett's famous quotes about how long to hold onto it is, "Our favorite holding period is forever."

Quality businesses that earn high returns and increase in value over time are hard to find. Because the fundamentals of a quality business can take years to impact that businesses' stock price, only the patient investor will be rewarded. Those people who are constantly buying and selling stocks will find that taxes and trading commissions will eat up their returns in the form of taxes and trading commissions. As Buffett says:

"The stock market is designed to transfer money from the active to the patient." – Warren Buffett

Diversification can be dangerous

"Opportunities come infrequently. When it rains gold, put out the bucket, not the thimble." – Warren Buffett

While many have preached that diversification is the best investment strategy Buffett believes that diversification should be spread over a smaller number of companies and industries than others recommend. Many mutual funds own hundreds of stocks in their portfolio. Contrary to these funds Buffett's major equity holdings are few. You will rarely find great companies at a reasonable stock price. So, what are the qualifications Buffett uses to find his 20-40 great companies? According to Buffett the qualifications you should judge companies by are these: (1) Purchase companies on a long-term basis. (2) Choose companies with favorable long-term economic characteristics. (3) Look for companies that have competent and honest management. (4) Select companies with a purchase price that is attractive when measured against the yardstick of value to a private owner. (5) Choose companies in an industry that you are familiar with and whose long-term business characteristics you feel competent to judge.

Buffett says, "It is difficult to find investments meeting such a test, and that is one reason for Berkshire's concentration of holdings." He says, "we simply can't find one hundred different securities that conform to our investment requirements. However, we feel quite comfortable concentrating our holdings in the much smaller number that we do identify as attractive."

Investing isn't rocket science

"You don't need to be a rocket scientist. Investing is not a game where the guy with the 160 IQ beats the guy with the 130 IQ." – Warren Buffett

Intelligence does not qualify you to be any better at choosing winning stocks than anyone else. One of the great misconceptions about investing is that it takes being smart to participate in the stock market.

While following Warren Buffett's investment philosophy doesn't take a genius, it also should be noted that there is no such thing as a magic formula, or an "Easy Button" that will guarantee you market-beating results. Buffett warns people against believing such a magic formula exist.

"Investors should be skeptical of history-based models. Constructed by a nerdy-sounding priesthood... these models tend to look impressive. Too often, though, investors forget to examine the assumptions behind the models. Beware of geeks bearing formulas." – Warren Buffett

Understand the difference between price and value

"Price is what you pay. Value is what you get." – Warren Buffett

Investors tend to be fixated on stock prices of companies rather than the value of companies. There are times when the stock price of a company have nothing whatsoever to do with its long term outlook. Anyone who pays more attention to stock prices, which are volatile, than the actual value of a company is bound to run into trouble in the long run. As an example, alert investors were able to find quite a few bargains during the financial crisis because people were selling off quality companies regardless of their long-term earnings potential. Even during the downturn plenty of companies continued to build upon good fundamentals to increase their competitive advantages over rivals and gain more market share. In spite of the financial crisis wise investors heeded Buffett's advice to, "buy quality when it is marked down in price."

"During the extraordinary financial panic that occurred late in 2008, I never gave a thought to selling my farm or New York real estate, even though a severe recession was clearly brewing. And, if I had owned 100% of a solid business with good long-term prospects, it would have been foolish for me to even consider dumping it. So why would I have sold my stocks that were small participations in wonderful businesses? True, any one of them might eventually disappoint, but as a group they were certain to do well." – Warren Buffett

Play it safe with Low-cost index funds

There are many actively managed investment funds that hit investors with excessive fees thereby eating away their returns and any dividend income they may have had coming. Such expensive index funds you may want to avoid. However, low-cost, passive indexing can prove to be a great strategy for investors. Most investors fail to beat the market often because of bad investing habits like trying to time the market, trading based on their emotions, taking excessive risks, getting involved with stocks that fall outside their area of knowledge, and other traits that all but guarantee bad results.

Showing his confidence in index funds Warren Buffett has given clear instructions to trustees who will be managing his Berkshire Hathaway shares once he passes away and those shares are given to charity.

"My advice to the trustee couldn't be more simple: Put 10% of the cash in short-term government bonds and 90% in a very low-cost S&P 500 index fund. (I suggest Vanguard's.) I believe the trust's long-term results from this policy will be superior to those attained by most investors – whether pension funds, institutions or individuals – who employ high-fee managers." – Warren Buffett

Chapter 12: Tomorrow Is Now

Beware of Dinosaurs

Now that you have the blueprint for success the last thing you want to do is waste your time walking down dead-end streets that lead nowhere. Technology is changing everything. Cloud computing, robotics, autonomous cars, and other technological advances are changing the way we work and live. Careers that were booming a few years ago may not even exist a few short years from now. Now that you are armed with these new skills and a wealth of valuable information let's take a look down the road to make sure that career destination you are moving toward will still be there when you arrive. Below are some careers you might want to avoid because they may soon become "extinct" or shall we say casualties of the age of technology. Also, we have a section called "Cash Money" for those of you who want to fire your job and get rich by building your own business empire. Some of the old tried and true business models no longer represent the way to succeed. Entrepreneurs are creating new models by using available technologies to create businesses and find their own profitable market niche. Let me show you a few new wrinkles you can use to fire your job and make some cold hard cash.

Be Your Own Boss And Make Cash Money

Print-On-Demand

Print on demand is a process where you create your own brand by working with a supplier to customize white-label products using your own designs which are then sold on a per-order basis. That means you don't pay for the products that are being produced for your company until after you've actually sold them. So, there's no need for you to buy products in bulk or stock any inventory yourself. No more spending a ton of money in advance to purchase a bunch of products then hoping and praying you can sell them. With print on demand you can create a design then have your supplier take that design, put it on white-label products (blank items like t-shirts, sweatshirts, baseball hats, tote bags, coffee mugs, etc.), and print these items only after you receive orders for them. If 10 items are ordered by your customers, your supplier prints 10 items. If 30 items are ordered, 30 items are printed. No money comes out of your pocket because your products are only printed after you sell them. Therefore, you can make profits off your products without the threat of losing money. It's an entrepreneur's dream come true. With print-on-demand services your supplier handles everything after the sale, from printing the product to shipping it to your customers. Once you set up your online store with an ecommerce platform like Shopify and connect it to a print on demand service like Printify, Printful, Zazzle, Redbubble, TeeSpring, Sunfrog, Threadless, Teefury, Design by Humans, Society6, or Fine Art America, it only takes a few clicks of the mouse for your customers to order your products. Once that order has been placed your print-on-demand supplier will print the item, fulfill the order, and ship it to your customer. Once that happens you just made money.

You can use print-on-demand services to do important things like:

Test a business idea or new product line for an existing business without the risks that comes with buying inventory.

Create original products for a small group of your customers. For example, you can design special apparel for pet lovers, or bookworms, or gamers, or foodies, or any number of people who are passionate about a specific topic.

You can monetize an audience you've built up on your website or blog. Print on demand is a great option for those who are YouTubers, cartoonist, or social media influencers who want to capitalize on their popularity by creating products for their followers without having to spend time dealing with manufacturers or fulfilling orders.

Print on demand companies or sites can be used to build your business based on a dropshipping model where products and shipping are handled by a third party. It's one of the easiest ways to produce products or start an online business.

As with any other business venture there are good things to take advantage of and some negative things to consider. So, before you go order that new Bentley, Mr. future business tycoon, here are some Pros and Cons about print-on-demand.

Pros

You can create products quickly: Once you have a design, you can create your product and put it up for sale in mere minutes.

All the tedious stuff is done for you. Shipping and fulfilment is handled by your supplier. Remember, after the sale you are still responsible for customer service.

Low investment, lower risk: Since you don't have to purchase and physically stock inventory, using print on demand is a low investment, low risk way for you to start and profit from business. POD also makes it easy for you to add or remove products from your online store, test new ideas, create new product, and change your sales or marketing strategy.

Cons

Lower margins: Naturally, your costs per item is going to be higher than if you buy product in bulk. Therefore, print-on-demand products may yield smaller profits, depending on how you price them.

Shipping costs could get complicated because it may vary from product to product. You don't have control over your packaging and some shipping options.

It may be costly to customize products. Customization costs and possibilities vary depending on the vendor and product. If you are considering using POD you'll need to consider profit margins, customization options, printing techniques, and available product sizes before designing or customizing items.

Dropshipping

Don't have a lot of money to invest but you still want to go into business for yourself? Dropshipping may be just the business model you need to get rolling. What exactly is dropshipping? Dropshipping is a retail fulfillment method where your online store doesn't keep the products it sells in stock. Instead, when your store sells a product from its online product listings, you then purchase the item from a third party (dropshipper) and have it shipped directly to the customer. This business model is so convenient because the merchant never sees or handles the product. The biggest difference between dropshipping and the standard retail model is that you won't have to stock or own inventory, and therefore you don't have to incur the cost of doing so. Instead, you purchase inventory as needed from a third party (wholesaler or manufacturer) whenever you get a sale to fulfill your orders. The dropshipper then packages and ships the item to your customer.

So, again, the most appealing thing about dropshipping is that it's possible to launch an ecommerce store without having to invest thousands of dollars in inventory up front. That gives your online store an advantage over traditional retailers who have to tie up huge amounts of their capital purchasing inventory. With the dropshipping model, you purchase a product only after you have already made the sale and been paid by the customer. By not having to pay for major up-front inventory, it's possible to start a successful dropshipping business with very little money. Your customer simply clicks the buy button on your online store site and your dropshipping supplier ships it, making you money on each sell.

You Can Get Started Right Away

Needless to say, running an ecommerce business is much easier when you don't have to deal with physical products. With dropshipping, you don't have to worry about things like, managing or paying for a warehouse, packing and shipping orders, tracking inventory, handling returns and inbound shipments, ordering products and managing stock levels. Because you don't have the expense of purchasing inventory or managing a warehouse, your overhead expenses and the cost of starting your business are very low. Dropshipping businesses are the perfect business to run from your home office with a laptop. You can run your dropshipping business from just about anywhere that has an internet connection. A successful dropship business can often be started for less than $100 per month. As you grow, your expenses will likely increase but they will still be lower than the cost of running a traditional brick-and-mortar business.

Imagine being able to offer your customers a wide selection of products because you don't have to pre-purchase the items you sell. If your dropship supplier stocks an item, you can list if for sale on your website without having to purchase it first.

Traditional businesses are labor intensive. The more items they sale the more labor there is to be done. By using a dropshipping supplier, the work it takes to process additional orders are taken care of by your supplier, allowing you to expand and scale up your business without the additional labor of you having to do customer fulfillment. With a growth in sales your extra work can be concentrated in the area of customer service. As you can see, these benefits make dropshipping very attractive for beginning entrepreneurs as well as some established merchants.

What Are the Negatives Of Dropshipping?

Low Margins: The biggest disadvantage to operating a dropshipping business is low margins. Because it's so inexpensive to get started with drop shipping and the overhead costs are so minimal it is worth it for some merchants to set up shop and sell items at rock-bottom prices so they can get their business started. The hope is that once they begin to increase sales they can grow their revenue to the point where the sheer volume of their sells generates profits. By investing so little in getting your business started you can afford to operate on low margins for a while.

Pricing: Cutthroat competition may be another disadvantage of dropshipping. Very often merchants who compete with you by selling the same items have low-quality websites and poor customer service, but customers will still compare their prices to yours. Cutthroat competition can destroy your profit margins by offering the same items you sell at lower prices than you. If the only thing of value you can offer is a low price, you'll soon be caught in a pricing war that will strip away all your profits. To guard against this, look for products that have MAP Pricing. Some manufacturers will set what's called a minimum advertised price (MAP) for their products. They require that all resellers price their products at or above certain levels. This pricing floor prevents those cutthroat price wars. MAP priced items help to ensure you as a merchant can make a reasonable profit by carrying that manufacturer's products.

Also, try to select items to sell that are popular, but unique, and well suited for dropshipping. The most common mistake new dropshipping businesses make is picking a product based on their personal interests or some passion they have. If your goal is to build a profitable dropshipping business it may be best to set your personal interest and passions aside when researching what products to sell.

Inventory: When you stock your own items it's easy to keep track of which items are in stock or out of stock. But, be aware when you're sourcing from multiple warehouses because they are also fulfilling orders for other merchants, so their inventory changes on a daily basis. You may not know whether a certain item is in stock or out. There are ways you can sync your store's inventory with your supplier's, but these solutions don't always work seamlessly. Furthermore, suppliers don't always support the technology required for this option.

Shipping: You may run into some complexities when you work with multiple suppliers, as most drop shippers do. The products on your website will most likely be sourced through a number of different drop shippers. This variety of suppliers complicates your shipping costs. Example: If a customer places an order for three items, that happen to come from three separate suppliers, you'll get three separate shipping charges for sending each item to the customer. Let me caution you here. You may have to eat some of that higher shipping cost. Why? It's probably not a good idea to pass this charge along to the customer, because in comparing the three prices your customer may believe he or she is being grossly overcharged for shipping. Automating these separate calculations is a headache as well.

Supplier Errors: If you don't like getting blamed for something that wasn't your fault, you may have to get used to it once you start a business based on dropshipping. Because even if a mistake was the fault of your dropshipping supplier the item was sold through your store, which means you will have to accept responsibility for the mistake. Even the best dropshipping suppliers make mistakes sometimes when fulfilling orders. When it happens, try to provide your customer with good customer service by making sure that whatever mistake occurred is quickly corrected. Apologize and take responsibility for supplier errors because bad reviews and word of mouth are worse than losing money on one bad transaction. Finally, try to avoid mediocre and low-quality suppliers because they will cause you endless frustration with missing items, shipping the wrong items, and low-quality packing which leads to damaged items and worse damage to your business reputation.

Dropshipping Suppliers

If you think you are ready to start an online store by using the dropshipping model here are a few of the best dropshipping suppliers:

Shopify, BigCommerce, SaleHoo, Alibaba, Doba, Worldwide Brands, Wholesale2B, Sunrise Wholesale, Inventory Source, Megagoods, and National Dropshippers.

Another way to find the best drop shipping suppliers is to attend trade shows. You can find local trade shows in drop shipping forums or through a Google search. Trade shows are an excellent way to meet established as well as up-and-coming companies. By attending trade shows you may also find good products to sell on your site that your competitors don't sell. Some drop shipping supplier directories publish a bestseller list. This is another way to see which items other competitors believe are the best items to sell. You might also see which items are popular by seeing how many Google searches have been made for it.

Build Wealth through Arbitrage

What is Arbitrage? Arbitrage is a practice in the economy of making risk-free profits by taking advantage of market fluctuations. This is done by buying an asset in one market at a lesser price and selling it immediately in another market at a higher price.

Real Estate

What if you observed someone who relocated from San Francisco to Portland because of his or her job and you witnessed them give up their Bay Area 2 bedroom home that cost $1,500,000 to buy a mansion in Portland for $400,000. After assessing that the person's salary in Portland is roughly the same as it was in San Francisco, and other characteristics like the topography, weather, diversity, and lifestyle, are also similar, how long would it take you to figure out that there is money to be made here?

It is only logical that many San Francisco homeowners would eventually cash in on their small million dollar properties to relocate to a much lower cost area if both areas are similar, especially if they are retiring. They can purchase the cheaper, larger home, and bank the money they profited on the move to live off of. This is a common occurrence now that technology has made working in a specific location less necessary. Over the past 10 years, places like Portland and Seattle have seen their property prices explode. With companies such as Amazon, Nike, Starbucks, and others headquartered in the Northwest plenty of people now call these two cities home. Think of the millions of dollars that were made by those wise enough to have purchased real estate in these cities while prices were more than reasonable and sold that real estate once prices skyrocketed by over 70%. Those smart people took advantage of a great arbitrage situation. The same thing happened in cities like Durham and Raleigh, North Carolina; Houston, Texas; Nashville, Tennessee; and many others. There are plenty of cities left that are going to see explosive growth in the near future. If major companies build or relocate to these places, rapid growth and higher real estate prices are not far behind. The key is to grab real estate before the companies arrive or shortly thereafter. Did you miss out on all the action? For Portland and Seattle, yes. But, arbitrage opportunities exist all over the place in various industries.

Real Estate Crowdfunding

Don't have enough capital to take advantage of such real estate arbitrage? Take advantage of real estate crowdfunding. Real estate crowdfunding is a multi-decade investment trend that is just starting to take off. By crowdfunding capital, you can easily own a portion of multi-million dollar commercial real estate projects in promising cities with lower valuations, strong job growth, and higher net rental yields. These real estate deals were once unavailable to you but laws changed in 2012 to make real estate crowdfunding possible. Real estate crowdfunding exploded onto the scene after the passage of the 2012 JOBS Act.

Real estate crowdfunding is an effective way for investors to pool their financial and intellectual resources to invest in properties and projects much bigger than they could afford or manage on their own. Real estate syndication has been around for decades. However, syndicated investments were difficult for individual investors to get into because of the high cost. Only ultra-high net worth investors or institutional investors with hundreds of millions, if not billions of dollars could invest in them and profit.

Now, real estate crowdfunding companies like Fundrise (for non-accredited investors) and RealtyMogul (mainly for accredited investors), allows you to access mid-market, commercial real estate deals that have provided above average real estate returns for decades. Crowdfunding is an exciting and growing way to take advantage of real estate arbitrage.

Classified Arbitrage

One of the simplest places to find arbitrage opportunities is in local classified markets. Buying goods from eBay or Craigslist and selling them for a profit is one of the most basic forms of arbitrage. Although this method most likely won't make you rich it can be a good source of additional income for you.

Although arbitrage is relatively risk-free, it is advisable for you to study your markets and current trends. Transaction costs are applied when you buy and sell products so do your research on the economics of your plan before dealing with any form of arbitrage.

Import/Export

Whenever it is legal, purchasing products in one country at a low price and selling it in another country at a higher price is an excellent way to build wealth. Import/export has been going on for thousands of years and it is still done because it is profitable. Just make sure you do your research to find reputable companies to deal with, understand the tariffs and taxes that may be added to your products, calculate insurance cost, and other cost of doing international business to make sure you are coming out way ahead profit wise.

Regional Opportunities

You may be able to find certain products that are popular in one region of the country but are not even sold in other regions of the country. If you can negotiate the rights to distribute that product in new geographic areas it could present a good arbitrage opportunity for you. With the use of the internet, online stores, social media marketing, and third party fulfilment, there are now thousands of arbitrage opportunities you can use to fire your job and get rich building your own business empire.

Make a Podcast That Pays

Podcasts are red-hot right now. All you really need to create one is a laptop and a good microphone. Since podcasts don't need to run daily, and don't have to be live, you can record multiple episodes at once. There are many ways to make money from a podcast, including commercial sponsorships or advertising products or services. You can record and broadcast a podcast from wherever you are in the world. It's simple, and it can be profitable.

Set Up an Online Course

If you have a skill you want to share you can set up an online course with written tutorials, PDF downloads and/or videos. Teaching online courses like home remodeling, furniture painting, math made easy, cooking made easy, yoga, and other courses where members can learn at their own pace is a good way to make money. Let's say you charge $60 four your course, and you enroll 40 students. That is $2400 earned. And that is just for one of the courses you can teach. If you teach only 3 such courses a month over a year's time that nets you $86,400. Some online course resources for teaching include TakeLessons, Udemy and Skillshare.

Write or Publish an E-Book

Speaking of e-books, it's a great way to turn your expertise into a platform that people will buy, creating a form of passive income. Kindle even has a step-by-step guide for how to create, publish and market an e-book. You can also write a guide or e-book for your online course. If you know anything really well, places to go, how to fix something, how to cook, where to shop for bargains, how to do a podcast, etc., you can write a guide that teaches it, then sell your guide as an e-book, offer it as a download for a fee on your site, or even reach out to other bloggers who feature similar content and ask if they will offer it as a paid download on their site and pay you part of the sell cost.

Another way to make money with e-books is to find a book that has already been published in print license it to publish online. The person who publishes the e-book gets the majority of money for online sells and pays the book's author the standard 8% to 15% royalties based on net sales. You can also pay some authors a one-time payment for the rights to publish their book online. like Vic Johnson. Paying as low as $200 Or $300 can get you the rights to a book that may over the years earn you thousands of dollars for the e-book. Statistics show that there are over 44 million print books on Amazon but only 2.6 million Kindle e-books. That is a lot of printed books waiting to be converted.

Create a Blog

If you are passionate about a certain subject or have an expertise in a certain field, you can create a blog about it. You may want to focus your writing on a topic that you personally feel passionate about or a subject you know enough about to write on consistently. The most popular blogs are those that provide information that is helpful to people, like how to become a micro-farmer, or how to start a business. Blogs can earn money through affiliate programs when people buy products through your blog. One of the biggest affiliate income programs is from Amazon. By signing up to become an Amazon Associate and connecting the Amazon store to your blog you can earn passive income 24/7.

Another way to earn money with your blog is to blog for AdSense Cash. AdSense Cash consists of ads that are put on your blog or site. These ads are matched with your blog content so whatever subject you are writing about is matched with ads that are promoting products that deal with the same type subject. For instance, your blog about health can be matched with ads that promote health products. It should be noted that blogs covering obscure subjects probably will not earn you as much income as those covering popular subjects. Therefore, consider what's trending by checking Google News and Trends when you are searching for suitable subjects to blog about.

Make A Podcast That Pays

Podcasts are red-hot. If you want to create one all you really need is a laptop and a good microphone. Because podcasts don't have to run daily, or be broadcast live, you can record multiple episodes at once and air them at later dates. Once you develop a following you can earn money with your podcast by having sponsorships or running commercials that advertise products or services. Before embarking on becoming a podcaster it would be wise to listen to some of the more popular podcasts.

If you are dreaming of launching your successful podcast and sharing your audio content with the world, you first have to host your audio files with a podcast hosting provider. There are over 100 million podcast listeners in the United States and more millions around the world. The podcast journey begins by choosing a podcast hosting provider and here are some of the best to choose from:

Buzzsprout, Podbean, Simplecast, Transistor, Spreaker, Captivate, Castos, Smart Podcast Player, and Audioboom.

Earn Money as A Writer

Writing is another way to earn income. Supplying marketing copy for companies, doing freelance writing for online media, and scores of other writing opportunities exist today. By using a laptop you can write from practically anywhere. There are a number of companies that hire online writers like iWriter, which pays up to $80 per 500 words once you're promoted up the writing ranks. You can also write that great novel you've always wanted to by using Amazon's Kindle Direct Publishing.

Use Your Freelance Designer Skills to Earn Money

If you are a talented designer with graphic design or web design skills you can get paid for your skills on websites like 99Designs.com, as well as many of the print-on- demand sites. There is a global community of designers on these sites who bid on design jobs and you can be one of them.

Craft Artists have Multiple Markets

If crafts happen to be your talent sites like Amazon Handmade, ArtFire, Cargoh and of course Etsy provide a place for those who make handmade items like jewelry and other accessories to market their products. These platforms make it possible for craft artists of all types to earn money from their creativity.

Bring in Revenue with Affiliate Programs

If you want to work from home you can make money by having a website or blog and promoting affiliate programs. One of the most high profile of these is the Amazon affiliate program which you can join by signing up to become an Amazon Associate. You promote Amazon items on your website or blog with links that lead back to the products on Amazon using your affiliate ID. Other affiliate programs work pretty much the same way. The success of making money with affiliate programs weighs heavily on how much traffic you can attract to your site and how closely the affiliate products may align with the content on your site. Another proven way to make money working from home is to sign up as an affiliate at ClickBank to promote their digital products. Before you use the ClickBank affiliate program it's smart to test the products you promote to better understand how they work. That way you'll be able to tell your customers what's good or not good about the products. How much you earn in commissions is based on what items you promote and how well they sell on your site.

Become A Social Media Influencer

Over the last decade social media has rapidly grown in influence and importance. According to 2019 statistics there are 3.2 billion social media users worldwide. That equates to about 42% of the current population. Influencers in social media are people who have built a reputation for their knowledge and expertise on a particular topic. They make regular posts about that topic on their preferred social media channels and generate large followings of enthusiastic engaged people who pay close attention to their views. More increasingly these days people look up to influencers in social media to guide them with their decision making. Brands love social media influencers because of their ability to create trends and encourage their followers to buy the products they promote.

Types of Influencers

The majority of influencers fit into four major categories: 1) Celebrities 2) Industry experts and thought leaders 3) Bloggers and content creators and $) Micro Influencers (this last category is becoming the most important category of influencers).

The bulk of social influencer marketing today occurs in social media, predominantly with micro influencers, and blogging. Industry experts and thought leaders such as journalists can also be considered influencers and hold an important position for brands. Surprisingly, celebrities, who were the original influencers, still play a role in influencing buyers but their importance as influencers is decreasing. Brands are now recognizing that bloggers and influencers in social media (predominantly micro-bloggers) have the most authentic and active relationships with their fans.

Compensation for Influencers

The pay range for influencers covers a wide span and is determined by a number of factors. Influencers can do deals for hundreds of dollars or hundreds of thousands depending on their level of influence. A single sponsored post can run from $50 to more than $50,000. According to Hopper HQ's 2018 Instagram Rich List, mega-stars like Selena Gomez and Kylie Jenner, who each have more than 100 million followers, pull in $800,000 and $1,000,000 per post, while those with the smallest following on the list (a mere one million) charge $1,300 to $3,000 per post.

In general, experts estimate the average pay for influencers is $1,000 per 100,000 followers, or roughly one cent per follower. The variables for these rates can depend upon such criteria as the influencer's quality of content, the influencer's following on their blog and the social media channels they use. Pay can also be determined by the influencer's engagement metrics, the number of deliverables, the allotted time frame and the agreed upon usage rights for their material. An influencer may be able to negotiate an increased rate if they agree to exclusivity (not working with a brand's competitors) or a deal that allows the brand to use the influencer's images and content in other avenues such as TV commercials, podcasts, print advertisements, or billboards.

For those who are still building their following, you don't have to wait until you have 50,000 followers to start monetizing. Influencers can begin monetizing from the moment they have followers. Most advertisers have public affiliate programs that allow anyone to partner with them to drive affiliate sales. When it comes to brand sponsorships, micro-influencers who have anywhere from 1,000 to 10,000 followers, according to influencer marketing platform IZEA are also very attractive to brands. Brands look at how many people influencers actually influence, not just how many followers they have. There are a lot of influencers who have thousands of followers but produce low engagement and poor results in driving sells.

In terms of impact, an influencer with 500 followers can be more successful in driving sales than an influencer who has 10,000 followers. A smaller following does not necessarily equal less selling power. Sometimes the opposite is true. When micro-influencers are extremely engaged with their audiences they can be significant drivers of product sells for advertisers.

Now you see that there are many ways to step off the traditional work path and build your own path. Blazing your own trail may not be easy but what is when it comes to starting something new, especially when that something is making a living by doing something you love? Social media influencers can earn a good living from becoming a key component in the new marketing mix.

Do Your Homework

Put in some work and find good products that you can purchase at a good price and sell at a better price, or preferably from a print-on-demand or dropshipping company so that you don't have to invest money up front. This chapter has shared a number of ways to earn income and get off the 9 to 5 treadmill. Learn your business, learn your market niche, build an attractive and well-functioning website, put out excellent products, market them well, and follow that with great execution, use affiliate marketing, create podcast, or make crafts. There are many ways to put yourself in position to fire your job. But, whichever path you choose remember to work hard, be smart, and tweak your processes when necessary. Then, Ba-Bam. Rake in the revenue.

You can also build your own business by providing services like social media marketing or promotional services for beauty salons, medical offices, personal therapists and other businesses. Where you may be asking does the RICH part come in? Answer. Once you open the floodgates to start the money rolling in simply duplicate your efforts. Then duplicate it again and again. McDonald's sells the same hamburgers at every restaurant. It's not the hamburger that makes them billions, it's selling billions of that hamburger at thousands of their restaurants. Perfect your success, then scale up my friend, Boom! If you are still on the 9 to 5 treadmill, use your job for money to keep your bills paid, and invest in your business until your business is profitable enough to sustain itself and you. Then you can finally tell your job, Sayonara, to begin building your business empire.

A Look At The Future

The Future of Cars

Automobile repair shops will vanish. Why? Consider this. A gasoline/diesel engine has 20,000 individual parts while an electrical motor has only 20. Electric cars are sold with lifetime guarantees and are repaired by dealers only. These dealers then send the malfunctioning electric motors to a regional repair shop that repairs them with robots. If you happen to be in a hurry here's some good news. It only takes 10 minutes to remove and replace an electric motor. When your electric motor repair light goes on all you'll have to do is drive up to what looks similar to a car wash, have a donut and latte as your car eases through and watch your car come out the other side with a brand new electric motor. Think the day of all electric cars is still far off? Starting with their 2019 model cars Volvo will start producing electric or hybrid vehicles only, doing away with internal combustion engines. It is the beginning of their strategy to phase out hybrid models and go totally electric. If you're an auto mechanic, you may want to start prepping for that next career now.

The future of transportation will belong to autonomous cars. Children born today will never own a driver's license or car. Driverless cars are already here and will begin to disrupt the transportation industry within the next two years. People wanting to go somewhere will simply use their phones to call for a car, it will show up at their location, and drive them to the destination. No stops for gas, and no need for parking. Passengers can choose to work while in transit or simply relax during the trip and then pay only for the distance they were driven. When that time arrives, the personal car is something you will only see in museums. No matter how innovative they try to be traditional car companies will disappear and the car industry will be ruled by tech companies who will build the smart cars of the future which will be nothing less than computers on wheels. Not only will these smart cars change lives, they will save lives as well. Around 1.2 million people die in car accidents each year worldwide. A very high percentage of these fatalities are caused by drunk or distracted drivers. Today there is about one accident for every 60,000 miles driven. With autonomous (driverless cars) that number will drop to 1 accident for every 6 million miles driven saving more than a million lives per year worldwide. With accidents no longer showing up in such staggering numbers insurance companies will fall on hard times. Those companies whose main business model is car insurance will quickly see their business evaporate.

Don't be Caught Sleeping

Don't get caught sleeping. Once upon a time Kodak and Polaroid were major companies in a booming market. Now they are part of a cautionary tale people use to illustrate how fast technology is disrupting industries. In 1998, Kodak had 170,000 employees. It also dominated its market by selling 85% of all the photo paper in the world. Polaroid was the inventor of the Polaroid instant camera, which was once the product everyone wanted to find under their Christmas tree. Then came digital. When digital cameras were invented in 1975, the first ones only boasted 10,000 pixels. Today, the digital cameras embedded in cell phones take pictures nearly as good as anything out there. Moore's Law strikes again. Consequently, within just a few years of their glory days, both Kodak and Polaroid became just shells of what they once were. Technology, including digital cameras in cell phones, mopped the floor with the business models of both companies. If these two companies would have moved quickly enough to lead the digital charge it may have been a different story. But, they didn't. The lesson here is, don't be caught sleeping.

Apps will become industries. UBER is just a software tool. They don't own cars and yet they have become the largest taxi company in the world! How many taxi drivers saw that coming? Airbnb does not own property but they are now the biggest hotel company in the world. The hotel industry was totally blindsided by that one.

Even Professionals are Not Safe

Just in case you thought becoming an attorney guarantees your job won't be taken away by technology there's this: There will be 90% fewer lawyers in the future. Why? Thanks to IBM's Watson, people can get legal advice within seconds with 90% accuracy. Compare this to 70% accuracy when the legal advice is given by humans. As of right now the legal advice given by computers is only for simple legal issues but very soon that advice will even cover complex legal issues. Don't laugh nurses. Watson already helps nurses by diagnosing cancer 4 times more accurately than human nurses. As artificial Intelligence makes computers exponentially better in understanding our world these career takeovers will become common. Don't believe it? The game Go is thought by some to be the most complicated game in the world. This year, a computer beat the best Go player on the planet. That little victory came 10 years earlier than experts expected.

Don't look now Doc but technology is coming for your job too. Remember Star Trek and their little machine called the Tricorder? There are companies who will build a medical device that works in conjunction with your phone. It will take your retina scan, your blood sample, and have you breathe into it. The machine will then analyze 54 bio-markers that will identify nearly every disease. If you think this prognosis is a little premature you should know that there are already dozens of phone apps out there right now being used for health purposes. And, by the way, the price on the Tricorder X will be announced this year. As electricity becomes cheaper and cities cleaner fossil energy companies will desperately try to limit access to the grid to fight off competition from home solar installations but no one can stop the march of technology.

Technology will Change Cities

Cities themselves will go through a radical transformation because of technology. With electric cars becoming dominant by 2030 cities will be less noisy, and with cars going from gas powered to electric cities will also have much cleaner air. Solar production and the use of solar energy has been increasing for the past 30 years, and in the very near future the majority of homes will produce and store electrical energy during the day then sell what they don't use back to the grid. The grid will store it and in return dispense it to companies in industries that are high volume electricity users. Some companies like Tesla whose roof is already a sea of solar panels are already ahead of the curve. The smart major auto manufacturers have already designated money to build new plants that build only electric cars. As electricity takes over this of course means that gas pumps will disappear. Gasoline/oil and coal industries will go away as well. There will be no need for drilling for oil because there will be no market for it. Bye-bye OPEC. In place of gas stations street corners will have electricity dispensing stations. Businesses will install electrical recharging stations for their fleets. As you can tell, the smart cities of the near future are certainly different than the cities we inhabit right now.

Technology innovations are already overthrowing industries left and right, and this is just the beginning of the upheavals. There is no denying how greatly the first three industrial revolutions transformed our society. Industrial revolution (1) occurred with the invention of the *steam engine;*

industrial revolution (2) was ushered in with *the age of science and mass production;* Industrial revolution (3) took place with *the rise of digital technology;* and industrial revolution (4) is now dawning. What makes Industrial Revolution Four different from 3IR? Mainly, three distinct concepts: extreme connectivity, extreme computing power, and extreme automation, all of which will make 4IR even more disruptive than the first three industrial revolutions.

Oh, How the World Will Change

What makes the Fourth Industrial Revolution (4IR) different from the Third Industrial Revolution (3IR)? Well, everything.

It is marked by exponential thinking where linear solutions no longer apply. The digital version replaces the analog version. Knowledge and invention are cumulative. Evolution is just the re-encoding of information, after all. Every person, culture, industry, and country is affected. All forms of production, management, systems, and governments will be transformed.

It is a time of endless possibilities. 3-D printing allows for faster prototyping and going from idea to product in no time. Diseases will be obliterated with the use of nanotechnology. Autonomous vehicles make transportation not only more convenient but safer as well. Advanced algorithms team with robo-advisors to offer micro-financing. Connected homes become more efficient as they become more affordable. These technological advances will be the result of a suitcase full of tech developments that include Artificial Intelligence (AI), machine learning, robotics, algorithms, and massively large data sets. The Fourth Industrial Revolution will be a time that disrupts individuals and industries, countries and cultures, companies and governments, management and the systems they use. Analog has given way to digital and linear solutions are history. Three key developments will usher in a host of changes that will make the future the present, they include extreme connectivity, extreme computing power, and extreme automation.

Extreme Connectivity is having 6 billion internet connected people and 1 trillion connected machines. How quickly will this happen? There are currently 5 billion people who are connected by cell phones and by 2025, that number will increase to 6 billion. The use of smart phones will explode when the cost of cell phones goes from $150 a month today to $150 a year by 2025. We are on track to have 1 trillion connected devices in (cars, homes, planes, etc.) the near future.

Extreme Computing Power is now possible for the masses who can rent almost endless processing power from Amazon AWS or Microsoft Azure. Quantum computing has been a possibility but the Fourth Industrial Revolution will make it a reality. Humans can no longer beat a computer at chess. Quantum computing has already reached 128 Qubits of processing capacity for a single system. How significant is this? Once we look at 1024 Qubits of quantum processing power, every door built by technology is suddenly vulnerable, from bank vaults to personal bank accounts to military weapon systems. It means all the traditional encryption codes in the world can be unlocked by a machine in near real time. Extreme computing? I'll say!

What would you call Extreme Automation? Automation that drives cars, cures cancer, teaches students, fights wars, replaces entire workforces, disrupts professions, litigates cases and diagnoses diseases. How about 5 billion Google searches a day, 2 billion daily worldwide Facebook subscribers, or 200 million daily orders on Alibaba. Or, maybe you think extreme automation is a combination of artificial intelligence, machine learning, algorithms; and 3-D printing that produces everything from cloths to prosthetics. All this equals the Fourth Industrial Revolution.

The First Industrial Revolution fueled by iron and steam engines and the Second Industrial Revolution which was powered by electricity, chemicals, and telecommunications both produced explosive growth and prosperity in business. The Third Industrial Revolution ushered in the Information Age bringing us world-changing innovations in computing, the internet, and mobile communications. Curiously enough, these innovations did not bring with it a massive increase in productivity. In fact, since 1970, productivity fell to roughly one-third the rate of the previous 100 years. This could be the result of many other factors like outsourcing work to other nations and businesses using computing to replace large workforces with smaller staffs. So, what should we expect from the Fourth Industrial Revolution?

A boom in business productivity and more wealth creation at least at the top of the food chain would seem to be on the horizon. Why? Because the same infrastructure technologies that fueled the first two industrial revolutions are leading the charge in this fourth industrial revolution, namely energy, transportation, health, and communication. Add to these the advantages of the digital age and the possibilities are staggering.

Digital energy combines smart power grids and meters into platforms that dynamically matches energy generation with demand for energy from both new and traditional sources. Digital transportation moves people and goods across land, oceans, and skies autonomously. Digital health enables connected health care to be remotely delivered from anywhere. Digital communication now connects billions of people and machines, allowing them to seamlessly interact with each other. These four foundational technologies will now be enhanced by a fifth, digital production that will cause a paradigm shift in how business is conducted changing production from being centralized to distributed, by combining cloud computing and 3D printing to create goods in almost real time.

By applying historical formulas and calculating when these digital technologies could reach their tipping points, Nokia Bell Labs has projected a significant productivity jump that could reach 30% to 35% in the United States, occurring somewhere between 2028 and 2033. That increase mirrors the leap in productivity that took place in the Second Industrial Revolution during the 1950s. This increase could add approximately $2.8 trillion to the U.S. economy. Similar increases can also be anticipated in china, and India. Cloud technologies and 5G will form the foundation of the networks that will soon accelerate the digitalization of various industries and creating opportunities across every segment of the economy. These innovations will give people more time and freedom to connect with each other and enjoy life. But, there will also be a down side to these technological advancements.

The Future of Entrepreneurship

WeWork was founded in New York in 2010 and offers coworking spaces to entrepreneurs, startup companies, freelancers and larger enterprises. The company has been growing rapidly ever since, and today it is one of the largest coworking space chains in the world with more than 2,000 employees and 580 office locations across 100 cities worldwide.

There are other companies that offer flexible space solutions such as Regus who prides itself on being a pioneer of the genre. Regus is the largest commercial space provider, with over 3,000 business centers in 120 countries. Like Regus, coworking provider WeWork is changing the way businesses think of workspace.

Technology has obviously changed the way business will be done in the future. New technologies have given Entrepreneurs a whole new basket of tools they can use to start and grow their business. Along with the changes technology has made to the future of business are changes companies like WeWork are making to how company's view building business infrastructure in the future.

Why do co-working real estate companies like WeWork represent the future of business infrastructure? WeWork says they are a company where all types of businesses can thrive: from freelancers to satellite sales teams, solo entrepreneurs to Fortune 500 companies, technology firms to financial advisers. While that may be impressive why does WeWork and their business model present a possible glimpse into the future of entrepreneurship? Using information from the WeWork website let's take a look at the WeWork model and how it could compel your business to do business their way.

Here are some particulars. Businesses pay **No Exorbitant Up-front Costs.** You can invest zero capital in office space and still have it tailored to your company's needs. **Greater Flexibility.** You can stay agile as you grow, with just a two-year minimum on member agreements. You can expand or contract as your business changes. **One Point of Contact.** You can reduce your operational headaches with consolidated support for cleaning, maintenance, IT, utilities, and more.

Choose Your Layout. Your company can select from various layout options that have proven results for companies of your size and locale. **Personalize Details.** You can upgrade technical gear based on your needs, and integrate your branding into the building interior's art and signage. **Move In Swiftly.** Thanks to a streamlined design and build process, you'll waste no time getting up and running.

WeWork Office Suites

For those companies looking for a private Office Suite that scales efficiently, you can configure your own branded layout from a menu of data-driven designs. **Engineered for Business at Scale.** If your company needs its own environment, but has a board that expects efficiency, you can select one of WeWork's recommended layouts for teams of 20-250, and get the best of both worlds. **Optimized for Focus.** By prioritizing natural light and power access, workstations maximize productivity, minimize distraction, and enable quality ROI. **Amenities All Your Own.** With private reception, conference rooms, executive offices, phone booths, and pantries, your company can enjoy exclusive access for a cohesive employee experience. **Meeting Essentials 2.0.** Equipped with high-end A/V and options for acoustic treatment, your private conference rooms will be future-state-of-the-art.

Standard Private Offices

WeWork rents enclosed spaces for teams of one to 100, with access to WeWork's shared meeting rooms, lounges, and amenities, like microbrewed coffee and printing services. WeWork standard private offices are move-in ready, lockable spaces that feel like home. They include desks, chairs, and storage cabinets so that all you need to do is get to work.

Privacy and security: You can be sure that all of your team's belongings are secure in a space that's all your own, with a lock and key. **Office essentials.** WeWork has all the basics covered, from bookable conference rooms to high-speed Wi-Fi, printing services, and even A/V equipment. **Simplified logistics.** They handle reception, cleaning, IT, mailroom services, kitchen restocking, and more so that you don't have to. **Networking and events. You can c**onnect and collaborate with other companies inside the WeWork network through in-person events and other networking activities.

Placing Your Headquarters at WeWork

If you want to headquarter your business at WeWork they can provide private offices on your own floor of an unbranded building. You can keep your business secure with your own private address, entrance, and network. Additional privacy and security options are also available.

Here's What You Get:

To sum up the possible advantages of using a real estate company like WeWork over normal real estate companies to provide for your business facility needs here is a review of what they provide.

Space: 24/7 building access, common areas and lounges, high-speed Wi-Fi, conference rooms, phone booths, kitchenettes. **Services:** Front-desk and guest reception, business-class printing, mail and package handling, cleaning services, building operations, streamlined billing process. **Perks:** Microbrewed coffee and herbal tea, fruit-infused water, events and conferences, unique spaces (e.g., rooftop lounges), desirable neighborhoods. **Above and beyond:** On-site support from a Community Manager, flexible membership agreements, access to book rooms at other locations, unlimited guests, connect with members through the Member Network, and an option to add space as you grow. **Member benefits and discounts:** As a WeWork member, you and your team will have access to their Services Store, an online portal offering you exclusive offers and pricing on business services like health insurance and lifestyle perks like gym memberships.

The Advent of Universal Basic Income

Autonomous cars, artificial intelligence, robotics, cloud computing, the digitalization of industries all add up to fewer jobs for human beings.

Researchers are already predicting mass unemployment in the new economy and politicians are already thinking about how to solve the problems that come with industries that no longer need large numbers of human capital to make their businesses profitable. One possible solution to the problem of mass unemployment that they are debating is "Universal Basic Income."

Hopeful United States 2020 presidential candidate Andrew Yang tossed his hat into the ring for the highest job in the nation using the promise of Universal Basic Income as his main campaign theme. For those who have never heard of UBI or are trying to learn more about what it is and how it works Yang's website gives one of the clearest explanations of the who, what, why, and how's of UBI. Yang call's his version of Universal Basic Income, The Freedom Dividend. Here are the particulars explained on the website and some questions and answers that shed some light on the subject:

THE FREEDOM DIVIDEND, DEFINED

In the next 12 years, 1 out of 3 American workers are at risk of losing their jobs to new technologies—and unlike with previous waves of automation, this time new jobs will not appear quickly enough in large enough numbers to make up for it. To avoid an unprecedented crisis, we're going to have to find a new solution, unlike anything we've done before. It all begins with the Freedom Dividend, a universal basic income for all American adults, no strings attached – a foundation on which a stable, prosperous, and just society can be built. **-Andrew Yang**

Andrew Yang wants to implement the Freedom Dividend because we are experiencing the greatest technological shift the world has ever seen. By 2015, automation had already destroyed four million manufacturing jobs, and the smartest people in the world now predict that a third of all working Americans will lose their job to automation in the next 12 years. Our current policies are not equipped to handle this crisis. Even our most forward-thinking politicians are unprepared.

How Can We Offset the Negative Results of Automation?

As technology improves, workers will be able to stop doing the most dangerous, repetitive, and boring jobs. This should excite us, but if Americans have no source of income—no ability to pay for groceries, buy homes, save for education, or start families with confidence—then the future could be very dark. Our labor participation rate now is only 62.7% – lower than it has been in decades, with 1 out of 5 working-age men currently out of the workforce. This will get much worse as self-driving cars and other technologies come online.

The Freedom Dividend—funded by a simple Value Added Tax—would guarantee that all Americans benefit from automation, not just big companies. The Freedom Dividend would provide money to cover the basics for Americans while enabling us to look for a better job, start our own business, go back to school, take care of our loved ones or work towards our next opportunity.

For more about why Andrew Yang believes so strongly in the Freedom Dividend, read his book 'The War on Normal People'.

Who Would Get the Dividend?

Every U.S. citizen over the age of 18 would receive $1,000 a month, regardless of income or employment status, free and clear. No jumping through hoops. Yes, this means you and everyone you know would receive a check for $1,000 a month every month starting in January 2021. What would you do with $1,000 a month on top of whatever you now make? Let's find out.

How Would We Pay for the Dividend

It would be easier than you might think. Andrew proposes funding the Freedom Dividend by consolidating some welfare programs and implementing a Value-Added Tax (VAT) of 10%. Current welfare and social program beneficiaries would be given a choice between their current benefits or $1,000 cash unconditionally – most would prefer cash with no restriction.

A Value-Added Tax (VAT) is a tax on the production of goods or services a business produces. It is a fair tax and it makes it much harder for large corporations, who are experts at hiding profits and income, to avoid paying their fair share. A VAT is nothing new. 160 out of 193 countries in the world already have a Value-Added Tax or something similar, including all of Europe which has an average VAT of 20 percent.

The means to pay for the Freedom Dividend will come from 4 sources:

1. Current spending. We currently spend between $500 and $600 billion a year on welfare programs, food stamps, disability and the like. This reduces the cost of the Freedom Dividend because people already receiving benefits would have a choice but would be ineligible to receive the full $1,000 in addition to current benefits.

Additionally, we currently spend over one trillion dollars on health care, incarceration, homelessness services and the like. We would save $100 – 200+ billion as people would take better care of themselves and avoid the emergency room, jail, and the street and would generally be more functional. The Freedom Dividend would pay for itself by helping people avoid our institutions, which is when our costs shoot up. Some studies have shown that $1 to a poor parent will result in as much as $7 in cost-savings and economic growth.

2. A VAT. Our economy is now incredibly vast at $19 trillion, up $4 trillion in the last 10 years alone. A VAT at half the European level would generate $800 billion in new revenue. A VAT will become more and more important as technology improves because you cannot collect income tax from robots or software.

3. New revenue. Putting money into the hands of American consumers would grow the economy. The Roosevelt Institute projected that the economy would grow by approximately $2.5 trillion and create 4.6 million new jobs. This would generate approximately $800 – 900 billion in new revenue from economic growth and activity.

4. Taxes on top earners and pollution. By removing the Social Security cap, implementing a financial transactions tax, and ending the favorable tax treatment for capital gains/carried interest, we can decrease financial speculation while also funding the Freedom Dividend. We can add to that a carbon fee that will be partially dedicated to funding the Freedom

Dividend, making up the remaining balance required to cover the cost of this program.

Won't People Stop Working?

Decades of research on cash transfer programs have found that the only people who work fewer hours when given direct cash transfers are new mothers and kids in school. In several studies, high school graduation rates rose. In some cases, people even work more. Quoting a Harvard and MIT study, "we find no effects of [cash] transfers on work behavior."

In our plan, each adult would receive only $12,000 a year. This is barely enough to live on in many places and certainly not enough to afford much in the way of experiences or advancement. To get ahead meaningfully, people will still need to get out there and work.

Isn't This Communism/Socialism?

No. Communism is, by definition, a revolutionary movement to create a classless, moneyless, and stateless social order built upon shared ownership of production. With Socialism, the core principle is the nationalization of the means of production – i.e. the government seizes Amazon and Google. The Freedom Dividend is none of those things and actually fits so seamlessly into capitalism, it is projected to grow the economy $2.5 trillion in eight years.

Really, the Freedom Dividend is necessary for the continuation of capitalism through the automation wave and displacement of workers. Markets need consumers to sell things to. The Freedom Dividend is capitalism with a floor that people cannot fall beneath.

Wouldn't Employers Just Start Paying Less?

Employers are already paying their employees less for doing more. Corporate productivity is up 72% since 1973, but American wages are up only 9%. UBI would put power in the hands of the worker—with consistent, unconditional cash to cover their expenses, Americans will be able to be more selective about the working conditions they're willing to accept.

With UBI, jobs that people naturally want to do — like being a teacher, or coach, or artist — might pay a little bit less. But jobs that people don't want to do will actually have to pay more because workers won't have to necessarily take that job.

What Are The Benefits of the Freedom Dividend?

The Freedom Dividend would transform society in many positive ways and evidence shows this. Trials of various UBI plans have led to all kinds of benefits—some expected, some surprising. Here are just a few of them:

UBI encourages people to find work. Many current welfare programs take away benefits when recipients find work, sometimes leaving them financially worse off than before they were employed. UBI is for all adults, regardless of employment status, so recipients are free to seek additional income, which most everyone does.

UBI reduces bureaucracy—with no-strings-attached coverage, determining who is eligible is far simpler and the cost of administering benefits is greatly reduced.

UBI increases bargaining power for workers because a guaranteed, unconditional income gives them leverage to say no to exploitative wages and abusive working conditions. Employers can't push workers around as much.

UBI increases entrepreneurship because it provides for basic needs in the early lean days of a company and acts as a safety net if the business fails. It also gives you more consumers to sell to because everyone has more disposable income. The Roosevelt Institute found that a UBI would create 4.6 million jobs and grow the economy by 12 percent continuously. UBI would be the greatest catalyst for new jobs, entrepreneurship, and creativity we have ever seen.

UBI improves the mental health of recipients because it reduces conditions of scarcity, poverty, and financial insecurity, major sources of stress for millions of people.

UBI helps people make smarter decisions. Studies have shown that people in straits of economic insecurity have a reduced cognitive ability equal to

13 IQ points. UBI would provide the security people need to focus on important things like their families.

UBI improves physical health. With increased economic security, people are less prone to stresses, disease, and self-destructive behavior. A UBI experiment in Canada saw hospitalization rates go down 8.5%.

UBI increases art production, nonprofit work and caring for loved ones because it provides a supplementary income for those interested in labor that isn't supported by the market.

UBI improves labor market efficiency because fewer workers are stuck in jobs that are a bad fit. National productivity will improve because people will be able to seek work that is more rewarding and promote higher job satisfaction.

UBI improves relationships by reducing domestic violence, child abuse, financial stresses, and sources of conflict. It ensures that everyone has an optimistic sense of his or her own future and has the mobility to get out of abusive relationships.

It's amazing what a steady source of money can do to transform people's lives. We can experience it here in America if we adopt the Freedom Dividend; we are the wealthiest and most technologically advanced society in human history. It's time to invest in our people.

Imagine your life and that of everyone you know with an extra $1,000 per month – how would you spend it? How would things change?

Other Thoughts on The Subject of UBI

Representative, Alexandria Ocasio Cortez (D.-N.Y.) who has floated Universal Basic Income as part of a Green New Deal, which is the umbrella name for a host of policies to tackle climate change and reduce inequality. Tech billionaires, among them Mark Zuckerberg and Elon Musk, have thrown their support behind UBI.

For those searching for actual examples of whether Universal Basic Income works there is some useful data from other countries and programs who have been experimenting with UBI.

A program in Kenya, run by the charity GiveDirectly, has been giving out unconditional money since 2016 to more than 21,000 people in villages across the country in a trial set to last 12 years. Initial results show a boost to the well-being of participants. In the U.S., a trial is about to kick off in Stockton, California, that will give $500 a month to 100 low-income families. And in Oakland, the tech incubator Y Combinator intends to start a UBI trial this year that would hand $1,000 a month with no strings attached to 1,000 people across two U.S. states for three years.

Matt Bruenig of the People's Policy Project, reminds us that there is an equivalent program already being used that can provide insight into the feasibility of using UBI in America.

"It's important to remember that there is a basic income program in the United States already that has been running for around 40 years: the Alaska Permanent Fund Dividend. So, it's not as hypothetical as some people seem to think," says Bruenig.

Through the program Alaska hands residents annual, unconditional checks of $330 to $2,000.

While the jury may still be out on Universal Basic Income as a solution to the increased use of automation in the workplace, it is one of the possible answers to what problems may occur in the future. Being that it is a possibility, it would be wise of you to start formulating a plan for what you would do with the money if UBI becomes a reality. Better to stay ahead of the curve than wait until it is upon you and then make a rushed decision on what to do with some unexpected cash. Spend it, invest it, use it to pay for education or training, give it as a gift, use it as supplemental income in addition to your main job, use it to retire and travel, there are many options that UBI makes possible. Now may be a good time to explore those options.

How Do You Prepare for the Future

In the future many industries will go through transformations because of technology. Take the field of finance where the field will soon be divided into those that understand technology and those that don't. If you can't explain what a blockchain is, describe how cloud computing impacts finance, or have no idea what fintech is you are ill equipped for the new world of finance. Finance professionals need to know how technology can be used, so that they can make use of it. Gaining this knowledge usually begins with education.

It should be no surprise to anyone with an eye on the future that the top in-demand degrees for the future will be found in careers that involve science, engineering and finance. Being that an emphasis is to be placed on careers that revolve around these technologies concentrating on design, monitoring, and maintenance in these areas should be the focus of those looking for college majors that can best prepare students for the future.

With this in mind here are the top growth career fields:

Engineering – software developers and engineers, Wind Turbine Service Technicians, Biomedical Engineers, Chemical Engineers, Civil Engineers, Environmental Engineers, Industrial Engineers, Marine Engineers and Naval Architects, Electrical and Electronics Engineers, and Solar Photovoltaic Installers.

Finance – Accountants, Economists, Actuaries, Financial planners, Investor Relations Associates, and Credit Analysts.

Information Technology – Cyber-Security, Application Software Developers, IT Security Specialists, Data Analysts, Computer Systems Analysts, Transformation Consultants, Biotechnicians, Network Analysts, Solar or Wind Energy Technicians, and Software Engineers.

What type of degrees will you need to get these jobs?

Healthcare – Healthcare Administrators, Clinical Research Administrators, Paramedics, Radiologic Technicians, Medical Technologists, Laboratory Technicians, Occupational Therapists, Physician's Assistants, Pharmacists, Physical Therapists, and Healthcare Information Technology Managers.

Carpe Diem

What would a surgeon be without a knowledge of anatomy? How can a coach be successful without a fundamental knowledge of the sport he or she is coaching? What chance does a pilot have of successfully flying a passenger plane from point A to point b without a knowledge of how to operate the plane's instrument panel? How can a home builder build a mansion from foundation to completion without having a knowledge of construction? All these professionals are dependent upon their knowledge to be successful in their chosen careers. You too are dependent upon knowledge to reach your goals of success. Not hype, not just motivation, not simply 5 easy steps, or some secret formula never before revealed, or any other get rich quick scheme is going to bring you the success you desire. People fail for two reasons, not knowing and not doing. Regardless of technology the path to success has remained the same over the centuries, knowledge, sweat equity, and flawless execution. This book has supplied you with the first ingredient Knowledge, it is up to you to add the final two ingredients. Success is waiting there for you to grasp it. I'm not here to tell you how to go about becoming successful. Your own mind is capable of that. My job has been to supply you with the knowledge you need to succeed and show you ways to use that knowledge.

Now, if knowledge truly is power, and the greatest among us have proven that it surely is, you should now be powerful enough to take what you have learned from this book and build a future for yourself that surpasses all you could ever hope and dream for. Whether it is unhitching your mind from the old beliefs that keep you from moving forward in life, decluttering your mind of the misinformation it has acquired over the years, bulking up on valuable new information you've learned, understanding where the world is headed and how you can meet it there, or embracing your ultimate self and refusing to settle for less ever again, you now have what it takes to "seize the day" and embrace success in ways you never could before. Remember, information and power only benefit you if you use them. You are now well equipped to face any obstacle the world throws at you. Be strong, be fearless, be courageous, and take the steps you must now take to become the success you were created to be. I wish you well and God's speed on your journey. All Love. - Charles Gentry

In Conclusion, congratulations on going the distance

Finally, whether you want to be a better employee, move into the executive suite, or go for the brass ring by starting your own business, if you read this book from cover to cover you are now more than ready to achieve your aims. Applauding you for going the extra mile to prepare yourself for the world to come (soon), I hereby leave you with these two companions: 10 motivational quotes to inspire you on your journey and The Blueprint, to re-engineer your life for success. Now that you are armed with the wealth of valuable information you need to succeed, I encourage you to pursue your destiny with all speed. Be bold, be brave, be crazy. The race to be who you were created to be is just beginning. Ladies and Gentleman, start your engines.

Words of Wisdom

"Every minute you spend in planning saves 10 minutes in execution; this gives you a 1,000 percent return on energy!" — **Brian Tracy, author and motivational speaker**

"Someone's sitting in the shade today because someone planted a tree a long time ago." — **Warren Buffett, investor**

"For CEOs today, it's all about achieving growth and efficiency through innovation. It's not about product innovation so much anymore as about innovating business models, process, culture, and management." — **Ginni Rometty, CEO IBM**

"Give me six hours to chop down a tree and I will spend the first four sharpening the axe." — **Abraham Lincoln, former U.S. President**

"Never begin the day until it is finished on paper." — **Jim Rohn, entrepreneur, author, and motivational speaker**

"I believe in destiny. But I also believe that you can't just sit back and let destiny happen. A lot of times, an opportunity might fall into your lap, but you have to be ready for that opportunity. You can't sit there waiting on it. A lot of times you are going to have to get out there and make it happen." — **Spike Lee, Award Winning Director**

"We need to accept that we won't always make the right decisions, that we'll screw up royally sometimes – understanding that failure is not the opposite of success, it's part of success." — **Arianna Huffington, Huffington Post Founder and CEO**

"I built a conglomerate and emerged the richest black man in the world in 2008 but it didn't happen overnight. It took me 30 years to get to where I am today. Youths of today aspire to be like me but they want to achieve it overnight. It's not going to work. To build a successful business, you must start small and dream big. In the journey of entrepreneurship, tenacity of purpose is supreme." — **Aliko Dangote, Richest Man in Africa**

"If everything was perfect, you would never learn and you would never grow." — **Beyoncé**

"Finally, I truly believe that each of us must find meaning in our work. The best work happens when you know that it's not just work, but something that will improve other people's lives." — **Satya Nadella, Chief Executive Officer   of   Microsoft**

Charles Gentry Social Media

Website: www.thecharlesgentry.com

Linkedin: https://www.linkedin.com/in/charles-gentry-542a72110/

Twitter: thecharlesgentry

Facebook: Charles Gentry

Instagram: thecharlesgentry

Pinterest: Charles Gentry

Email: charlesgentry6000@yahoo.com